Advanced Methods of Power Load Forecasting

Advanced Methods of Power Load Forecasting

Editors

**J. Carlos García-Díaz
Óscar Trull**

MDPI • Basel • Beijing • Wuhan • Barcelona • Belgrade • Manchester • Tokyo • Cluj • Tianjin

Editors
J. Carlos García-Díaz
Department of Applied Statistics, Operational Research and Quality
Universitat Politècnica de València
Valencia
Spain

Óscar Trull
Department of Applied Statistics, Operational Research and Quality
Universitat Politècnica de València
Valencia
Spain

Editorial Office
MDPI
St. Alban-Anlage 66
4052 Basel, Switzerland

This is a reprint of articles from the Special Issue published online in the open access journal *Applied Sciences* (ISSN 2076-3417) (available at: www.mdpi.com/journal/applsci/special_issues/advanced_forecasting).

For citation purposes, cite each article independently as indicated on the article page online and as indicated below:

LastName, A.A.; LastName, B.B.; LastName, C.C. Article Title. *Journal Name* **Year**, *Volume Number*, Page Range.

ISBN 978-3-0365-4218-8 (Hbk)
ISBN 978-3-0365-4217-1 (PDF)

© 2022 by the authors. Articles in this book are Open Access and distributed under the Creative Commons Attribution (CC BY) license, which allows users to download, copy and build upon published articles, as long as the author and publisher are properly credited, which ensures maximum dissemination and a wider impact of our publications.

The book as a whole is distributed by MDPI under the terms and conditions of the Creative Commons license CC BY-NC-ND.

Contents

Preface to "Advanced Methods of Power Load Forecasting" vii

Changchun Cai, Yuan Tao, Tianqi Zhu and Zhixiang Deng
Short-Term Load Forecasting Based on Deep Learning Bidirectional LSTM Neural Network
Reprinted from: *Appl. Sci.* **2021**, *11*, 8129, doi:10.3390/app11178129 1

Sylwia Henselmeyer and Marcin Grzegorzek
Short-Term Load Forecasting Using an Attended Sequential Encoder-Stacked Decoder Model with Online Training
Reprinted from: *Appl. Sci.* **2021**, *11*, 4927, doi:10.3390/app11114927 17

Abdulla I. Almazrouee, Abdullah M. Almeshal, Abdulrahman S. Almutairi, Mohammad R. Alenezi, Saleh N. Alhajeri and Faisal M. Alshammari
Forecasting of Electrical Generation Using Prophet and Multiple Seasonality of Holt–Winters Models: A Case Study of Kuwait
Reprinted from: *Appl. Sci.* **2020**, *10*, 8412, doi:10.3390/app10238412 33

Nikos Andriopoulos, Aristeidis Magklaras, Alexios Birbas, Alex Papalexopoulos, Christos Valouxis and Sophia Daskalaki et al.
Short Term Electric Load Forecasting Based on Data Transformation and Statistical Machine Learning
Reprinted from: *Appl. Sci.* **2020**, *11*, 158, doi:10.3390/app11010158 53

Oscar Trull, Juan Carlos García-Díaz and Angel Peiró-Signes
Forecasting Irregular Seasonal Power Consumption. An Application to a Hot-Dip Galvanizing Process
Reprinted from: *Appl. Sci.* **2020**, *11*, 75, doi:10.3390/app11010075 75

Abdulla I. Almazrouee, Abdullah M. Almeshal, Abdulrahman S. Almutairi, Mohammad R. Alenezi and Saleh N. Alhajeri
Long-Term Forecasting of Electrical Loads in Kuwait Using Prophet and Holt–Winters Models
Reprinted from: *Appl. Sci.* **2020**, *10*, 5627, doi:10.3390/app10165627 99

Preface to "Advanced Methods of Power Load Forecasting"

Advanced societies are characterized by the intensive use of energy produced, distributed and consumed in an uninterrupted, reliable and safe manner. The liberalization of the markets has meant that the entities participating in the electricity system do not have a vertical structure, differentiating in this way between the entities that produce energy from the sellers, all going to an energy pool. Consequently, price competition has increased. In other words, energy systems aim to produce and consume energy efficiently and economically.

A case of special importance is the electricity obtained as a result of a combination of fossil, nuclear and renewable energy sources. The current trend at a global level is to have more and more resources of clean and non-polluting, renewable energy, but with the limitations that this entails, since on many occasions, production does not depend exclusively on human planning, but also on environmental conditions. Both planning, programming and the cost of energy are based on a correct estimate of the electrical load, both in the short term (STLF) and in the medium and long term (MTLF and LTLF).

For the proper functioning of the energy system within today's liberalized energy markets, predicting the energy load has therefore become a crucial task. Improving the accuracy of forecasting energy load, as well as peak loads to ensure energy supply from the energy system to final consumers, has been of increasing interest to researchers in recent years. Responsibility for the system rests with the transmission system operators (TSO). The system works based on the work carried out by the TSO, which manages the transmission of energy in the countries (and the continents, like the ENTSO), and is therefore in charge of making the predictions that the electricity market will use to establish not only the price of energy, but also the units of production.

This concept of forecasting is not exclusive to the TSO. Production units, lower systems such as local and domestic, or any entity participating in the electrical system must have a good load forecasting system. Even industries with high energy needs. The perception of a consumer who is oblivious to electricity prices, and whose consumption is established, has changed radically. High-energy consumers pay much more attention to their consumption and the way they consume. Their studies allow consumption to be improved while accompanying contracts with electricity marketers, with planning according to anticipated energy consumption and needs.

The prediction methodology for power load used in the literature has been advancing over time. From the use of the simplest methods to the most modern ones based on artificial intelligence, always going through statistical methods. Their evolution has always been gradual, and in general with few advances in strategies to deal with the problem of accuracy and safety in predictions. However, as a result of deregulation, the system has radically changed for everyone, from the generator to the consumer. Monitoring consumption and prices is necessary for better management of resources. This has caused an explosion of proposals that try to channel efforts to improve the ways of predicting and achieve more accurate predictions for both the STLF and the LTLF.

The objective of this Special Issue is to present new emerging methodologies that improve the traditional tools used in load forecasting. Artificial intelligence, machine learning, deep learning and hybrid models are some of the new methods that can help improve decision-making in today's energy markets, characterized by high uncertainty and volatility.

The articles presented here are very interesting and innovative. We have made a brief summary of the most important points of all of them.

Cai et al. present a prediction method based on multi-layer stacked bidirectional LSTM for the STLF. The proposed methodology uses a typical Deep Learning structure such as the LSTM neural network. It introduces the combination of two layers, one to compute the hidden vector from front to back, and one in the opposite direction combined, in order to reduce the accumulated error. This structure is repeated in multiple layers connected sequentially that allow information to be filtered and predictions to be made. The efficiency of the predictions is checked using data from an AC power station in southwest China and is measured in terms of MAPE, RMSE and MAE. The results show efficiency around 0.45% of MAPE.

Helsenmeyer and Grzegorzek present an application for electricity load forecasting (STLF) at the NYISO. They use LSTM neural networks with the SESDA architecture (sequential encoder-stacked decoder architecture). The encoder-decoder structure is especially suitable for time series prediction, where the encoder shows a compressed representation of the input information that the decoder will later use to make predictions. The results of the predictions are compared with other methods, and the MAPE reported is 1.52%.

Andriopoulos et al. present a new prediction method based on convolutional neural networks, where the use of statistical methods allow to optimize the obtaining of the hyperparameters of the network. It makes its application to three different types of load (household demand, from a local electricity company in northern Italy, and from an office) with different frequencies. The results show that the use of the LSTM-CNN models improve the results with respect to the LSTM, of proven efficiency.

Trull et al. present Holt-Winters models with discrete moving interval seasonalities (DIMS) applied to a forecast of electricity demand with irregular seasonality. Specifically, it is the demand for a galvanized steel production factory located in Spain. The use of DIMS makes it possible to circumvent existing problems by not having regular seasonality. A comparison is made with other common methods, such as neural networks, ARIMA models, exponential smoothing models. The results show that the prediction efficiency is better than all of them, and that it is at the same level as those made by NARX neural networks.

Almazrouee et al. proposes the use of Facebook's Prophet method for the prediction of long-term electricity load in Kuwait. In his paper, he describes the Prophet method and applies it to electricity demand data from the Kuwait National Control Center. It uses a seasonality of P=365.25 days and uses the holiday function $h(t)=Z(t)\kappa$ with the matrix of regressors $Z(t)=[1(t\ infoNumberD1),\ldots,1(t\ infoNumberD\_L)]$ considering D as the holidays, $\kappa\ N(0,\ \hat{}2)$, where is the holiday smoothing parameter and t measured in days.

Almazrouee et al. uses the Prophet method to determine the maximum long-term peak electrical load, and applies it to the consumption data. It uses 354.25 days as annual seasonality and 7 days for weekly seasonality. He then compares the results with a Holt-Winters model with annual seasonality. The comparison is made using different indicators (MAPE, MAE, RMSE, CVRMSE and R2). In all cases, it is observed that the new proposal improves the results, which are in the order of 1.75% in ASM.

The results shown by the articles presented here contribute to the improvement of electricity load predictions in many areas, and encourage research in all the areas worked on. In addition, the coexistence between modern methods, based on artificial intelligence, with methods considered traditional is verified. With the publication of this Special Issue, a new range of possibilities opens up that the electricity load forecaster can use.

Future research will be more focused on combining the fundamental aspects of traditional models with artificial intelligence models, creating a symbiosis between both models. One of the fundamental aspects to take into account is the volatility of demand due to the introduction of renewable energies, as well as the need for a fast calculation that can deal with sudden and unexpected changes in the power load. This aspect will be developed in future editions of this Special Issue.

We want to thank all the authors who have contributed to this Special Issue and congratulate them for their good work.

J. Carlos García-Díaz and Óscar Trull
Editors

Article

Short-Term Load Forecasting Based on Deep Learning Bidirectional LSTM Neural Network

Changchun Cai [1,2,*], Yuan Tao [1,2], Tianqi Zhu [1,2] and Zhixiang Deng [1,2]

[1] Jiangsu Key Laboratory of Power Transmission and Distribution Equipment Technology, Hohai University, Changzhou 213022, China; Taoy@hhu.edu.cn (Y.T.); Zhutq@hhu.edu.cn (T.Z.); Dengzx@hhu.edu.cn (Z.D.)
[2] College of The Internet of Things Engineering, Hohai University, Changzhou 213022, China
* Correspondence: 20031690@hhu.edu.cn

Abstract: Accurate load forecasting guarantees the stable and economic operation of power systems. With the increasing integration of distributed generations and electrical vehicles, the variability and randomness characteristics of individual loads and the distributed generation has increased the complexity of power loads in power systems. Hence, accurate and robust load forecasting results are becoming increasingly important in modern power systems. The paper presents a multi-layer stacked bidirectional long short-term memory (LSTM)-based short-term load forecasting framework; the method includes neural network architecture, model training, and bootstrapping. In the proposed method, reverse computing is combined with forward computing, and a feedback calculation mechanism is designed to solve the coupling of before and after time-series information of the power load. In order to improve the convergence of the algorithm, deep learning training is introduced to mine the correlation between historical loads, and the multi-layer stacked style of the network is established to manage the power load information. Finally, actual data are applied to test the proposed method, and a comparison of the results of the proposed method with different methods shows that the proposed method can extract dynamic features from the data as well as make accurate predictions, and the availability of the proposed method is verified with real operational data.

Keywords: bidirectional long short-term memory; multi-layer stacked; neural network; short-term load forecasting; power system

1. Introduction

A reliable and accuracy short-term load forecasting system is the basis of energy trade between the customers and electrical utility companies [1,2]. With the increasing penetration of distributed generations and consumer energy systems, the randomness and variability of load profiles bring more challenges for short-term load forecasting systems. Researchers around the world have focused on short-term load forecasting in recent years and tried to get a more accuracy forecasting result using variable new technologies.

The traditional load forecasting method uses statistics [1,3,4], which has appeared in former studies. However, large amounts of precise historical data are needed, which increases the challenges of accurate prediction. Artificial neural network-based methods are the most popular among the data-driven methods due to their strong capability of nonlinear approximation and self-learning. Different types of neural networks such as back propagation (BP) [5], radial basis function (RBF) [6], and extreme learning machines (ELM) [7,8] have been proposed and applied in short-term load forecasting. Furthermore, a regularizing term and the combination of multiple ELM is added to reduce the randomness of traditional ELM in photovoltaic power forecasting in [8]. However, low convergence speed is always an obstacle to the large-scale application of neural networks.

The rapid development of a deep learning framework and artificial intelligence (AI) technology brings more choices for the power system load forecasting. In recent years, convolutional neural network (CNN) [9,10], deep belief network (DBN) [11–13], and deep residual networks (DRN) [14] have been developed and applied in load forecasting, which shows a promising prospect in load forecasting areas. These methods can extract the key elements of the load profile. A multiple-input deep convolutional neural network (CNN) model is proposed and applied in the short-term photovoltaic power forecasting in [9], in which solar radiation and ambient temperature combined with the historical output power of a PV system are collected as the input data of the forecasting model. In [10], a deep convolutional neural network-based forecasting method is proposed for the short-term PV power forecasting; here, the original meter data are decomposed into a two-dimensional timescale by convolution kernels and refined into advanced features by a CNN model. Deep belief network is applied in photovoltaic power forecasting in [11]; the proposed methodology is focused on real data capturing to establish the optimum architectural of deep belief network. An improved deep belief network is applied in load forecasting considering demand-side response in [12]; three aspects of the DBN are optimized to dispose the predictive accuracy. The deep belief network method is incorporated into a feed-forward neural network in [13], in which the layer-by-layer unsupervised training procedure is combined with parameters' fine-tuning based on a supervised back-propagation training method. In [14], a two-stage ensemble strategy of deep residual network is formulated to enhance the generalization capability of load forecasting.

Due to its advantages to solve the vanishing gradient issues, LSTM is more effective than a recurrent neural network to deal with industrial problems that are highly related to time series [15–17]. A LSTM neural network has been successfully deployed in many practical applications; it can learn longer-term dependencies due to the associated memory units [18–20]. An LSTM architecture-based method is used in a distributed network in [18], in which the LSTM-based structure is used for the linear regression of each node and receives a variable length data sequence with its neighbors to train the LSTM architecture. A video-captioning method based on adversarial learning and LSTM is proposed in [19]; it is used to handle the temporal nature of video data exponential error accumulation. In [20], an attention-based LSTM model with semantic consistency is used to transfer videos to natural sentences. An LSTM neural network is used in multimodal ambulatory sleep detection in [21], and the proposed method can synthesize temporal information accuracy. In [22], nonuniformly sampled variable length sequential data are classified, which is followed by regression by LSTM.

The LSTM neural network also shows significant potential in the prediction field. The authors in [23,24] proposed an LSTM-based framework for the single energy customer load forecasting. In [25], a multi-layer bidirectional RNN based on LSTM and a gated recurrent unit (GRU) is proposed for short-term load forecasting; the proposed method can match different types of load data and is shown to be more accurate. In [26], a forecasting model based on LSTM-DNN is proposed for the photovoltaic power output, available temperature data, and statistical features extracted from the historical photovoltaic output data using stationary wavelet transform. An LSTM neural network is proposed for the prediction of solar irradiance one hour in advance and one day in advance [27,28]; the clearness index was used to classify the type of weather by k-means. A k-means LSTM network model for wind power spot prediction is proposed in [29]; the wind power factors are clustered to generate a new LSTM sub-prediction model.

In [30], the authors proposed five LSTM-based forecasting methods for photovoltaic power prediction, and the prediction capacity is improved by stacking LSTM layers on top of each other. In [31] a one-dimensional convolutional stacked LSTM for load disaggregation is proposed; the deep learning framework is created by stacking several LSTM layers within the hidden layers. The hidden layers are joined reconnections in the LSTM cell. There is no gradient disappearance or gradient explosion problem in the prediction model of the stacked LSTM neural network. However, the long-distance data transmission will cause data loss, which will result in accumulated errors in the process prediction. In order to solve this problem, reverse computing combined with forward computing are introduced to solve the unidirectionality of the memory process in the process of training the data. A feedback mechanism is introduced to improve the front and back association. Combined with the reverse computing, the LSTM neural network has the ability of bidirectional computing, which can overcome the defection of data loss in long-distance transmission. Furthermore, forward and backward propagation prediction make data more dependent and reliable. A multi-layer stacked deep learning style is built for the data training process to improve the information communication between the dataset sequentially.

The main contributions of this paper are as follows: (1) A bidirectional LSTM short-term load forecasting framework model is proposed in this paper, in which reverse computing is combined with forward computing to retrieve the important information hidden in the load profiles and improve the forecasting ability of the time-series problem. (2) A multi-layer stacked bidirectional LSTM prediction structure based on deep learning technology is proposed. The advantages of the multi-layer structure are applied to analyze the load profiles and extract the data essential features. (3) Last, the multi-layer stacked bidirectional LSTM prediction model is approved by using real operational cases, and the evaluation results are compared with other methods.

2. LSTM Neural Network

2.1. LSTM Neural Network

The LSTM neural network was proposed in 1997, which is a time-domain deep learning neural network. Compared with traditional recurrent neural network, there are two special parts: the forget gate and the memory unit in the hidden layer of the LSTM neural network. A long-term information stream from the input to output can improve the memory capacity of the neural network in the process of training. The structure of the LSTM cell is shown in Figure 1. It consists of four computing units: namely, the output gate, forget gate, memory unit, and input gate, respectively.

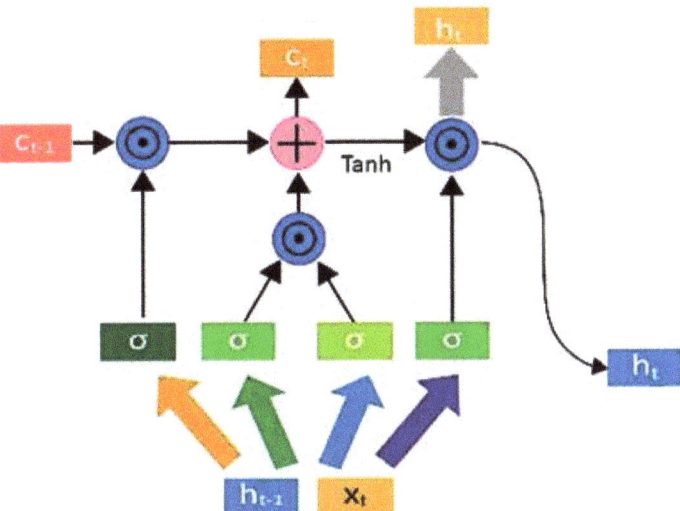

Figure 1. LSTM cell structure.

Based on the output h_{t-1} of the last hidden layer and the current input x_t, a new value of f_t is generated based on the activation function "Sigmoid", which determines whether to let the information C_{t-1} learned in the last moment pass through; that is, how much of the last cell state C_{t-1} is saved to the current time C_t. The function between h_{t-1}, x_t and f_t can be written as:

$$f_t = \sigma \left(W_f \cdot [h_{t-1}, x_t] + b_f \right) \tag{1}$$

where σ is the "Sigmoid" function, and the range of the output value of the "Sigmoid" function is [0,1]. W_f is the weight matrix of the forget gate, b_f is the bias of the forget gate, f_t is the value of the forget gate which decides the forgetting factor of long-term memory information. The value of f_t is between [0,1].

The threshold of LSTM consists of a sigmoid activation function and dot multiplication operation. After the hidden layer of the previous moment enters the forget gate, the function gives the judge information about whether it is updated or not. However, the cell state rolls continuously and runs in the horizontal direction.

$$I_t = \sigma(W_t \cdot [h_{t-1}, x_t] + b_i) \tag{2}$$

$$\widetilde{C}_t = \tanh(W_c \cdot [h_{t-1}, x_t] + b_c) \tag{3}$$

$$C_t = f_t * C_{t-1} + I_t * \widetilde{C}_t \tag{4}$$

where tanh is the hyperbolic tangent activation function, $\widetilde{C}_t$ is the temporary unit state of C_t, W_c is the weight matrix of the memory unit, b_c is the bias of the memory unit, and I_t is the output value of the input gate. The current cell state C_t is the sum of the original state and the updated state.

$$o_t = \sigma(W_o \cdot [h_{t-1}, x_t] + b_o) \tag{5}$$

$$h_t = o_t * \tanh(C_t) \tag{6}$$

where W_o is the weight matrix of the output gate, o_t is the output value of the output gate, and b_o is the bias of the output gate. The initial output h_t is obtained through the sigmoid layer, $\tanh(C_t)$ is between -1 and 1.

The signal passes through the input gate, output gate, and forget gate in turn, and it realizes information storing and maintaining in the current time period. The LSTM structure of the neural network shows that the input variable is transmitted horizontally from input to output directly. Hence, the prediction error will accumulate continuously and suddenly swell in direct proportion with the previous time in the prediction model. Figure 2 shows the LSTM prediction accumulation error in the power load forecasting in one day. The short-term load forecasting method usually takes a day or a week as the training dataset. Three days' data are taken as sample forecast in Figure 2. The error accumulation occurs in the LSTM prediction results with the increase in the step of the prediction data, and the error will become larger and larger as time goes on.

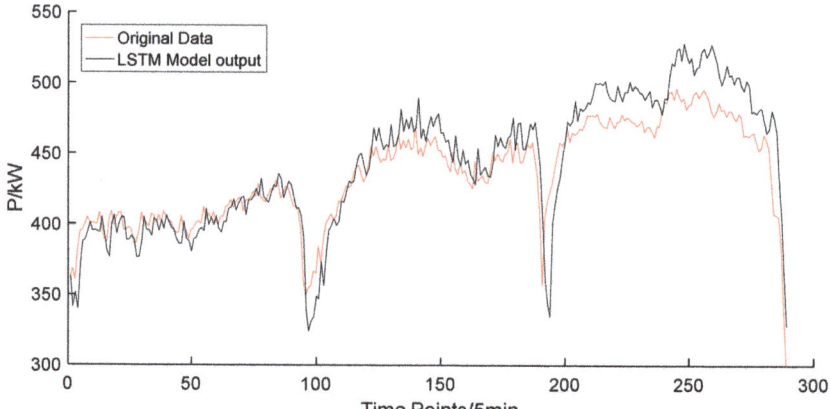

Figure 2. Accumulate error of the forecasting model.

2.2. Bidirectional LSTM Neural Network

In order to overcome the accumulative error problem, a bidirectional LSTM is proposed here, which is shown in Figure 3. The bidirectional LSTM neural network consists of two layers of LSTM structure; one is used to calculate the hidden vector from the front to the back, and the other is used to calculate the hidden vector from the back to the front. The output of the bidirectional LSTM neural network is determined by these two layers.

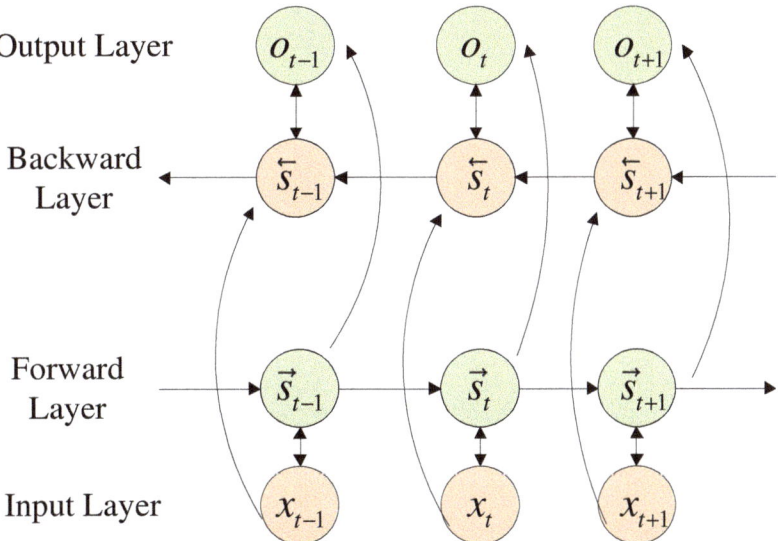

Figure 3. Basic structure of bidirectional LSTM.

The bidirectional LSTM neural network is different from the traditional feed-forward mechanism neural network. The internal nodes in each layer do not connect with each other in bidirectional LSTM. A directional loop is introduced in the connection of hidden layers, foregoing information; results are memorized and stored in the memory unit, which can improve the association of single pieces of information in different time series. The current output of the neural network is determined by combining the previous output and the current input. However, with the increasing amount of input data in the time series, there will be gradient disappearance and gradient explosion problems due to the lack of delay window width.

Based on the traditional LSTM model, the bidirectional LSTM neural network will fully consider the front and back correlation of the load data in time series and improve the model performance for the sequence classification problem especially. During the training process, the input data sequence of the forward layer is the training data, and the backward layer is the reverse copy of the input data sequence. The results of bidirectional structure prediction are determined by the previous input and the latter input, which increases the dependence between the training data to avoid the forgetting of the order information.

Figure 3 shows that the forward layer calculates the forward direction from 1 to t, and it saves the output of the forward hidden layer at each moment. The backward layer calculates the reverse time series and saves the output of the backward hidden layer at each moment. Finally, the output of the bidirectional LSTM neural network is calculated by combining the corresponding output results of the forward layer and backward layer at each time point. The bidirectional LSTM neural network can be written as:

$$s_t = f(Ux_t + Ws_{t-1}) \tag{7}$$

$$s'_t = f(U'x_t + W's'_{t+1}) \tag{8}$$

$$o_t = g(Vs_t + V's'_t) \tag{9}$$

where s_t is the state variable of the hidden layer at time t, o_t is the state variable of the output layer at time t, s'_t is the state variable of the reverse hidden layer at time t, x_t is the input vector, g and f are activation functions, V, W, and U are the weight matrix from the hidden layer to the output layer, the hidden layer, and the input layer to the hidden layer, and V', W', and U' are the corresponding reverse weight matrix. The state weight matrix of the forward layer and the backward layer is not shared information between the two. The forward layer and backward layer are calculated in turn and give the result of each time. The final output o_t depends on the sum of the forward calculation result s_t and the reverse calculation result s'_t.

3. Multi-Layer Stacked Bidirectional LSTM Neural Network for Short-Term Load Forecasting

The power load profile is affected by the residential electricity behavior, temperature, humidity, etc. It is a multi-dimension nonlinear problem. The bidirectional LSTM neural network solves the accumulated error problem in the training process. Furthermore, the multi-layer bidirectional LSTM neural network is the fusion of a bidirectional neural network based on a deep learning mechanism. A multi-layer forward structure and reverse structure constitute the multi-layer stacked bidirectional LSTM. The multi-layer stacked bidirectional LSTM neural network expands the depth of the bidirectional LSTM neural network. The input data can be learned repeatedly to get an in-depth understanding of the data characteristics and improve the accuracy of load forecasting.

3.1. Multi-Layer Stacked Bidirectional LSTM Neural Network

The system structure of the multi-layer stacked bidirectional LSTM is shown in Figure 4. In the multi-layer stacked structure, every two layers of the LSTM neural network are composed of forward and reverse LSTM networks. The second layer receives the sum of the output results of the first layer of forward and reverse LSTM.

Figure 4 specifies the multi-layer bidirectional LSTM neural network system structure; the output of the multi-layer stacked bidirectional LSTM neural network is determined by the forward and backward results of each layer, and its model can be expressed as follows.

$$o_t = g\left(V^{(j)}s_t^{(i)} + V^{(i)}s_t^{(i)}\right) \tag{10}$$

$$o_t = g\left(V^{(j)}s_t^{(i)} + V^{(i)}s_t^{(i)}\right) \tag{11}$$

$$s_t^{(i)} = f\left(U^{*(i)}s_t'^{(-1)} + W^{(i)}s'_{t+1}\right) \tag{12}$$

$$s_t^{(1)} = f\left(U^{(1)}x_t + W^{(1)}s_{t-1}\right) \tag{13}$$

$$s_t'^{(1)} = f\left(U'^{(1)}x_t + W'^{(1)}s'_{t-1}\right) \tag{14}$$

where s_t^i and s_{t-1}^i are the state variables of the ith hidden layer at $t-1$ and t time, respectively. The forward and reverse calculations do not share the weight information. $V^{(i)}$, $U^{(i)}$, and $W^{(i)}$ are the weight matrix between the input layer, hidden layer, and output layer. In the reverse calculation, $V'(i)$, $U'(i)$, and $W'(i)$ are the corresponding inverse weight matrix, respectively. i is the number of bidirectional LSTM layers, and $i = 0, 1, 2 \cdots \infty$ represents the value of the output layer.

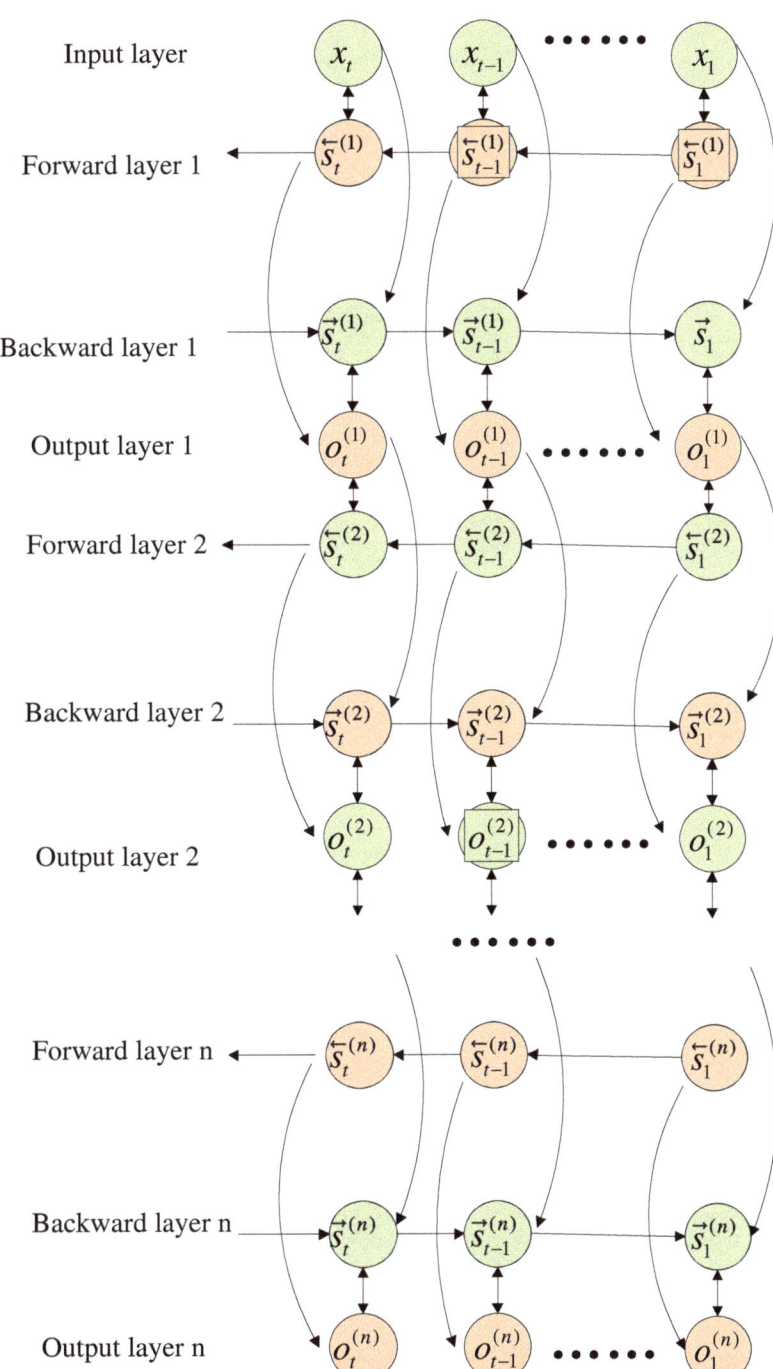

Figure 4. Multi-layer stacked bidirectional LSTM neural network.

3.2. Multi-Layer Stacked Bidirectional LSTM Based Load Forecasting

The essential concept of the proposed improved LSTM neural network consists of obtaining the statistical analysis of the power load by reconstructing the training sample data. The multi-layer stacked bidirectional LSTM network is trained to perform the forecast of the power load for the next 24 h. The prediction process of the proposed model can be divided into the follow steps and shown in Figure 5.

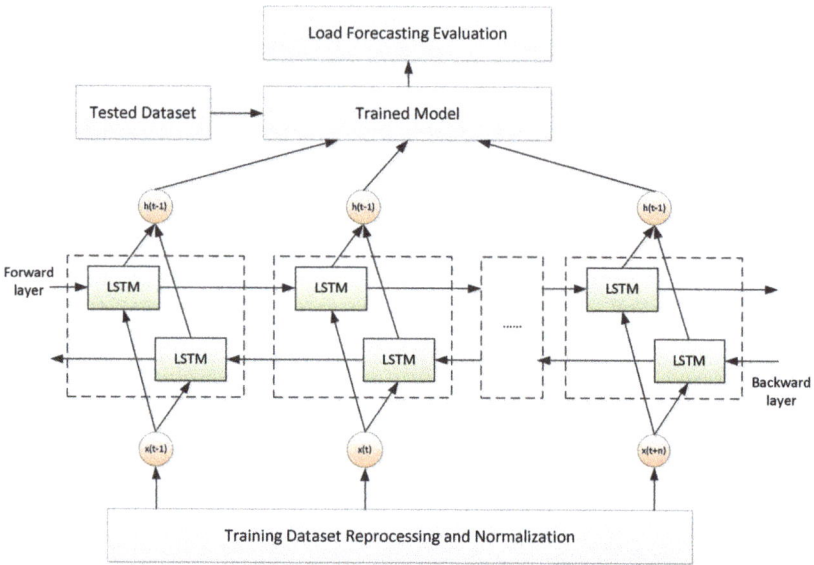

Figure 5. The framework of the proposed method for load forecasting.

Step 1: Data preparation. Historical data of the power load profiles are collected and pre-processed to remove any outlier or incorrect data before the training process. However, the original data are not standard enough to use directly. Normalization is a common method to normalize original data structures in system modeling, and the original data become dimensionless after normalization, which can increase the convergence speed of the neural network. After normalization, the value of the original data is between the range of [0,1]. There are many normalization methods such as min–max scaling, Z-score standardization method, and decimal scaling. In this paper, a linear normalization method based on min–max scaling is used, which can be written as follows:

$$x^* = \frac{x - x_{min}}{x_{max} - x_{min}}. \tag{15}$$

x_{max} and x_{min} are the maximum and minimum values of the sample data of power load, x is the original value of the sample data, and x^* is the normalized value of the original data.

Step 2: Network training. The forward value of input at $t = 1$ and the reverse state value of input at $t = T$ (T is the last sampling time of the training dataset) are unknown, which are generally set to a fixed value (0.5) in the training process. Additionally, the derivative of the forward value of input at $T = t$ and the original value of the reverse state of $t = 1$ are generally set to zero. It is assumed that the later information is not very important for the current information updated. The process of network training contains the following:

(1) Forward transfer. With the time sequence of $1 < t <= T$, training data are input from the cell of the bidirectional LSTM, and the predicted outputs are determined. Forward

passes are only for forward states (from t = 1 to t = T) and backward states (from t = T to t = 1). The output cells were transferred forward, and the n-th layer forward predicted output is calculated.

(2) Backward transfer: The derivative of the partial objective function is calculated for the forward transfer time period with 1 < t <= T. The backward LSTM cells are calculated based on the forward value of 1 < t <= T and the reverse value of 1 < t <= T. The reversed prediction output is calculated.

(3) Weight matrix updating. Based on the loss function of the neural network during the training process, the weight matrix is calculated and updated.

(4) Result output. Based on the bidirectional calculation, the parameters of the prediction model of LSTM neural network are estimated.

3.3. Evaluation Index

In this paper, the mean absolute error (MAE), root mean square error (RMSE), and mean absolute percentage error (MAPE) are used to evaluate the error of prediction results. MAPE, RMSE, and MAE are common indicators to evaluate the accuracy of the proposed model based on the measurement value and estimated value. The definition of the indicators is shown in Equations (16)–(18). MAE is the estimated indictor, which is used as the measurement value. RMSE is used to evaluate the deviation between the observed value and the true value; it is sensitive to outliers. MAPE is used to evaluate the relative errors between the average observed value and the true value on the test. MAE can reflect the error distribution during the time series, while MAPE normalizes the error at different points and reduces the effect of the absolute errors of the outliers.

$$MAPE = \frac{1}{n}\sum_{i=1}^{n}\frac{|x_i - \hat{x}_i|}{x_i} \times 100\% \tag{16}$$

$$RMSE = \sqrt{\frac{1}{n}\sum_{i=1}^{n}|x_i - \hat{x}_i|^2} \tag{17}$$

$$MAE = \frac{1}{n}\sum_{i=1}^{n}|x_i - \hat{x}_i| \tag{18}$$

n is the number of sample data, x_i is the real value, and $\hat{x}_i$ is the predicted value.

4. Simulation and Experimental Analysis

In this section, we evaluate the performance of the proposed multi-layer stacked bidirectional LSTM neural network for short-term load forecasting, and the key parameters of the model are discussed as well. Moreover, the comparison between the proposed method and previous work are also assessed. All models were executed in a computer with a CPU clock speed of 3.0 GHz and 8 GB of RAM. The hidden layer of the proposed model is 100, the hidden node is 8, the initial value of training learning rate is 0.01, and the number of model training iterations is 100.

4.1. Dataset for Load Forecasting

The databases used in the paper were obtained from the station in the southwest of China with an AC power voltage of 35 kV. The dataset contains a 3-year power load profile with the sampling time of 15 min. The dataset is a mixed dataset that contains different types of loads such as resident load, commercial load, and industrial load. The dataset was pre-processed in order to separate the relevant data and select the predictive features in the models. Here, we separated the dataset into different types for the load forecasting based on days and season characteristics. The pre-processing of the dataset is shown in Section 3.2, and the forecasting models were trained and tested using a 1-year sample dataset where the first 80% is used for model training and the remaining 20% is used to test the performance of the proposed model.

4.2. Neural Network Structure Determine

Prediction accuracy has a significant relationship with the depth of the bidirectional LSTM neural network. The dynamic characteristics of the load data will be extracted based on the interaction of the different layers of the neural network. The internal relevance information of the load profiles will be deep learned with the different stacked layers, and the nonlinearity of the load sequence can be described in different dimensions. The parameters of the input units, forget units, and output units of the proposed model are shown in Table 1.

Table 1. The parameters of the equivalent model.

	0.023	0.020	0.120	0.127	0.033	0.975	0.044	0.037	0.579	0.035
Input Gate	0.044	0.049	0.017	0.012	0.034	0.025	0.041	0.001	0.043	0.037
	0.027	0.025	0.135	0.128	0.070	0.975	0.049	0.043	0.540	0.007
	0.025	0.047	0.042	0.029	0.034	0.025	0.048	0.043	0.005	0.040
	0.024	0.006	0.030	0.008	0.032	0.015	0.050	0.016	0.024	0.005
Forget Gate	0.012	0.015	0.013	0.046	0.013	0.045	0.041	0.048	0.050	0.019
	0.049	0.044	0.046	0.005	0.000	0.023	0.015	0.046	0.019	0.037
	0.007	0.014	0.030	0.007	0.043	0.016	0.044	0.025	0.047	0.037
	0.030	0.002	0.043	0.038	0.005	−0.033	0.049	0.001	0.012	0.014
Output Gate	0.006	0.024	0.012	0.001	0.046	0.043	0.049	0.036	0.039	0.014
	0.008	0.048	0.029	0.037	0.038	−0.044	0.023	0.012	0.002	0.035
	0.021	0.045	0.002	0.017	0.006	0.048	0.019	0.020	0.023	0.012

The prediction accuracy of the different layers of the LSTM neural work is shown in Figure 6. It can be seen that the proposed multi-layer bidirectional LSTM neural network is an effective method and is accurate enough for the load forecast problem. Furthermore, with the increasing numbers of layers, the prediction result will be more accurate. However, when there are four layers, the prediction accuracy will increase, on the contrary. It is said that three layers is suitable for the prediction of the load sequence data in this paper. Table 2 shows the prediction errors of MAPE between the different layers of the different neural network model.

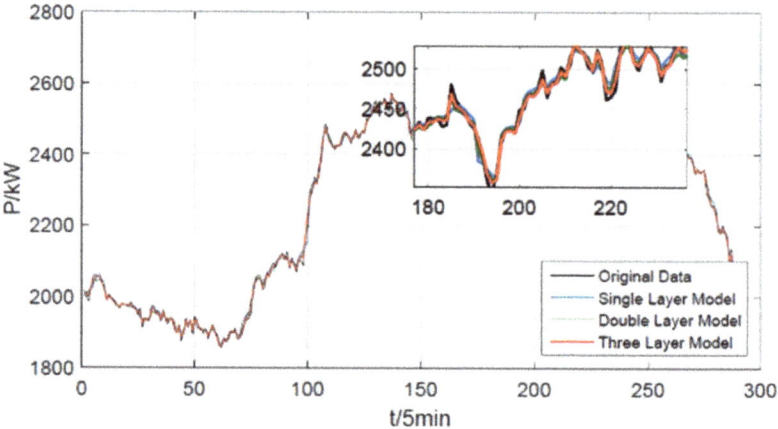

Figure 6. The load forecasting of different layers of LSTM.

Table 2. Error of different stacked layers of bidirectional LSTM.

Bi-LSTM Layers	1	2	3	4	5
MAPE (%)	0.51	0.465	0.405	0.41	0.41

4.3. Method Comparison

In order to show the high performance of the multi-layer stacked bidirectional LSTM neural network in short-term load forecasting, different methods that contain a BP neural network, ELM, traditional LSTM, and multi-layer stacked bidirectional LSTM model are discussed in this paper. The prediction results all the methods tested in this paper followed the same trend with the real load power shown in Figure 7. It can be seen that the multi-layer stacked bidirectional LSTM neural network will be more competitive, and the error comparison of those methods is shown in Table 3, where the MAPE, RMSE, and MAE index are calculated and compared for one day over 24 h. From Table 3, the average MAPE of the proposed method prediction model is 0.4137%; however, the average MAPE values of the BP, LSTM, and ELM models are 1.485%, 1.030%, and 0.77%, respectively. The average RMSE of the proposed method prediction model is 0.706, and those of the BP, LSTM, and ELM models are 2.95, 1.921, and 1.369, respectively.

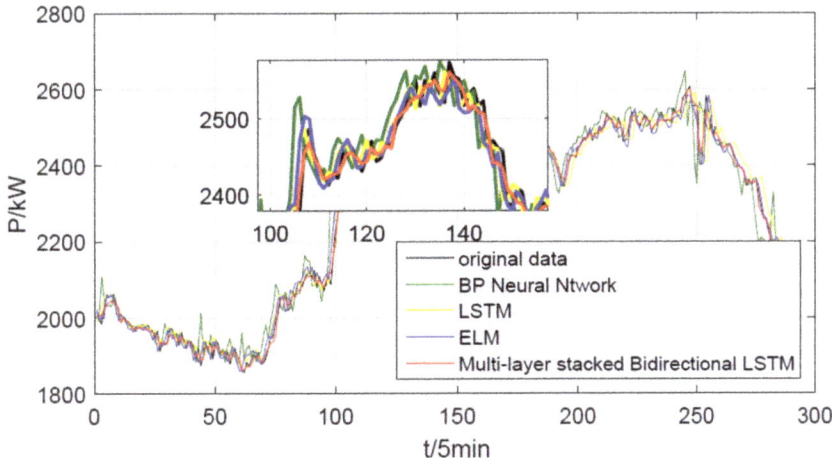

Figure 7. Load power of different forecasting methods.

Table 3. Error comparison of different prediction models.

Prediction Model	BP	LSTM	ELM	Proposed Method
MAPE (%)	1.485	1.03	0.77	0.405
RMSE	2.95	1.921	1.369	0.706
MAE	33.564	23.236	17.07	9.341

Different time interval errors are calculated between ELM, LSTM, BP, and the proposed method in Table 4. The two-hour interval forecasting results fluctuate in different evaluation indexes. However, the total evaluation indexes of the proposed method are at the minimum in one day, and the quantitate analysis forecasting errors are calculated and shown in Figure 8. Here, it can be seen that proposed method based on the multi-layer bidirectional LSTM prediction model better grasps the prediction sample information and has a more competitive forecasting performance. The multi-layer stacked bidirectional LSTM neural network model can retain the original characteristics of the load sequences and reduce the data error by incorporating errors in unsupervised training, which can enhance the robustness of the predictive model.

Table 4. Error comparison of different prediction models in a two-hour interval.

Forecast Time Interval	BP [6]			LSTM [21]			ELM [8]			Proposed Method		
	MAPE%	RMSE	MAE	MAPE%	RMSE	MAE	MAPE%	RMSE	MAE	MAPE%	RMSE	MAE
0–2 h	0.73	28.53	14.76	0.59	15.94	11.79	0.58	14.21	11.58	0.35	9.36	7.13
2–4 h	0.92	33.16	17.71	1.18	26.11	22.66	1.11	25.33	21.56	0.49	10.8	9.39
4–6 h	1.62	40.76	30.47	1.01	23.14	19.18	1.08	23.17	20.49	0.41	9.09	7.7
6–8 h	1.71	40.38	35.08	1.03	25.62	21.21	0.92	23.4	18.96	0.52	12.96	10.66
8–10 h	2.67	90.05	60.54	1.22	38.12	28.11	1.26	41.67	28.95	0.49	14.95	11.43
10–12 h	1.1	30.61	27.58	0.79	24.86	19.93	0.65	21.26	16.38	0.39	11.89	9.96
12–14 h	1.27	36.6	30.36	0.66	22.32	15.65	0.57	18.78	13.51	0.43	12.9	10.41
14–16 h	1.05	32.59	25.15	0.56	18.35	13.4	0.61	17.76	14.67	0.39	11.73	9.51
16–18 h	0.95	28.58	23.3	0.78	23.36	19.12	0.43	13.44	10.37	0.27	7.96	6.54
18–20 h	1.09	33.3	27.2	1.0	30.51	25.11	0.56	17.02	14.01	0.32	9.82	8.03
20–22 h	2.27	78.7	57.12	1.85	65.6	46.68	0.93	31.81	23.52	0.48	16.9	11.99
22–24 h	2.42	73.32	54.88	1.57	41.71	35.33	0.48	13.01	10.8	0.42	12.76	9.56

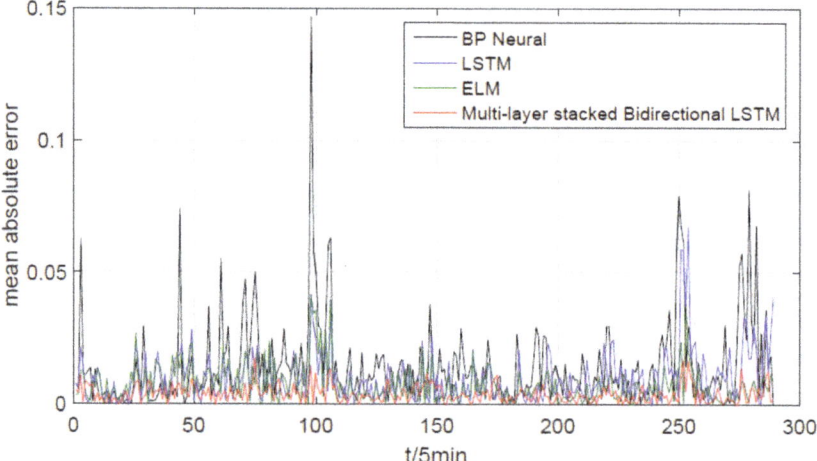

Figure 8. Comparison of different prediction mode.

Different samples of training data will significantly affect the robustness of the load forecasting model. The load will be more accurate with a smaller sample in the training dataset. With 48 or 24 measurement points, the training dataset will be more random, which will increase the difficulty of the load prediction. In this paper, a sample dataset with 48 measurement points is used for the training of the proposed method to verify the robustness of the proposed method and compare it with other methods. Figure 9 shows the comparison of the load forecasting results with a half-hour training dataset; the proposed method is accurate enough to track the load profiles based on deep learning, which can extract the internal characteristics of the discrete sample load data and improve the robustness of the proposed method with the multi-layer bidirectional training mechanism. The MAPE of the proposed method is 2.39%, as shown in Table 5.

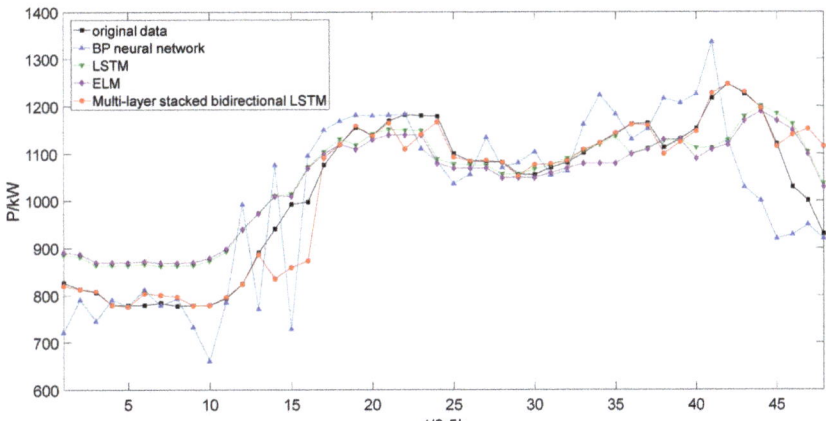

Figure 9. Load forecasting of different methods.

Table 5. The error between different methods.

Prediction Model	BP	LSTM	ELM	Proposed Method
MAPE (%)	6.77	5.44	5.61	2.39
RMSE	91.9627	64.244	67.237	50.827
MAE	69.535	51.158	56.03	23.763

Furthermore, in order to verify the generalization ability of the proposed method for the more complex environments on special days such as the weekend or a holiday, study cases are tested with the historical day based on different measurement points; these are shown in Figures 10 and 11. It can be seen that the prediction results of the load profile can track the measurement data accuracy in different sample time intervals, and the sampling time will influence the prediction results. The results in Figures 10 and 11 show that the proposed multi-layer stacked bidirectional LSTM method is more accurate than the other methods mentioned such as the BP neural network, ELM, and traditional LSTM neural network.

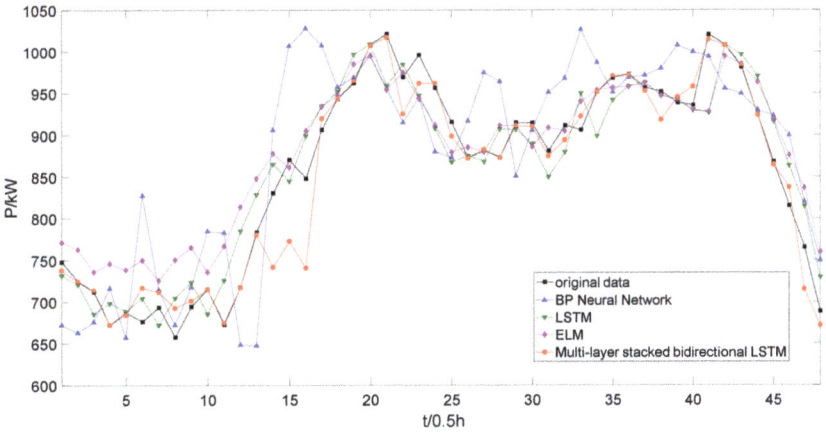

Figure 10. The load forecasting for a weekend with a 0.5 h sample training dataset.

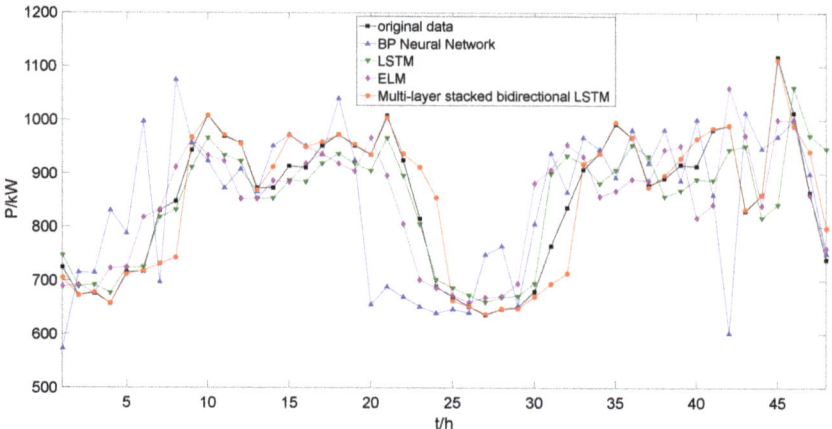

Figure 11. The load forecasting for a weekend with a 1 h sample training dataset.

5. Conclusions

Accurate short-term load forecasting is a huge challenge due to the complexity of the electrical load composition in modern power systems. In this paper, based on the traditional LSTM neural network, a multi-layer stacked type short-term load forecasting method is proposed. Reverse computing combined with forward computing is designed to solve the unidirectionality of the memory process during the training period. The output gate can collaborate the implied information in the historical load series. Furthermore, a multi-layer stacked deep learning style for the neural network is proposed to perceive a low-level features form of power load and form a more abstract high-level representation of load characteristics. At last, a load forecasting frame based on the multi-layer bidirectional LSTM neural network is proposed that contains neural network model construction, historical load profile training, and load forecasting. In the experiments, the real operational load data of a substation are tested, and the performance of the proposed method is tested and evaluated. The results show that the proposed multi-layer stacked bidirectional LSTM neural network method has high performance and is more accurate than the others. The proposed method can retain the original information as much as possible and has a strong memory function to extract the relevant information from historical load sequences.

However, with the increase in the sequence length of the problem, the efficiency of the proposed method will reduce because the capacity of the memory units is limited. There are four fully connected layers in each cell in the LSTM neural network; it needs a lot of computing time in a deep stacked LSTM neural network. Future works will focus on the industrial application of the proposed method with a more complex dataset. (1) We built an online load forecasting system. The application of load forecasting is employed for the dispatch of the power system, which is working all the time. Hence, an online and rolling load forecasting system using the historical load data is the basis of this work. (2) We corrected the load forecasting results. If the load forecast results deviate greatly, the forecast points are corrected based on the data before and after time points.

Author Contributions: Conceptualization, C.C. and Y.T.; methodology, Y.T., T.Z.; validation, C.C. and Y.T.; writing—review and editing, C.C. and Y.T. and Z.D. All authors have read and agreed to the published version of the manuscript.

Funding: This research was funded by "National Natural Science Foundation of China, grant number 51607057", "The Fundamental Research Funds for the Central Universities, grant number 2020B22514"and "The open funding of Jiangsu Key Laboratory of Power Transmission & Distribution Equipment Technology, grant number 2021JSSPD07".

Institutional Review Board Statement: Not applicable.

Informed Consent Statement: Not applicable.

Conflicts of Interest: The authors declare no conflict of interest.

References

1. Quilumba, F.L.; Lee, W.J.; Huang, H.; Wang, D.Y.; Szabados, R.L. Using smart meter data to improve the accuracy of intraday load forecasting considering customer behavior similarities. *IEEE Trans. Smart Grid* **2014**, *6*, 911–918. [CrossRef]
2. Xu, D.; Wu, Q.; Zhou, B.; Li, C.; Bai, L.; Huang, S. Distributed multi-energy operation of coupled electricity, heating and natural gas networks. *IEEE Trans. Sustain. Energy* **2019**, *11*, 2457–2469. [CrossRef]
3. Al-Hamadi, H.M.; Soliman, S.A. Short-term electric load forecasting based on Kalman filtering algorithm with moving window weather and load model. *Electr. Power Syst. Res.* **2004**, *68*, 47–59. [CrossRef]
4. Ceperic, E.; Ceperic, V.; Baric, A. A strategy for short-term load forecasting by support vector regression machines. *IEEE Trans. Power Syst.* **2013**, *28*, 4356–4364. [CrossRef]
5. Kaur, A.; Nonnenmacher, L.; Coimbra, C.F. Net load forecasting for high renewable energy penetration grids. *Energy* **2016**, *114*, 1073–1084. [CrossRef]
6. Cecati, C.; Kolbusz, J.; Rozycki, P.; Siano, P.; Wilamowski, B.M. A novel RBF training algorithm for short-term electric load forecasting and comparative studies. *IEEE Trans. Ind. Electron.* **2015**, *62*, 6519–6529. [CrossRef]
7. Teo, T.T.; Logenthiran, T.; Woo, W.L. Forecasting of photovoltaic power using extreme learning machine. In Proceedings of the IEEE Innovative in Smart Grid Technologies-Asia (ISGT ASIA), Bangkok, Thailand, 3–6 November 2015; pp. 1–6.
8. Teo, T.T.; Logenthiran, T.; Woo, W.L.; Abidi, K. Forecasting of photovoltaic power using regularized ensemble extreme learning machine. In Proceedings of the IEEE Region 10 Conference (TENCON), Singapore, 22–25 November 2016; pp. 455–458.
9. Huang, C.J.; Kuo, P.H. Multiple-input deep convolutional neural network model for short-term photovoltaic power forecasting. *IEEE Access* **2019**, *7*, 74822–74834. [CrossRef]
10. Zang, H.; Cheng, L.; Ding, T.; Cheung, K.W.; Liang, Z.; Wei, Z.; Sun, G. Hybrid method for short-term photovoltaic power forecasting based on deep convolutional neural network. *IET Gener. Transm. Distrib.* **2018**, *12*, 4557–4567. [CrossRef]
11. Neo, Y.Q.; Teo, T.T.; Woo, W.L.; Logenthiran, T.; Sharma, A. Forecasting of photovoltaic power using deep belief network. In Proceedings of the 2017 IEEE Region 10 Conference (TENCON), Penang, Malaysia, 5–8 November 2017.
12. Kong, X.; Li, C.; Zheng, F.; Wang, C. Improved deep belief network for short-term load forecasting considering demand-side management. *IEEE Trans. Power Syst.* **2019**, *35*, 1531–1538. [CrossRef]
13. Dedinec, A.; Filiposka, S.; Kocarev, L. Deep belief network based electricity load forecasting: An analysis of Macedonian case. *Energy* **2016**, *115*, 1688–1700. [CrossRef]
14. Chen, K.J.; Chen, K.L.; Wang, Q.; He, Z.; Hu, J.; He, J. Short-term load forecasting with deep residual network. *IEEE Trans. Smart Grid* **2018**, *10*, 3943–3953. [CrossRef]
15. Ergen, T.; Kozat, S.S. Efficient online learning algorithms based on LSTM neural networks. *IEEE Trans. Neural Netw. Learn. Syst.* **2017**, *29*, 3772–3783. [PubMed]
16. Greff, K.; Srivastava, R.K.; Koutník, J.; Steunebrink, B.R.; Schmidhuber, J. LSTM: A search space odyssey. *IEEE Trans. Neural Netw. Learn. Syst.* **2016**, *28*, 2222–2232. [CrossRef]
17. Feng, Y.; Zhang, T.; Sah, A.P.; Han, L.; Zhang, Z. Using appearance to predict pedestrian trajectories through disparity-guided attention and convolutional LSTM. *IEEE Trans. Veh. Technol.* **2021**, *70*, 7480–7494. [CrossRef]
18. Ergen, T.; Kozat, S.S. Online training of LSTM networks in distributed systems for variable length data sequences. *IEEE Trans. Neural Netw. Learn. Syst.* **2017**, *29*, 5159–5165. [CrossRef]
19. Yang, Y.; Zhou, J.; Ai, J.; Bin, Y.; Hanjalic, A.; Shen, H.T.; Ji, Y. Video captioning by adversarial LSTM. *IEEE Trans. Image Process.* **2018**, *27*, 5600–5612. [CrossRef]
20. Gao, L.; Guo, Z.; Zhang, H.; Xu, X.; Shen, H.T. Video captioning with attention-based LSTM and semantic consistency. *IEEE Trans. Multimedia* **2017**, *19*, 2045–2055. [CrossRef]
21. Sano, A.; Chen, W.; Martinez, D.L.; Taylor, S.; Picard, R.W. Multimodal ambulatory sleep detection using LSTM recurrent neural networks. *IEEE J. Biomed. Health Inform.* **2018**, *23*, 1607–1617. [CrossRef]
22. Sahin, S.O.; Kozat, S.S. Nonuniformly sampled data processing using LSTM networks. *IEEE Trans. Neural Netw. Learn. Syst.* **2018**, *30*, 1452–1462. [CrossRef]
23. Mohan, N.; Soman, K.; Kumar, S.S. A data-driven strategy for short-term electric load forecasting using dynamic mode decomposition model. *Appl. Energy* **2018**, *232*, 229–244. [CrossRef]
24. Tang, X.; Dai, Y.; Wang, T.; Chen, Y. Short-term power load forecasting based on multi-layer bidirectional recurrent neural network. *IET Gener. Transm. Distrib.* **2019**, *13*, 3847–3854. [CrossRef]
25. Wang, Y.; Shen, Y.; Mao, S.; Chen, X.; Zou, H. LASSO and LSTM Integrated Temporal Model for Short-Term Solar Intensity Forecasting. *IEEE Internet Things J.* **2018**, *6*, 2933–2944. [CrossRef]
26. Ospina, J.; Newaz, A.; Faruque, M.O. Forecasting of PV plant output using hybrid wavelet-based LSTM-DNN structure model. *IET Renew. Power Gener.* **2019**, *13*, 1087–1095. [CrossRef]

27. Yu, Y.; Cao, J.; Zhu, J. An LSTM short-term solar irradiance forecasting under complicated weather conditions. *IEEE Access* **2019**, *7*, 145651–145666. [CrossRef]
28. Hong, Y.Y.; Martinez, J.J.F.; Fajardo, A.C. Day-ahead solar irradiation forecasting utilizing gramian angular field and convolutional long short-term memory. *IEEE Access* **2020**, *8*, 18741–18753. [CrossRef]
29. Zhou, B.; Ma, X.; Luo, Y.; Yang, D. Wind power prediction based on LSTM networks and nonparametric kernel density estimation. *IEEE Access* **2019**, *7*, 165279–165292. [CrossRef]
30. Abdel-Nasser, M.; Mahmoud, K. Accurate photovoltaic power forecasting models using deep LSTM-RNN. *Neural Comput. Appl.* **2019**, *31*, 2727–2740. [CrossRef]
31. Quek, Y.T.; Woo, W.L.; Logenthiran, T. Load disaggregation using one-directional convolutional stacked long short-term memory recurrent neural network. *IEEE Syst. J.* **2019**, *14*, 1395–1404. [CrossRef]

Article

Short-Term Load Forecasting Using an Attended Sequential Encoder-Stacked Decoder Model with Online Training

Sylwia Henselmeyer [1,*] and Marcin Grzegorzek [2]

1 Siemens AG, Humboldtstr. 59, 90459 Nuremberg, Germany
2 Institute of Medical Informatics, University of Lubeck, 23562 Lubeck, Germany; marcin.grzegorzek@uni-luebeck.de
* Correspondence: sylwia.henselmeyer@siemens.com

Abstract: The paper presents a new approach for the prediction of load active power 24 h ahead using an attended sequential encoder and stacked decoder model with Long Short-Term Memory cells. The load data are owned by the New York Independent System Operator (NYISO) and is dated from the years 2014–2017. Due to dynamics in the load patterns, multiple short pieces of training on pre-filtered data are executed in combination with the transfer learning concept. The evaluation is done by direct comparison with the results of the NYISO forecast and additionally under consideration of several benchmark methods. The results in terms of the Mean Absolute Percentage Error range from 1.5% for the highly loaded New York City zone to 3% for the Mohawk Valley zone with rather small load consumption. The execution time of a day ahead forecast including the training on a personal computer without GPU accounts to 10 s on average.

Keywords: short-term load forecast; Artificial Neural Network; deep neural network; recurrent neural network; attention; encoder decoder; online training

1. Introduction

Load forecasts are substantial in several areas of power network operation independently of the voltage level. With the increasing number of renewables and thus more volatility and dynamics in the network, the task of load forecasting becomes even more important. Errors in forecasts have direct financial consequences on the utilities and in the long-term on their customers. They also may lead to an inexcusable waste of the green power in the case it has to be curtailed due to network congestions.

Load forecasts are usually subdivided into three categories concerning the length of the prediction horizon:

- short-term: from a few minutes until one week ahead
- mid-term: from one week until one year ahead
- long-term: from one year until several years ahead

Short-term load forecasts are used to guarantee a safe and optimal real-time network operation (prevention of network violations, unit commitment, and economic dispatch). Mid-term load forecasts are more important for planning maintenance tasks, load redispatch, and securing a balanced load and generation. Long-term forecasts are mainly relevant for network reassembling and expansion.

In the area of short-term load forecasting, two basic groups of methods have been established, i.e., methods based on statistics and so-called intelligent approaches [1]. Statistical methods are usually easy to implement and provide quick results. A standard method from the group of statistical approaches is multiple regression [2,3]. It can cope with changes in the load data due to trending or seasonal impacts and it can include in the forecast model different kinds of independent variables such as weather and calendar or the load data from previous time instances. To guarantee good prediction results, training

data from at least one year before the forecast begins is required. Other well-established statistical forecast methods are General Exponential Smoothing with inclusion of seasonality (Holt-Winters) [4] and autoregressive integrated moving average (ARIMA) [5,6] and combination of ARIMA and Artificial Neural Networks [7]. They can consider influences resulting from changing trends, seasonal differences and irregularities in load data and work well with a limited amount of training samples. However, external variables such as weather cannot be included in their models.

Statistical methods expect an exact mathematical model of load and its influencing factors. Parameters of the model are estimated from the historical data samples. Fuzzy logic approaches from the class of intelligent techniques get along with a high-level model specification expressed with the "IF"-"THEN" statements [8,9]. Another group of intelligent approaches are Artificial Neural Networks (ANNs) [10,11]. They require the definition of the neural network to be used and pairs of input and output data. Since they can approximate any function hidden in the data, they are very well suited for tasks where an explicit model description is too complicated or the underlying function undergoes frequent changes which are difficult to capture such as for example in load forecasting in electric power networks with a high number of renewable sources.

With the advances in the research and the application of neural networks, the classical multi-perceptron networks (MPN) [12,13] are more and more replaced by recurrent or convolutional networks or combinations of these. Recurrent neural networks can represent time dependency by sharing the hidden layers of subsequent time steps. From this category, especially Gated Recurrent Units (GRU) [14] and the even more powerful Long Short-Term Memory (LSTM) networks [15] and their combined usage with convolutional networks [11,16], the Genetic Algorithm (GA) and Particle Swarm Optimization (PSO) for hyperparameter search [17,18] shall be mentioned. Different than simple recurrent networks, these architectures do not experience the so-called gradient vanishing or exploding problems [19] and are to some extent able to memorize longer time series sequences and provide therefore superior results over MPLs or simple recurrent architectures.

Lately, originated from the research on machine translation problems also encoder-decoder architectures are being applied to the load forecast problem. Ref. [20] used it for the prediction of the load heat. The basic idea is to encode the information required for the forecast execution before passing it to the actual forecast model. This decoupling is crucial for machine translation and shows however good effects while applied to time series prediction problems. An extension of this architecture is the incorporation of the attention mechanism as introduced by Bahdanau in [21] in the area of natural language processing. The attention approach allows for choosing those encoder states which may be most influential for the prediction of the next decoder state. Ref. [22] applied the attention model with Bahdanau attention [21] to the load forecasting using Vanilla, GRU, and LSTM cells achieving in general superior results over non attended sequence to sequence models. In [23] multi-headed attention together with a seasonal decomposition and trend adjustment is used. Ref. [24] uses the classic combination of attended encoder-decoder model with GRU cells as proposed by [21]. Additionally, to simplify the choice of the hyperparameters the Bayesian optimization is applied.

The goal of the presented approach is the development of an improved attended encoder-decoder architecture and its application to the problem of short-term load forecasting considering the increasing number of renewable sources. Before passing to the model, the inputs of the encoder and decoder are weighted using a one-dimensional convolutional neural network. This operation allows for filtering out features that have a temporarily lower correlation with the load power to predict. Additionally, a novel online training based on its core of the concept of transfer learning is presented [25–27].

The scientific contribution of the presented paper is therefore an improved attended sequential encoder-stacked decoder model applied to the problem of short-term load prediction with:

- a novel and simplified definition of the attention scoring function

- a novel online training procedure for sequence data on the base of transfer learning. This training procedure is especially important in the field of very dynamically changing load patterns.
- a high accuracy achieved on real data provided by NYISO
- an evaluation with different methods including linear regression, Hidden Markov Models and different recurrent neural network architectures

In the next Section 2.1, the data set is discussed along with the feature selection. In Sections 2.2 and 2.3 the definitions of a recurrent network, an LSTM, encoder-decoder model and attention are compiled. Using these definitions, the method is described in Section 2.4. The results obtained by the proposed approach are evaluated together with the results available from NYISO and with additional benchmark methods in Section 3. The conclusions can be found in the final Section 4.

2. Materials and Methods

2.1. Data Used

The data used for training and evaluation of the approach is owned by the New York Independent System Operator (NYISO) and can be freely accessed [28]. It has been already used in [29] and therefore it will be possible to compare the results of both approaches. NYISO's data consists of integrated hourly load forecasts and corresponding measurements of active load power. Moreover, load information, NYISO additionally offers time series representing the price for power delivery, losses, and congestion in USD and forecasts of ambient and wet bulb temperature in Fahrenheit produced by different weather stations.

The NYISO data set is almost complete (with a few missing inputs) for all eleven zones. Because it includes also the forecast results of the utility, it is very adequate for research purposes.

The training, test, and evaluation data used in the presented approach contain load, temperature, and wet bulb time series from the years 2013 until 2015, 2016, and 2017 respectively. The decision to not consider price information was motivated by the very low correlation between load and price data. More details related to the data set are in [29].

The most strongly correlated features are the load power and the ambient temperature. However, this relationship differs concerning the season as described in [29] and varies strongly depending on the temperature range. Figure 1 shows daily load curves for subsequent working days in May 2017 in the New York City data. Remarkable are strongly different daily peak values causing different load curve shapes. The peak values increase from 6 [GW] on 15.05.17, over 6.5 [GW] on 16.05.17 until 8 [GW] on 17.05.17.

The corresponding daily temperature curves shown in Figure 2 document the same order of increase of the peak values from 15.05.17 until 17.05.17 indicating a relationship between both variables.

Figure 3 shows this relationship which is non-linear and differs strongly for each day discussed. Because of this fact, the conclusion is self-evident, which is that the commonly used sliding window approach for the choice of the training data such as for example in [24] cannot be successful here. Instead, the choice of the training is based on similar-day approach [12,30]. The reason is that following days can have strongly differing load patterns due to changing weather conditions. Therefore, the similar day approach seems to be superior.

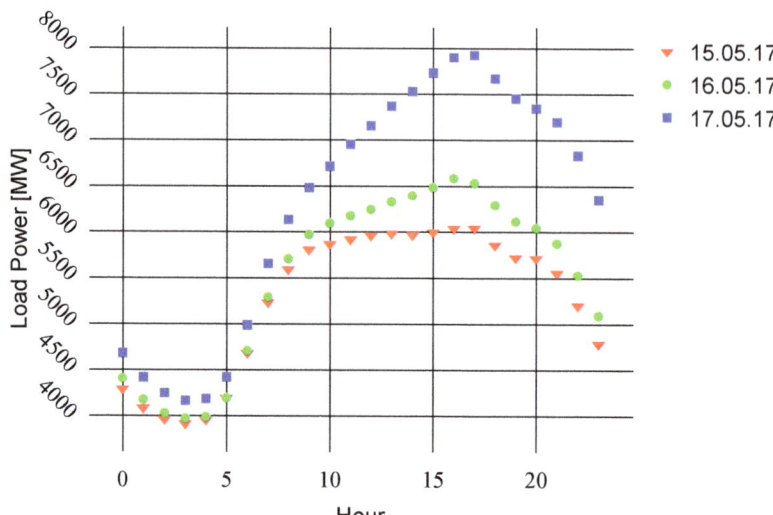

Figure 1. Load curves on subsequent days in May 2017 for the New York City data.

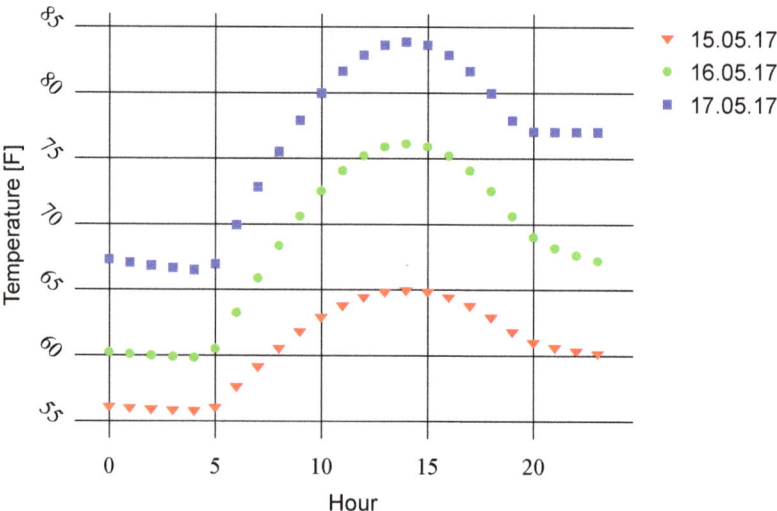

Figure 2. Temperature curves on subsequent days in May 2017 for the New York City data.

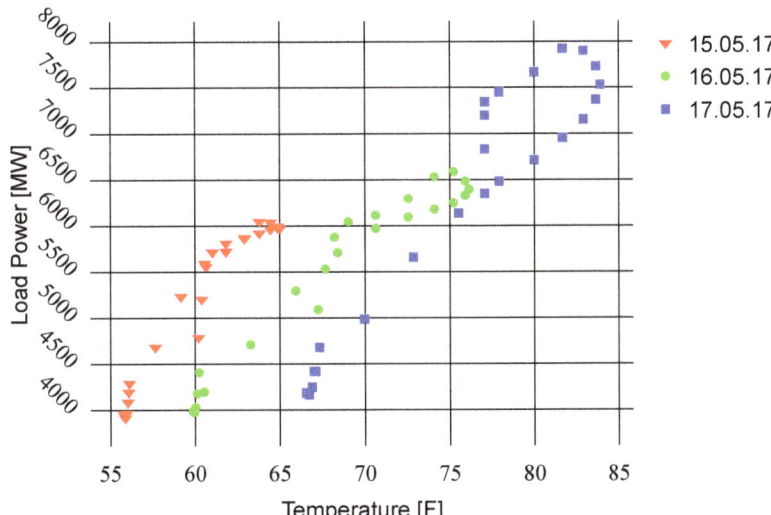

Figure 3. Correlation between temperature and load on subsequent days in May 2017 for the New York City data.

Before the training, time series with missing entries or outlier values are excluded from the data set. The training, test, and evaluation are executed on the z-score normalized data according to Equation (1) with μ the feature mean and σ feature standard deviation. For the calculation of the accuracy of the method, the data are however transformed back to the original value space.

$$z_i = \frac{x_i - \mu}{\sigma}. \qquad (1)$$

2.2. Recurrent Network with Long Short-Term Memory Cell

Recurrent networks are a group of neural networks which is developed to support the dealing of the temporal aspects in the data [31]. This is achieved while conditioning the hidden state from a time instance t not only on the input for time t but also on the hidden state at the time instance $t-1$. In simple recurrent networks also called Elman networks, three matrices are shared over all time instances. A matrix W which stores weights connecting input x_t and hidden state h_t, a matrix U containing the weights between the hidden states of subsequent time instances and the matrix V which transforms the hidden states to the network output. Accordingly, the hidden state h_t is obtained from the application of an activation function g on the weighted input and previous hidden state (2). The network output y_t is calculated using an activation function f on the weighted hidden state h_t as specified in (3).

$$h_t = g(Uh_{t-1} + Wx_t) \qquad (2)$$

$$y_t = f(Vh_t) \qquad (3)$$

One of the problems of Elman networks is that information inserted early time instances may become lost at later ones. A solution to that problem is Long Short-Term Memory (LSTM) cells which can filter out information not required at further time steps and keep the one that may be needed later on. This is achieved by adding a recurrent context layer and several weight matrices and gates in combination with the usage of the sigmoid activation function as presented in Figure 4.

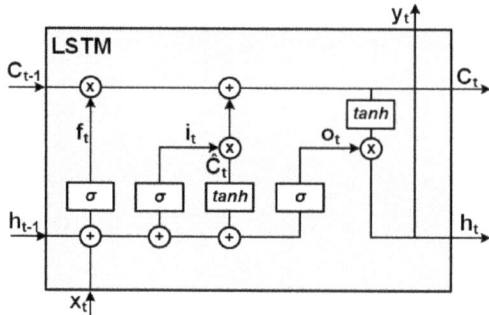

Figure 4. A Long Short-Term Memory cell.

A Long Short-Term Memory cell consists of the forget gate (4), the input gate (5), the cell update gate (6) and the output gate (7). The context C_t is obtained from the sum of the pointwise multiplication ($\otimes$) of the context from time instance $t-1$ and the forget gate and the cell update gate and the input gate (8). The output for the time instance y_t is calculated through the pointwise multiplication of the context at time instance t and the output gate (9).

$$f_t = \sigma(U^f x_t + W^f h_{t-1}) \tag{4}$$

$$i_t = \sigma(U^i x_t + W^i h_{t-1}) \tag{5}$$

$$\hat{C}_t = tanh(U^g x_t + W^g h_{t-1}) \tag{6}$$

$$o_t = \sigma(U^o x_t + W^o h_{t-1}) \tag{7}$$

$$C_t = \sigma(C_{t-1} \otimes f_t + \hat{C}_t \otimes i_t) \tag{8}$$

$$h_t = y_t = tanh(C_t \otimes o_t) \tag{9}$$

2.3. Encoder-Decoder and Attention

The encoder-decoder architecture developed in the domain of machine translation is constructed of two separated mostly recurrent networks called the encoder and the decoder. Figure 5 shows an example of such architecture using LSTM networks. The goal of the encoder network is to provide a compressed representation of the input sequence which is then passed to the decoder as the initial state. The decoder creates the output sequence subsequently one by one using the output from the preceding time instance as the input at the following one. Because of this, the encoder-decoder architecture is very well suited for time series problems.

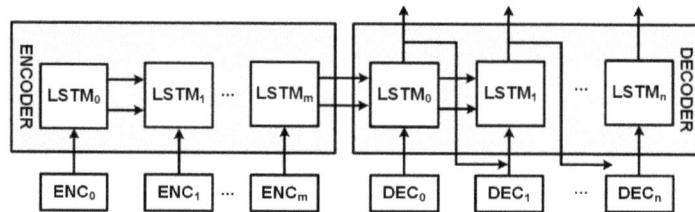

Figure 5. An example of the encoder-decoder architecture with Long Short-Term Memory cells.

The encoder-decoder model is very powerful but has however one significant limitation. While encoding the input sequence, often the information relevant for the creation of a correctly decoded output becomes lost. This is solved using the attention mechanism. At its core, the attention concept evaluates the similarity score between each encoder output and the currently produced decoder output. The goal is to draw attention to those encoder sequence parts which are most significant for the current decoder output. In [21] first the similarity score between each encoder state stored in h_j and the previous decoder output s_{t-1} is calculated (10). The softmax function is applied to the similarity coefficients (11). From that, the context vector is calculated (12) which is then concatenated with the decoder hidden state of the time instance $t-1$.

$$e_{ij} = v_a^T tanh(W_a s_{t-1} + U_a h_j) \tag{10}$$

$$\alpha_{ij} = \frac{exp(e_{ij})}{\sum_{k=1}^{T_x} exp(e_{ik})} \tag{11}$$

$$c_i = \sum_{j=1}^{T_x} \alpha_{ij} h_j \tag{12}$$

Using these equations, the attention is drawn to those parts of the encoder which are most significant while decoding the ith element of the sequence.

2.4. Application of the Attended Encoder-Decoder to the Short-Term Load Forecasting

2.4.1. Training Data

As mentioned in Section 2.1, the training data consists not of n recent days like it is established through the sliding window approach. It contains n most similar days to the day under forecast. The similarity of two days day_i and day_j is expressed by the Equation (13) and it considers the weighted Euclidean distance $d(day_i, day_j)$ between the features measured at that days. Most similar days have the smallest distance between the respective features.

$$d(day_i, day_j) = \sqrt{\sum_{k=0}^{N} w_k (f_{i,k} - f_{j,k})^2} \tag{13}$$

The weight allows for larger differences in features that are wider spread and for smaller differences in those which are contained within a narrow interval.

$$w_k = \frac{1}{|f_k^{max} - f_k^{min}|} \tag{14}$$

The feature set used for filtering of the most similar days consists of:

- daily minimum ambient temperature and wet bulb
- daily maximum ambient temperature and wet bulb
- daily minimum next day ambient temperature and wet bulb
- load power one hour before the intended forecast start before forecast start
- the type of the day (working day, weekend or holiday)
- the length of the day
- the type of the day concerning the ambient temperature (hot, cold, regular day)

To predict the hourly load curve for the next day, data of 96 most similar training days is used.

2.4.2. Application of Encoder-Decoder Architecture

The encoder accepts inputs for the last 24 h before the forecast day as shown in Figure 6. The decoder is fed with hourly chunks of the time-series data related to hourly ambient temperature, hourly wet bulb, the type of the day, etc. at the forecast day and the output of the decoder cell at the previous time instance (except the first decoded time step).

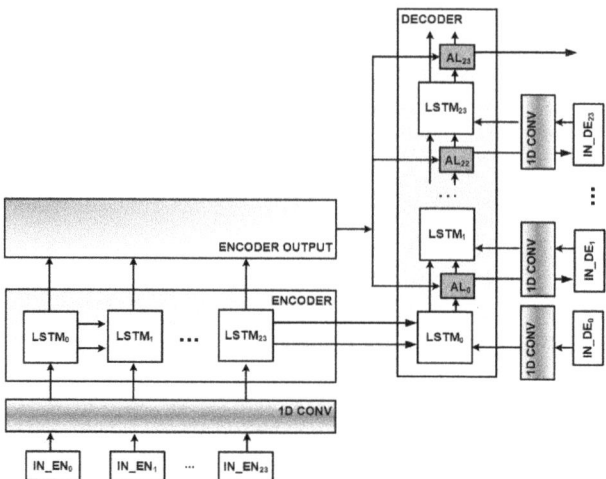

Figure 6. Artifitial neural network architecture for load forecasting.

Each encoder and decoder input consists of:

- the hour h,
- the load power from hour $h-1$ (for decoder the previous predicted value),
- the ambient temperature and wet bulb from hour h,
- the day of the week (0–6),
- the type of the day concerning the temperature (hot, cold, regular),
- the type of the day concerning holiday or working day,
- the length of the day

The usage of the load power alone as encoder input as done in [24] increased the prediction error, therefore it was not applied here. The encoder and decoder input is processed with a 1D convolutional filter to account for changing relevance of the input data depending on temperature and day type.

The encoder is used as a sequential model, the decoder as a stacked architecture as shown in Figure 6. During the test, it turned out that it is beneficial concerning the forecast error to apply a separate convolution and attention layer for each decoded instance. This might be related to the varying correlation between the encoder outputs and the decoder output at time t.

2.4.3. Attention Score Function

During the development of the algorithm, a simplified score function showed slightly better results. In Equation (15), the absolute difference between the encoder output h of the dimension N and the last decoder output s_{t-1} adjusted to the dimension of the encoder is calculated. Afterwards the softmax function is applied twice (16) and (17). The first time, to map the differences obtained from Equation (15) to the interval $[0, 1]$. The second time, to assign small differences between the decoder and encoder output to the upper part of the interval $[0, 1]$ and larger differences to the lower part (17). The final context vector is obtained in (18) as a sum over the time dimension. The decoder state for which the attention is applied is concatenated with the context vector. Finally, a dense layer is used to adjust the size of the concatenated vector to the output produced by the LSTM cell.

$$e_{ij} = |h - s_{t-1 \times N}| \tag{15}$$

$$\alpha_{ij} = \frac{exp(e_{ij})}{\sum_{k=1}^{T_x} exp(e_{ik})} \tag{16}$$

$$\beta_{ij} = \frac{exp(1-\alpha_{ij})}{\sum_{k=1}^{T_x} exp(1-\alpha_{ik})} \tag{17}$$

$$c_i = \sum_{j=1}^{T_x} \beta_{ij} h_j \tag{18}$$

In this formulation, only one weight matrix is required instead of three matrices as specified in (10). The forecast error while using both formulations of attention is however similar.

2.4.4. Online Training—A Piecewise Learning of the Underlying Function

The standard training approach as applied for example in natural language processing consists of a choice of representative training and validation data. The goal is to learn the approximation of the underlying function in one training procedure and to use the model for a longer period. The validation data are used to control the progress and the quality of the training. Such holistic training procedures can be quite a time-consuming one depending on the complexity of the function to be learned expressed in the network architecture and the number of training data required. Additional problems arise if there is not enough representative training data available or there is a sudden change in the underlying function which is not captured in the chosen training data. In load forecasting, holidays and abnormal days (very cold or very hot) are usually underrepresented and there is no simple method to create artificial data without prior knowledge of the underlying function. Due to the increasing number of renewables and prosumers, load patterns are subject to further unexpected changes. Therefore, there must be a possibility to train the network fast with a limited amount of training data.

In the presented approach, transfer learning [25,26] in combination with online training is being used to cope with time-consuming training procedure, the insufficient amount of training data especially for weekends and hot days, and changing load patterns. Figure 7 shows an overview of the training and inference procedure.

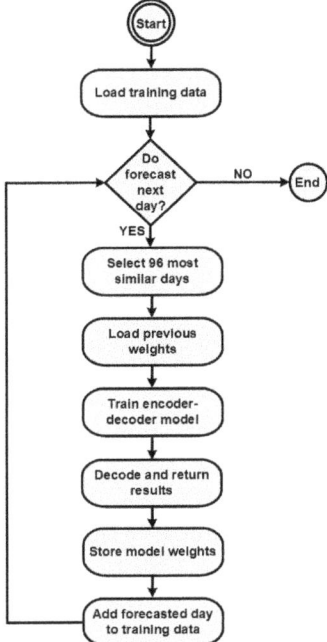

Figure 7. Overview of the applied algorithm for training and inference.

The preprocessed training data are loaded. If the forecast for the next day's load power shall be executed, the most similar days are picked. If available, the weights from the previous day are loaded into the model. The encoder-decoder model is trained for 50 epochs in one batch using the ADAM optimizer. Each training data related to the day day_j is weighted according to the Euclidean distance to the time series under prediction day_i as calculated by Equation (13) shown in (19).

$$w_j^{train} = 100 * \left| \frac{max(d(day_i, day_{1:n})) - d(day_i, day_j))}{max(d(day_i, day_{1:n}))} \right| \qquad (19)$$

No validation data are used but an early stopping criterion is applied if the value of the loss function falls below the threshold of 0.0001. The approximated piece of the underlying function follows the data in the training data set. The prediction results are decoded and returned. The weights are stored so that they can be reused as a starting point for the next training. The data of the forecasted day is added to the training data set. Using this approach, the training time is distributed in small chunks on each day to be forecasted. Additionally, the most recent data can be easily included in the training procedure capturing the most recent changes in the load pattern.

3. Results

The evaluation of the approach has been executed on the data from 2017 and it includes all NYISO zones. Table 1 compiles the name, the abbreviation, and the average load for each zone. The power consumption is varying because the zones differ concerning the size of the area, the number of residents, and the type of housing (cities, villages, rural areas). New York City is the zone with the highest number of residents. The power consumption for that area is accordingly high. Mohawk Valley on the other side, has a relatively large area, a small number of residents and therefore a significantly smaller load [28].

Table 1. NYISO load zones.

Zone Name	Zone ID	Average Load [MW]
Capital	CAPITL	1450
Central	CENTRL	1900
Dunwoodie	DUNWOOD	780
Genese	GENESE	1200
Hudson Valley	HUD VL	1200
Long Island	LONGIL	2500
Millwood	MILL VD	770
Mohawk Valley	MHK VL	980
New York City	NYC	6000
North	NORTH	590
West	WEST	1800

The results obtained from the sequential encoder-stacked decoder with attention (SESDA) are evaluated together with the results of three other methods. First of them is the Hidden Markov Model approach from [29]. The Hidden Markov Models used there were created online using the data directly without any training procedure. Additionally, the results of the NYISO are taken into account [28,32]. The third benchmark is a linear regression method from [3] and is named Tao's Vanilla Benchmark. It already has served as a benchmark for the GEFCom2012 load forecast competition and was under the first 25% best results of that competition [33].

The prediction error is measured by the Mean Absolute Percentage Error (MAPE) which is specified by Equation (20), with M as measured value and P as the predicted value.

$$MAPE = \frac{100\%}{n} \sum_{t=1}^{n} \left| \frac{M_t - P_t}{M_t} \right| \qquad (20)$$

Figure 8 compiles the forecast error for 2017 delivered by all considered methods for each NYISO load zone. The attended sequential encoder-stacked decoder (SESDA) achieves the best results for all zones. It is, however, closely followed by the Hidden Markov Model with no training. The NYISO approach which combines regression with the usage of neural networks outperforms Tao's Vanilla Benchmark but seems to have some problems with the low load zone MHK VL. For this zone, all approaches deliver relatively high error which may be related to quite a wide area (15,230 square kilometers) and a small population of that zone.

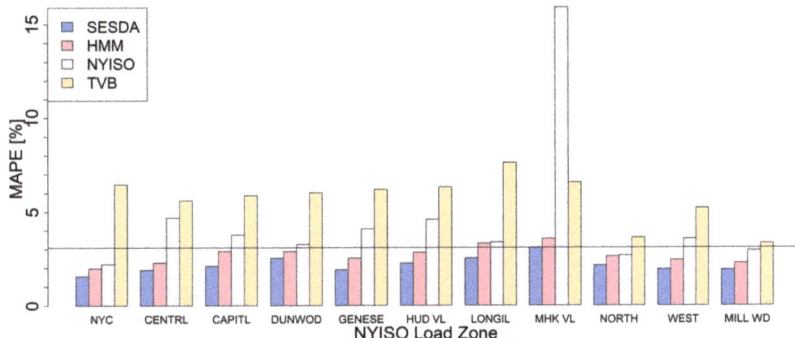

Figure 8. Evaluation of the 24 h ahead forecast error in 2017.

Figure 9 compares the daily MAPE for 2017 in New York City calculated using the two best approaches: SESDA and HMM. The SESDA approach returns a smaller error. The largest MAPE value for HMM is around 20% around 139th day of the year. Generally, the highest HMM errors are concentrated between May and September. The highest attended sequential encoder-stacked decoder error is around 10%. It occurs on holidays, on 4 July 2017 and 25 December 2017. Moreover, the higher forecast error on average, the HMM approach delivers also more and higher error peaks on problematic days.

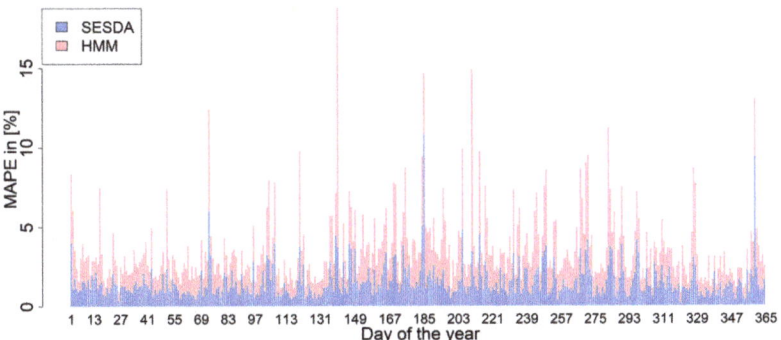

Figure 9. Daily MAPE of a 24 h ahead forecast in NYC for 2017.

Figure 10 compiles the results of SESDA and HMM evaluated for each day of 2017 in the load zone Mohawk Valley (MHK VL). The highest error delivered by the SESDA approach is around 10% and occurs on around the 165 and the 275th day of the year. The HMM produces the highest error of around 20% also around 165. day of the year. On several days of the year, the MAPE returned by the HMM exceeds the 10% limit. The SESDA approach delivers therefore more stable results with significantly smaller error peaks.

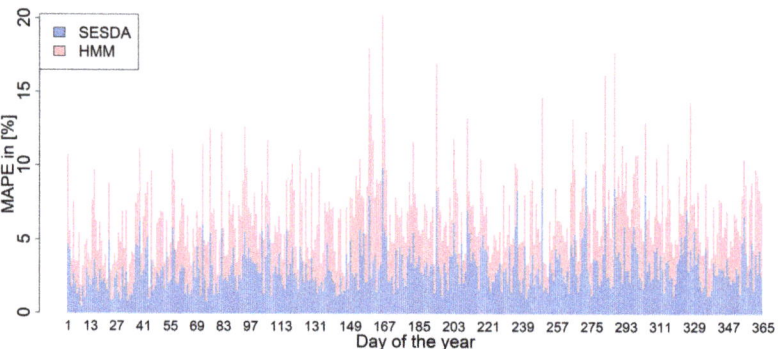

Figure 10. Daily MAPE of a 24 h ahead forecast in MHK VL for 2017.

Figure 11 shows forecast errors in New York City according to the hour of the day. For each hour the SESDA model outperforms the HMM reducing significantly the forecast errors.

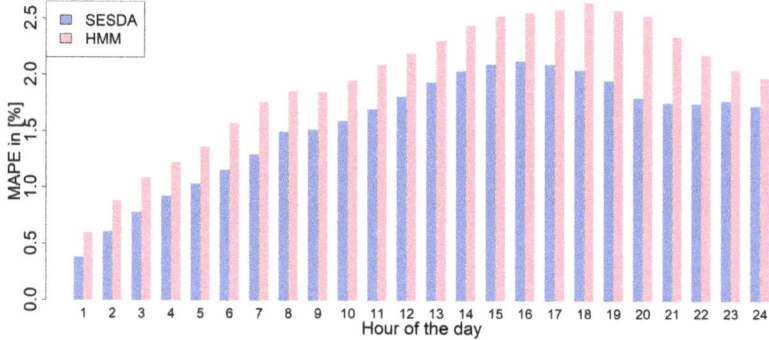

Figure 11. Hourly MAPE of 24 h ahead forecast in NYC for 2017.

Table 2 shows the evaluation of different ANN approaches on the NYC data set. Among all approaches, the best results are achieved with the sequential encoder and stacked decoder architecture. Sequential encoder-decoder with attention performs only a little better than the sequential encoder-decoder without attention because it shares the attention layer for all time instances. Sequential encoder-decoder without attention performs only slightly better than the LSTM network. The reason is too strong context vector compression in a 24 instances encoder. The LSTM network used for the evaluation consists of 24 inputs. The 24th input is the predicted one. The model is trained for each prediction hour separately. The Nonlinear Autoregressive Network with Exogenous inputs (NARX) [19] shows the worst results. It has been implemented using 24 dense networks for every prediction hour each.

The encoder-decoder method has been evaluated on a personal computer with Intel Core i5-6300U CPU@2.40 GHz and 32 GB RAM. For the implementation, the Python programming language along with the Tensorflow [34] and Keras libraries [35] has been used. An average execution time for 24 h ahead forecast took around 10 s (including loading test data, picking the most similar data, loading the weights into the model, training, and inference). The required amount of time is around 5 times larger in comparison to the HMM approach [29].

Table 2. Results of different ANN approaches for NYC zone.

Method Name	MAPE
Sequential Encoder Stacked Decoder with Attention	1.52
Sequential Encoder-Decoder with Attention	1.66
Sequential Encoder-Decoder	1.72
LSTM	1.75
NARX	2.16

4. Conclusions

The presented approach uses a sequential encoder-stacked decoder architecture in combination with attention (SESDA) to predict load power 24 h ahead. The training data are collected using the smallest Euclidean distance between the daily features of the forecasted day and the days in the past. For each forecast day, a fast online training is executed using the filtered most similar past data. The features included in the encoder-decoder model range from hourly weather parameters, calendar data to the load demand from the previous hour.

The algorithm achieves the best results in comparison with the benchmark methods which include Linear Regression, a combination of Linear Regression and the usage of Neural Networks, and the Hidden Markov Model approach. Although the difference between the MAPE values of HMM and the encoder-decoder model is not as large as the difference between HMM and Linear Regression, the HMM seems less stable than the proposed architecture. However, the error reduction comes at a cost of the increased forecast execution time.

One of the limitations of the algorithm is the requirement of the availability of pairs of consecutive daily data for the training due to the network architecture (encoder-decoder model). For data with many gaps related to whole days, the algorithm may perform less successfully. Additionally, the algorithm requires on average 96 historical time series including the previous days for the training. If the requirement is not fulfilled, the prediction error will increase depending on the number of data provided. However, today's utilities have mostly access to the required amount of data.

The approach can be extended to support longer time horizons. However, in this case some modifications of the architecture must be applied. First of all, the length of the encoded sequence must be adjusted to the length of the forecast sequence. Additionally, the self-attention mechanism inside of the decoder has to be used to consider the impact of the preceding predicted values on the following ones due to the longer time horizon.

In future work, the authors will draw their attention to the application of reinforcement learning to the area of short-term load forecasting.

Author Contributions: Conceptualization, S.H.; methodology, S.H. and M.G.; software, S.H.; validation, S.H. and M.G.; formal analysis, S.H. and M.G.; writing-original draft preparation, S.H.; writing-review and editing, S.H. and M.G. All authors have read and agreed to the published version of the manuscript.

Funding: This research received no external funding.

Institutional Review Board Statement: This article does not contain any studies with humans or animals.

Informed Consent Statement: This article does not contain any studies with humans or animals.

Data Availability Statement: https://www.nyiso.com/load-data (accessed on 26 May 2021).

Conflicts of Interest: The authors declare no conflict of interest.

Sample Availability: A prototype of the attended encoder-decoder is provided at https://github.com/sylwia-lab/LoadForecastEncoderDecoder/ (accessed on 26 May 2021).

References

1. Srivastava, A.K.; Pandey, A.S. Short-term load forecasting methods: A review. In Proceedings of the 2016 International Conference on Emerging Trends in Electrical Electronics & Sustainable Energy Systems (ICETEESES), Sultanpur, India, 11–12 March 2016; pp. 130–138.
2. Papalexopoulos, A.D.; Hesterberg, T.C. A regression-based approach to short-term system load forecasting. *IEEE Trans. Power Syst.* **1990**, *5*, 1535–1547. [CrossRef]
3. Hong, T. *Short Term Electric Load Forecasting*; North Carolina State University: Raleigh, NC, USA, 2010.
4. Trull, O.; García-Díaz, J.C.; Troncoso, A. Application of Discrete-Interval Moving Seasonalities to Spanish Electricity Demand Forecasting during Easter. *Energies* **2019**, *12*, 1083. [CrossRef]
5. Shilpa, G.; Sheshadri, G. Short-Term Load Forecasting Using ARIMA Model For Karnataka State Electrical Load. *Int. J. Eng. Res. Dev.* **2017**, *13*, 75–79.
6. Mpawenimana, I.; Pegatoquet, A.; Roy, V.; Rodriguez, L.; Belleudy, C. A comparative study of LSTM and ARIMA for energy load prediction with enhanced data preprocessing. In Proceedings of the 2020 IEEE Sensors Applications Symposium (SAS), Sundsvall, Sweden, 2–4 August 2020; pp. 1–6.
7. Singhal, R.; Choudhary, N.K.; Singh, N. Short-Term Load Forecasting Using Hybrid ARIMA and Artificial Neural Network Model. In *Advances in VLSI, Communication, and Signal Processing*; Lecture Notes in Electrical Engineering; Dutta, D., Kar, H., Kumar, C., Bhadauria, V., Eds.; Springer: Berlin/Heidelberg, Germany, 2020; pp. 935–947.
8. Ganguly, P.; Kalam, A.; Zayegh, A. SHORT TERM LOAD FORECASTING USING FUZZY LOGIC. In Proceedings of the 2016 International Symposium on Electrical Engineering (ISEE), Hong Kong, China, 14 December 2017; pp. 1–7.
9. Al-Kandari, A.M.; Soliman, S.A.; El-Hawary, M. Fuzzy short-term electric load forecasting. *Int. J. Electr. Power Energy Syst.* **2004**, *26*, 111–122. [CrossRef]
10. Ding, N.; Benoit, C.; Foggia, G.; Besanger, Y.; Wurtz, F. Neural Network-Based Model Design for Short-Term Load Forecast in Distribution Systems. *IEEE Trans. Power Syst.* **2016**, *31*, 72–81. [CrossRef]
11. Tian, C.; Ma, J.; Zhang, C.; Zhan, P. A Deep Neural Network Model for Short-Term Load Forecast Based on Long Short-Term Memory Network and Convolutional Neural Network. *Energies* **2018**, *11*, 3493. [CrossRef]
12. Peng, T.M.; Hubele, N.F.; Karady, G. Advancement Short-Term in the Application of Neural Networks for Load Forecasting. *Trans. Power Syst.* **1992**, *7*, 250–257. [CrossRef]
13. Kiartzis, S.; Bakirtzis, A.; Petridis, V. Short-term load forecasting using neural networks. *Electr. Power Syst. Res.* **1995**, *33*, 1–6. [CrossRef]
14. Wu, W.; Liaob, W.; Miaoa, J.; Du, G. Using Gated Recurrent Unit Network to Forecast Short-Term Load Considering Impact of Electricity Price. In Proceedings of the 10th International Conference on Applied Energy (ICAE2018), Hong Kong, China, 22–25 August 2018; pp. 3369–3374.
15. Zheng, J.; Xu, C.; Zhang, Z.; Li, X. Electric Load Forecasting in Smart Grid Using Long-Short-Term-Memory based Recurrent Neural Network. In Proceedings of the 2017 51st Annual Conference on Information Sciences and Systems (CISS), Baltimore, MD, USA, 22–24 March 2017; pp. 1–6.
16. Kuo, P.H.; Huang, C.J. A High Precision Artificial Neural Networks Model for Short-Term Energy Load Forecasting. *Energies* **2018**, *11*, 213. [CrossRef]
17. Bouktif, S.; Fiaz, A.; Ouni, A.; Serhani, M.A. Optimal Deep Learning LSTM Model for Electric Load Forecasting using Feature Selection and Genetic Algorithm: Comparison with Machine Learning Approaches. *Energies* **2018**, *11*, 1636. [CrossRef]
18. Bouktif, S.; Fiaz, A.; Ouni, A.; Serhani, M.A. Multi-Sequence LSTM-RNN Deep Learning and Metaheuristics for Electric Load Forecasting. *Energies* **2020**, *13*, 391. [CrossRef]
19. Bianchi, F.M.; Maiorino, E.; Kampffmeyer, M.C.; Rizzi, A.; Jenssen, R. *Recurrent Neural Networks for Short-Term Load Forecasting. An Overview and Comparative Analysis*; Springer: Cham, Switzerland, 2017.
20. Lu, K.; Meng, X.R.; Sun, W.X.; Zhang, R.G.; Han, Y.K.; Gao, S.; Su, D. GRU-based Encoder-Decoder for Short-term CHP Heat Load Forecast. *IOP Conf. Ser. Mater. Sci. Eng.* **2018**, *392*, 1–7. [CrossRef]
21. Bahdanau, D.; Cho, K.H.; Bengio, Y. Neural Machine Translation by Jointly Learning to Align and Translate. *arXiv* **2015**, arXiv:1409.0473.
22. Sehovac, L.; Grolinger, K. Deep Learning for Load Forecasting: Sequence to Sequence Recurrent Neural Networks with Attention. *IEEE Access* **2020**, *8*, 36411–36426. [CrossRef]
23. Meng, Z.; Xu, X. A Hybrid Short-Term Load Forecasting Framework with an Attention-Based Encoder–Decoder Network Based on Seasonal and Trend Adjustment. *Energies* **2019**, *12*, 4612. [CrossRef]
24. Jin, X.B.; Zheng, W.Z.; Kong, J.L.; Wang, X.Y.; Bai, Y.T.; Su, T.L.; Lin, S. Deep-Learning Forecasting Method for Electric Power Load via Attention-Based Encoder-Decoder with Bayesian Optimization. *Energies* **2021**, *14*, 1596. [CrossRef]
25. Pan, S.J.; Yang, Q. A Survey on Transfer Learning. *IEEE Trans. Knowl. Data Eng.* **2010**, *22*, 1345–1359. [CrossRef]
26. Hooshmand, A.; Sharma, R. Energy Predictive Models with Limited Data using Transfer Learning. *arXiv* **2019**, arXiv:1906.02646. .
27. Ribeiro, M.; Grolinger, K.; ElYamany, H.; Higashino, W.A.; Capretz, M. Transfer learning with seasonal and trend adjustment for cross-building energy forecasting. *Energy Build.* **2018**, *165*, 352–363. [CrossRef]
28. NYISO. Load Data. 2019. Available online: https://www.nyiso.com/load-data (accessed on 26 May 2021).

29. Henselmeyer, S.; Grzegorzek, M. Short-term load forecasting with discrete state Hidden Markov Models. *J. Intell. Fuzzy Syst.* **2020**, *38*, 2273–2284. [CrossRef]
30. Mandal, P.; Senjyu, T.; Urasaki, N.; Funabashi, T. A neural network based several-hour-ahead electric load forecasting using similar days approach. *Electr. Power Energy Syst.* **2006**, *28*, 367–373. [CrossRef]
31. Yurafsky, D.; Martin, J. *Speech and Language Processing*; Prentice Hall: Upper Saddle River, NJ, USA, 2008.
32. Operations, N.E.M. Day Ahead Scheduling Manual. 2017. Available online: https://www.nyiso.com/documents/20142/2923301/dayahd_schd_mnl.pdf/0024bc71-4dd9-fa80-a816-f9f3e26ea53a (accessed on 26 May 2021).
33. Liu, B. *Short Term Load Forecasting with Recency Effect: Models and Applications*; ProQuest, UMI Dissertation Publishing: Ann Arbor, MI, USA, 2016.
34. Abadi, M.; Agarwal, A.; Barham, P.; Brevdo, E.; Chen, Z.; Citro, C.; Corrado, G.S.; Davis, A.; Dean, J.; Devin, M.; et al. TensorFlow: Large-Scale Machine Learning on Heterogeneous Systems. *arXiv* **2015**, arXiv:1603.04467.
35. Chollet, F. Keras. 2015. Available online: https://keras.io (accessed on 26 May 2021).

Article

Forecasting of Electrical Generation Using Prophet and Multiple Seasonality of Holt–Winters Models: A Case Study of Kuwait

Abdulla I. Almazrouee [1,*], Abdullah M. Almeshal [2], Abdulrahman S. Almutairi [3], Mohammad R. Alenezi [2], Saleh N. Alhajeri [1] and Faisal M. Alshammari [4]

1. Department of Manufacturing Engineering Technology, College of Technological Studies, P.A.A.E.T., P.O. Box 42325, Shuwaikh 70654, Kuwait; sn.alhajeri@paaet.edu.kw
2. Department of Electronics Engineering Technology, College of Technological Studies, P.A.A.E.T., P.O. Box 42325, Shuwaikh 70654, Kuwait; am.almeshal@paaet.edu.kw (A.M.A.); mr.alenezi@paaet.edu.kw (M.R.A.)
3. Department of Mechanical Power and Refrigeration Technology, College of Technological Studies, P.A.A.E.T., P.O. Box 42325, Shuwaikh 70654, Kuwait; asa.almutairi@paaet.edu.kw
4. Engineering and Environmental Department, Ministry of Electricity and Water, Ministries Zone 12010, Kuwait; fmnalshammari@mew.gov.kw
* Correspondence: ai.almazrouee@paaet.edu.kw

Received: 31 October 2020; Accepted: 23 November 2020; Published: 26 November 2020

Abstract: Electrical generation forecasting is essential for management and policymakers due to the crucial data provided for resource planning. This research employs the Prophet model with single and multiple regressors to forecast the electricity generation in Kuwait from 2020 to 2030. In addition, multiple seasonality Holt–Winters models were utilized as a benchmark for comparative analysis. The accuracy, generalization, and robustness of the models were assessed based on different statistical performance metrics. The triple seasonality Holt–Winters model achieved superior performance compared with the other models with $R^2 = 0.9899$ and MAPE = 1.76%, followed by the double seasonality Holt–Winters model with $R^2 = 0.9893$ and MAPE = 1.83%. Moreover, the Prophet model with multiple regressors was the third-best performing model with $R^2 = 0.9743$ and MAPE = 2.77%. The forecasted annual generation in the year 2030 resulted in 92,535,555 kWh according to the best performing model. The study provides an outlook on the medium- and long-term electrical generation. Furthermore, the impact of fuel cost is investigated based on the five forecasting models to provide an insight for Kuwait's policymakers.

Keywords: prophet model; multiple seasonality; Holt–Winters model; long-term forecasting

1. Introduction

Accurate electrical generation forecasting is essential for the management and policymakers of local and national power plants. Electric power generation is one of the complex processes where many parameters are involved and need to be optimized to deliver the electricity continuously and efficiently to the whole population [1]. On the other hand, power generation is faced with many challenges, such as environmental legislation, fluctuations in fuel prices, and the need to optimize the available resources. Moreover, different sources for power generation are used nowadays. These sources include nuclear energy, fossil fuel such as coal, natural gas, crude oil, other gasses, and renewable energy such as hydropower, solar, wind, municipal solid waste, and geothermal. Therefore, appropriate forecasting is a need for these power plants in order to support continued prosperity.

Forecasting horizons vary from short-term to mid-term and long-term horizons [2–6]. Long-term forecasting is the most complex and critical due to the different parameters involved [6,7]. Parameters include population, gross domestic product (GDP), consumer behavior, the advancement of technology, and weather temperature. Long-term forecasting is facilitated to predict the future maximum peak loads and/or annual demand and generation [3]. The forecast of maximum peak loads helps make significant decisions such as constructing new power plants and/or any expansion. On the other hand, forecasting the annual electrical generation provides critical data to define future power needs and assess logistics, such as fuel and personnel needed for the specified generation. Accurate forecasting guarantees efficient resource planning for the growing population and increasing demand for electricity that avoids over or underestimating the procurement of resources such as fuel.

Different kinds of approaches are employed for electrical load demand forecasting in the literature with several parameters in various complexity degrees to attain the best electricity demand forecasting accuracy. The methods can be categorized into two main categories: conventional models and artificial intelligence (AI) models [2–6]. Conventional methods include time series models, exponential smoothing, regression models, and gray models [2,3,8]. In contrast, artificial intelligence models include models such as machine learning (ML) models, deep learning (DL) models, genetic algorithm (GA) models, artificial neural networks (ANN) based models, and support vector regression (SVR) [2,3,8].

Various studies investigated the long-term forecasting of electricity demand from different angles using multiples approaches. Perez-Garcia and Moral-Carcedo [9] developed long-term forecasting for electricity demand in Spain until 2030, based on a simple growth decomposition scheme to identify other key factors. Torrini et al. [10] used a fuzzy logic approach to forecast Brazil's long-term annual electricity demand and extract rules from the input variables. Pessanha and Leon [11] decomposed the total electricity residential consumption in Brazil into three variables: the number of households, the average consumption of customers, and the electrification rate, and found the forecast by the product of the forecast of the three variables. Mohamed and Bodger [12] used multiple linear regression analyses to investigate the electricity consumption correlation of GDP, population, and the average price of electricity during the period 1965–1999 of New Zealand. Ardakani and Ardehali [13] developed an artificial neural network (ANN) and optimized regression models with improved particle swarm optimization (IPSO) to forecast electrical energy consumption of Iran and the U.S. for 2010–2030. Bianco et al. [14] presented different regression models based on co-integrated or static data using historical data from 1970 to 2007 to develop a long-term consumption forecasting model for Italy. Chen and Wang [15] implemented a collaborative principal component analysis and fuzzy feed-forward neural network (PCA-FFNN) methodology in addition to the partial-consensus fuzzy intersection and radial basis function network (PCFI-RBF) approach to forecast the electrical loads of Taiwan. Silva et al. [16] presented a methodology that associates hierarchical models with the bottom-up approach and the inclusion of the Bayesian inference to develop forecasting of electricity consumption for the pulp and paper industry in Brazil ranging from 2015 until 2050.

A relatively new methodology is introduced by researchers from Facebook called Prophet model [17]. It is a simple yet robust for estimation because of its structure of adjusting parameters without investigating the original model's details. It contains a decomposable time series model with three main model components: trend, holidays, and seasonality. In a recent study [18], the Prophet model outperformed the well-established Holt–Winters model in Kuwait's long-term peak load forecasting. The use of this method in forecasting is expected to spread due to its robustness and accuracy. On the other hand, recent advances are employed on the Holt–Winters model [19], which probably improves its accuracy. A recent study by Jiang et al. [20] predicted the electricity consumption of a city in China by proposing a hybrid forecasting model and using the fruit fly optimization algorithm to select the optimum smoothing parameters.

One of this study's main contributions is to explore the use of the Prophet forecasting model, with single and multi-regressors, and the multi-seasonality Holt–Winters model for the long-term forecasting of electricity generation. The dataset is based on the State of Kuwait as a case study with a historical dataset from January 2015 to May 2020.

Kuwait is a country in the Middle East, and its economy is dependent on oil. The major commodities in Kuwait, such as electricity, are supported financially and owned by the government, aiming to keep them as low as possible for customers. Kuwait has eight conventional power plants located in different cities with a total installed 19,673 megawatts [21]. Electricity peak demand in Kuwait varied dramatically in the last 70 years with a generally decreasing trend. The average annual increase in the fifties was around 32%, then it decreased to 26% in the sixties to 15% in the seventies and reached around 8% in the nineties. The annual increase rate has decreased during the last twenty years and reached around 3.68% in 2019 [22–24]. There is a dramatic increase in the population and consumption per capita, as depicted in Table 1 below. The increase in electricity generation is attributed to population growth and economic development [25]. The annual energy use per capita in 2018 is 14,235 kWh, which is considered very high and among the world's highest. [21–24,26]. The average household in Kuwait consumed is reported [27] in 2014 to be about 38 MWh, which is the highest globally. The severe hot weather in summer and historically low prices are considered the main reasons for this increase. However, other factors, such as people's lifestyles, inefficient construction practices, and installed equipment, might also contribute [26].

Table 1. The growing population and per capita consumption in three decades [21].

Year	Population	Per Capita Consumption kWh/Person	Mean Annual Rate of Growth during 10 Years %
1989	2,048,000	10,295	-
1999	2,148,032	12,552	3.87%
2009	3,484,881	13,372	0.65%
2019	4,776,407	14,002	0.51%

One of the main points proposed [28] for fixing the high generation's need is to tackle the subsidized energy prices, which inspire greater electricity. Another viable idea is the use of dynamic pricing [29], which can change the pattern or reduce the quantity of people's electricity consumption. Increasing electricity tariffs is expected to be a significant contributor to change the consumption pattern of people. However, there are some difficulties in implementing these reforms due to their political nature [28]. Alajmi [30] used energy audit techniques and implemented non-retrofitting and retrofitting on a two-story educational facility that results in more than 50% annual total saving for governmental buildings. The Ministry of electrical and water, especially with the need to mitigate climate change, aims to reach a generation of 15% of renewable energy by 2035 [31]. Moreover, the government is encouraging people to use renewable energy and new technology, which might lead to decentralize the power systems and might also reduce the effect on government [22]. The introduction of new sustainable buildings and cities that implement renewable energy and efficiently use the electricity, especially with new residential cites in Kuwait, is feasible and efficient [22]. Digitalization through the use of smart meters and smart grid is also believed to provide more reduction and sustainable use of the electricity and are discussed by the Ministry of electrical and water and should come into action [22]. However, remedies for the increase in the generation and their consequences are out of this study's scope.

The continuous increase in electricity generation and the different plans of government necessitate carrying out more studies in forecasting. Studies are needed to estimate the total electricity generation for the coming years to assist the policymakers in achieving the proper decisions regarding the future. Several studies were carried out regarding long-term forecasting for Kuwait. However, most of them were about peak load forecasting [18,32–37]. Alajmi and Phelan [32] used a bottom-up approach to create a baseline for the residential sector's end-use energy profile in Kuwait until 2040. Recently, Alhajeri et al. [35] investigate the effects of COVID-19 on electrical consumption from 1st March to 30th

May. Atalla and Hunt [37] studied high residential electricity demand drivers in the Gulf Cooperation Council countries (GCC) using the time series model and suggested some recommendations to reduce the demand.

To the best of authors' knowledge, limited studies have investigated the Prophet model's use in forecasting the electricity generation. The originality of this study is that it explores the performance of prophet model with multi-regressors in long-term forecasting of electricity generation. The multi-regressors are the historical daily maximum and minimum load, temperature and population. In addition, comparative quantitative analyses with multi-seasonality Holt–Winters model is presented to assess the forecasting performance. Furthermore, the generalizability and robustness of the Prophet and Holt–Winters methods for forecasting long-term electricity generation are explored and presented. Various factors of the future are changing, such as population, weather temperatures, and peak loads, directly or indirectly related to electricity generation were taken into account in the forecasting. The study also provides and discusses the estimation of the expected future fuel consumption cost until 2030.

The paper is structured as follows. Section 2 presents a description of the Prophet and the multi-seasonality Holt–Winter models. Section 3 illustrates the results and analyses based on the performance indicators. In addition, Section 3 provides insight for policymakers on the implications of electrical generation on fuel costs.

2. Methodologies

The electrical generation's real data between January 2015 and July 2020 was attained from the Ministry of Electricity and Water (MEW) is used in this research. The data is plotted in Figure 1, showing the daily generation for approximately six years. A vivid seasonality of the data is observed with an annual maximum generation in the hot summer, especially June to August. There is an increasing trend of the generation, as noticed from Figure 1, due to the growth of population, the building of new cities, as well as economic development, and this is expected to continue in the upcoming years.

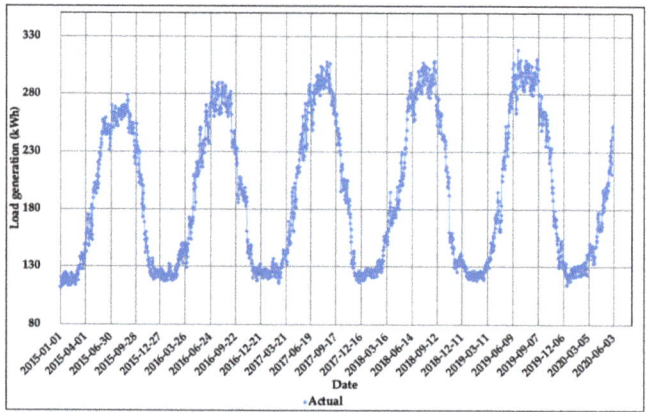

Figure 1. The actual data of generated daily loads data in Kuwait between January 2015–May 2020.

The data consists of five years with daily observations for electrical generation from January 2015 to May 2020 with 1978 data points. Taking a closer look at Figure 1, a yearly seasonality occurring within July–August, can be observed. During these months, the high electricity demand is due to Kuwait's hot summer, with temperatures reaching 55 °C. The data also reveals a weekly seasonality with low demand on Fridays and Saturdays each week due to the factories' and industries' closure on weekends. Furthermore, the third seasonality corresponds to the year's meteorological seasons and will be addressed hereafter as quarters to avoid the confusion with methods' seasonality patterns.

In this study, long-term forecasting for electrical generation for the coming ten years is aimed. Therefore, a search for models that comprise data with time-series nature with different seasonality resulted in choosing the relatively new Prophet model from Facebook and the Holt–Winters model for this work.

The relatively new Prophet model possesses some features such as tunable parameters by an expert during the analysis, which allows for fine-tuning and the ability to reach robust forecasting. The model's automatic tuning does not require a full understanding of the underlying model, making it easier to use. Limited studies are reported to use this model and proved to achieve vigorous results [18,38]. Whereas the Holt–Winters model, with different variations, is used extensively for long-term forecasting and providing excellent results [39,40].

One of the Prophet model's points of superiority is its ability to deal with missing data and reach outstanding results. The Prophet model's flexibility for complex data can be achieved using an analyst-in-the-loop feature by integrating multiple-seasonality of different periods. The availability of single and multivariate forecasting in a straightforward manner adds a new strength for the Prophet model. On the other hand, Holt–Winters deals only with univariate forecasting. There exist different Holt–Winters model variations in the literature where it was generalized to include double and triple seasonalities [41,42]. The Holt–Winter model was then generalized and introduced in literature to include n-seasonalities and was therefore known as nHWT [38]. Initialization methods of nHWT were proven to have a crucial impact on the accuracy of the forecast [19].

In this research, the multivariate Prophet forecasting model is utilized to forecast the annual load generation needed in Kuwait for the upcoming 10 years and is compared with the univariate nHWT forecasting model with initialization methods. In the next sections, the implementation of the various Prophet and Holt–Winters forecasting methods is presented in detail.

2.1. Prophet Forecasting Method

A Prophet model is used with simple or complicated time-series data that includes single or multiple seasonality, holidays, and data trends. Multiple seasonality can include different patterns, such as days, weeks, months, and years. As reported by Taylor and Letham [17], the mathematical representation of the decomposed time series model:

$$y(t) = g(t) + s(t) + h(t) + \varepsilon_t \qquad (1)$$

where $g(t)$ denotes the data trend function, $s(t)$ denotes the seasonality, and $h(t)$ denotes holidays effect that can be added within specific points of the data and as an extra regressor. The error term, ε_t, denotes any distinctive features of the data that are not fitted by the model.

Prophet trend function, $g(t)$, can be signified by a piecewise linear growth model or a saturating growth model. Since the electrical generation does not exhibit a saturating growth, a piecewise linear growth model is utilized as:

$$g(t) = (k + a(t)^T \delta)t + (m + a(t)^T \gamma) \qquad (2)$$

where k represents the growth rate, δ represents adjustment rate, m represents the offset parameter, and γ is the trend changepoints, s_j, and is set as $-s_j \delta_j$, with $a(t)$ defined as:

$$a_j(t) = \begin{cases} 1 & if\ t \geq s_j \\ 0 & otherwise \end{cases} \qquad (3)$$

The change points allow the analyst in the loop to adjust the resulting forecast based on a previous experience. Therefore, the trend of the forecast can be hence fine-tuned and results in an enhanced forecast. The seasonality function $s(t)$ can be modelled by Fourier series to represent daily, weekly, and yearly seasonality as well as to incorporate more complex seasonality patterns by higher order Fourier series. The seasonality function is hence written as:

$$s(t) = \sum_{n=1}^{N}\left(a_n \cos\left(\frac{2\pi nt}{P}\right) + b_n \sin\left(\frac{2\pi nt}{P}\right)\right) \quad (4)$$

where P is assumed to be 365.25 for yearly seasonality pattern. Furthermore, Prophet model allows adding extra regressors to enhance the forecast results. The holiday effects, as example, can be incorporated using $h(t)$ function and define a list of holiday dates as a matrix of regressors $Z(t)$ defined as:

$$Z(t) = [1(t \in D_1), \ldots, 1(t \in D_L)] \quad (5)$$

$$h(t) = Z(t)\kappa \quad (6)$$

with D as the set of holiday dates, $\kappa \sim \text{Normal}(0, v^2)$ with v as the holiday smoothing parameter. In this work, additional regressors were utilized and defined as the temperature, the maximum load, the minimum load, and the population to result in a more reliable forecast that reflects the growth in population and Kuwait's average temperatures.

2.2. Holt–Winters Forecasting Model

Holt–Winters models are well-established models that have two seasonal variations: additive and multiplicative types. The additive method is appropriate for fitting a time series data with a constant seasonal variation. Whereas multiplicative method is appropriate for a time series with an increasing seasonal pattern relative to the data level. The generalized Holt–Winters model was reported in literature [19,41,43]. In this research, the generalized Holt–Winters model with multiple seasonality and initialization methods is used for forecasting the electrical generation of Kuwait until 2030.

The Holt–Winters model consists of forecast equation and smoothing equations of the level, trend, and seasonality of the time series. Assuming that S_t represents the seasonality, T_t to represent the trend and that I_t corresponds seasonality, the additive trend multiplicative seasonality HW model can be defined as:

$$S_t = \alpha\left(\frac{X_t}{\prod I_{t-s_i}^i}\right) + (1-\alpha)(S_{t-1} + T_{t-1}) \quad (7)$$

$$T_t = \gamma(S_t - S_{t-1}) + (1-\gamma)T_{t-1} \quad (8)$$

$$I_t^i = \delta^i\left(\frac{X_t}{S_t \prod_{j\neq 1} I_{t-s_j}^i}\right) + (1-\delta^i)I_{t-s_i}^i \quad (9)$$

$$\hat{X}_t(k) = (S_t + kT_t)\prod_i I_{t-s_i+k}^i + \varphi_{AR}^k\left(X_t - (S_{t-1} + kT_{t-1})\prod_i I_{t-s_i}^i\right) \quad (10)$$

where S_t represents the level, T_t as the trend, I_t^i to correspond to multiple seasonality and $\hat{X}_t(k)$ is the k-step ahead forecast. The smoothing parameters are defined as α for the level smoothing, γ as the trend smoothing parameter, and δ^i as the smoothing parameters of each seasonal pattern with cycle length of S_i. The term φ_{AR}^k is an adjustment for the first autocorrelation error.

There exist various initialization methods for the level, trend, and seasonality in order to enhance the forecast accuracy [19]. The trend is initialized as $T_0 = 0$ for an additive trend. Whereas the level equation is initialized by the moving average value of the dataset and is obtained by:

$$S_0 = \frac{1}{S_m}\left[\frac{X_{1+s_m} - X_1}{s_m} + \frac{X_{2+s_m} - X_2}{s_m} + \cdots + \frac{X_{2s_m} - X_{s_m}}{s_m}\right] \quad (11)$$

The seasonality is initialized by the method presented by Brockwell and Davis [39] and adopted by the National Institute of Standards (NIST) which depends on calculating the weights of the data series against the multiple seasonality pattern values. The proposed method is presented in the following steps:

Step 1: Compute the yearly average as A_m^i for each seasonality of length s_m and has a pattern of n_q times in the dataset

$$A_m^i = \frac{\sum_{j=1}^{s_i} X_{(m-1)s_i+j}}{s_i} \quad \text{for } m = 1, 2, \ldots, n_q$$

Step 2: Divide the observations by the yearly averages as:

index	1	2	...	q
1	$\frac{X_1}{A_1^i}$	$\frac{X_{s_i+1}}{A_2^i}$	...	$\frac{X_{s_i+1}}{A_q^i}$
...	...	...	...	...
s_i	$\frac{X_{s_i1}}{A_1^i}$	$\frac{X_{2s_i}}{A_2^i}$	...	$\frac{X_{m_1 s_i+1}}{A_{m_i}^i}$

Step 3: Write each seasonality as:

$$I_{1-s_i}^{*(i)} = \frac{\frac{X_1}{A_1^i} + \frac{X_{s_i+1}}{A_2^i} + \cdots + \frac{X_{(m_i-1)s_i+1}}{A_{m_i}^i}}{m_i}$$

$$I_{1-s_i}^{*(i)} = \frac{\frac{X_1}{A_1^i} + \frac{X_{s_i+1}}{A_2^i} + \cdots + \frac{X_{m_i s_i+1}}{A_{m_i}^i}}{m_i}$$

Step 4: Write the seasonal indices as:

$$I_{1-s_i}^{*(i)} = \begin{cases} I_{t-s_1}^{*(i)} & i = 1, t = 1, \ldots, s_i \\ \dfrac{I_{t-s_1}^{*(i)}}{\prod_{j=1}^{i-1} I_{t-s_j}^{*(i)}} & i > 1, t = 1, \ldots, s_i \end{cases}$$

The simulation parameters are presented in Table 2 with the values of level, trend and seasonality smoothing parameters as α, γ, δ^i respectively. The seasonality smoothing parameters are presented as δ^y, δ^q and δ^w that corresponds to the yearly, quarterly, and weekly seasonality smoothing parameter values.

Table 2. Multi-seasonality Holt-Winter parameters.

Method and Seasonality	α	γ	δ^i
HWSS—yearly	0.048	0.023	$\delta^y = 0.3$
HWDS—weekly, yearly	0.039	0.029	$\delta^y = 0.32$ $\delta^w = 0.28$
HWTS—daily, weekly, yearly	0.042	0.025	$\delta^y = 0.3$ $\delta^q = 0.29$ $\delta^w = 0.35$

2.3. Performance Indicators

In order to evaluate the performance of each model in terms of accuracy, various statistical metrics were adopted, such as root mean square error (RMSE), the mean absolute percentage error (MAPE), coefficient of determination (R^2), mean absolute error (MAE), and coefficient of variation of root mean square error (CVRMSE) that can be expressed as in the following equations:

$$\text{RMSE} = \frac{\sqrt{\sum_{i=1}^{n}(\hat{y}_i - y_i)^2}}{n} \tag{12}$$

$$\text{CVRMSE} = \frac{\sqrt{\sum_{i=1}^{n}(\hat{y}_i - y_i)^2}}{\breve{y}} \tag{13}$$

$$\text{MAE} = \frac{1}{n}\sum_{i=1}^{n}|y_i - \hat{y}_i| \tag{14}$$

$$\text{MAPE} = \frac{1}{n}\sum_{i=1}^{n}\left|\frac{\hat{y}_i - y_i}{y_i}\right| \times 100\% \tag{15}$$

$$R^2 = 1 - \frac{\sum_{i=1}^{n}(y_i - \hat{y}_i)^2}{\sum_{i=1}^{n}(y_i - \breve{y})^2} \tag{16}$$

where y, $\hat{y}$, and $\breve{y}$ represent the measured, predicted, and averaged values respectively.

3. Results and Discussion

Different models are employed to forecast the electrical generation for Kuwait up to 2030 using real data from the Kuwait Ministry of electrical and water. The simulations were carried out within Rstudio and Matlab software environments. The period between January 2015 to December 2018 was used for estimation and adjustment, while the period from January 2019–May 2020 was used for the validation, and the forecasting horizon is between June 2020 to December 2030.

Single (PSR) and multiple (PMR) regressors were used for Prophet model, and three methods of seasonality Holt–Winters models: single (HWSS), double (HWDS), and triple (HWTS). Each model's performance is assessed from different angles by accuracy indicators. The future electrical generation forecasting of Kuwait until the year 2030 using the five models is plotted in Figure 2a,b. The models are assessed in the following section and then discussed, and different fuel cost scenarios are investigated.

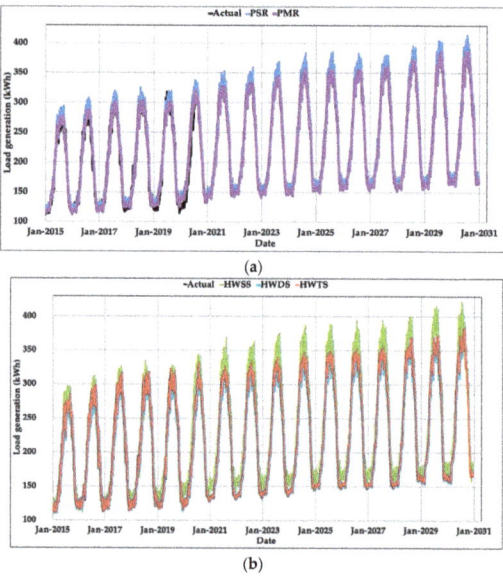

Figure 2. The generation of daily loads data in Kuwait: the trained, predicted, and forecasted data using the five models of (**a**) two types of the Prophet model and (**b**) three types of the Holt-Winters model.

3.1. Model Assessments

Several performance indicators were employed to investigate the reliability of the forecasting of the used models. These indicators are discussed in this section to assess the accuracy and generalization of the used models. Five accuracy performance statistical metrics were employed in this study. These metrics include MAPE, MAE, RMSE, CVRMSE, and R^2. Each of the metrics shed light on one angle of the accuracy of the data. MAPE can be considered one of the utmost used tools for evaluating the accuracy of models. MAE reveals the difference between the estimated value and the real value using the absolute error. RMSE assesses the variability of model response regarding variance and sensitivity to large errors. CVRMSE standardizes the forecasted error and provides a unit-less metric that evaluates the variability of the errors between predicted and real values.

Table 3 presents the calculated values of various statistical performance metrics (MAPE, MAE, RMSE, CVRMSE, and R^2) for the used models. Five different models were used: The single Prophet, multiple Prophet models, single, double, and triple seasonality Holt–Winters models. Abbreviations are used to denote the different models used: PSR denotes a Prophet single regressor model. PMR denotes Prophet multiple regressors model, HWSS denotes Holt–Winters with single seasonality model, HWDS denotes Holt–Winters with double seasonality model, and HWTS denotes Holt–Winters with triple seasonality model. The triple seasonality Holt–Winters model achieved a superior value of accuracy in comparison with other model's performance metrics. The double seasonality Holt–Winters model was the second with all performance measures comparable to the triple seasonality model. MAPE was proposed as a reference indicator for assessing energy forecasting performance at different horizons [2]. All models achieved a low MAPE value of less than 5%, which indicates the models' high accuracy. It is benchmarked [40] that When MAPE is less than 10%, it is considered a highly accurate model. Highly accurate models were then categorized into four levels, with the best model denoted by I level when MAPE is ≤1.2%. Other levels are as follows: II (1.2–2.8%), III (2.8–4.6%), and IV (4.6–10%) [2]. Three of the used models, namely the multiple Prophet model and the double and triple seasonality of Holt–Winters models, fall in the II level of this rating, whereas the other two, namely single Prophet and single seasonality of Holt–Winters model, fall in the III level. The triple seasonality Holt–Winters model outperforms all the other models in MAPE value. Superiority is also observed for both double and triple seasonality Holt–Winters models in MAPE values compared to other models. The MAPE values were 1.76% and 1.83% for triple and double seasonality Holt–Winters models, respectively.

Table 3. The calculated values of different performance statistical metrics for the used models.

Indicator	PSR	PMR	HWSS	HWDS	HWTS
MAPE	3.18%	2.77%	3.29%	1.83%	1.76%
MAE	120.10	78.23	127.82	54.01	46.82
RMSE	153.81	104.38	165.08	75.09	67.05
CVRMSE	22.92	16.26	24.50	11.22	10.45
R^2	0.9709	0.9743	0.9641	0.9893	0.9899

The coefficients of determination, R^2, of the five models are plotted with excellent values in Figure 3, showing small differences among the forecasted and real data values. The best-fitting was for the Holt–Winters model's triple seasonality with $R^2 = 0.9899$, then to the Holt–Winters model's double seasonality $R^2 = 0.9893$ followed by multiple Prophet model with $R^2 = 0.9743$. The least values of R^2 were 0.9709 and 0.9641 for the single Prophet model and single seasonality of the Holt–Winters model, respectively. The MAE of the best model, which is the triple seasonality of Holt–Winters, was found to be 47.82, whereas the value of MAE for the least model, which was the single seasonality Holt–Winters model, was 127.82, which is approximately three times of the triple model.

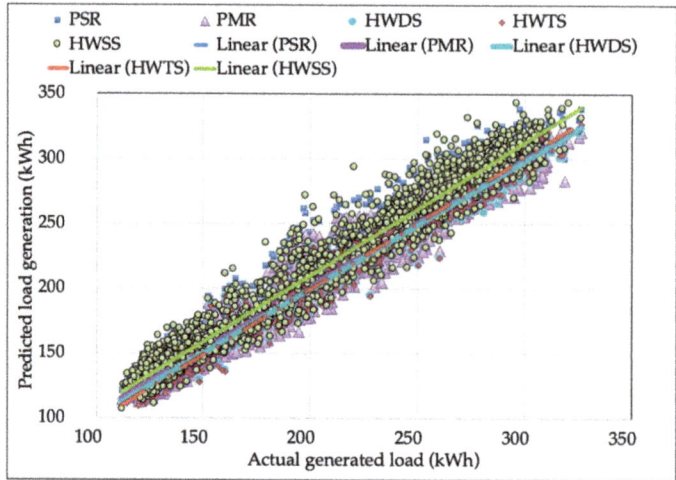

Figure 3. The coefficient of determination R^2 and the fitting characteristics of real and simulated data for all the models.

The RMSE value of the Holt–Winters model's triple seasonality was also the lowest with a value of 67.05 among the other models, followed by the double seasonality with a value of 75.09, whereas the single seasonality of the Holt–Winters model was the maximum with a value of 165.06. Similarly, the CVRMSE percentage of the Holt–Winters model's triple seasonality was the least compared to other models, followed by the double seasonality. Therefore, based on the statistical performance metrics, it is vividly clear that the triple seasonality of the Holt–Winters model has a superior fitting and better accuracy compared to other used models followed by the double seasonality of the Holt–Winters model.

A model's generalization is measured by a model's capability to estimate samples beyond the training zone. The five models' relative error variations are shown in Figure 4 with a maximum relative error value of less than 40% for all models. The triple seasonality of the Holt–Winters model values was less than 21%, and the maximum was for the single seasonality of the Holt–Winters model. The worst relative error was for the single seasonality of the Holt–Winters model.

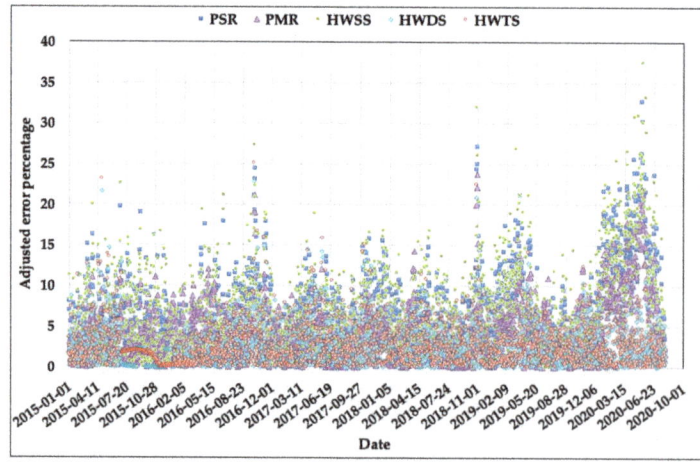

Figure 4. Relative errors percentage for the five models.

The models' robustness is assessed by incorporating different Gaussian white noise intensities into the real tested data similar to relevant previous studies [44–46]. The data were divided into a training dataset and several testing sets with each set corresponding to a different noisy intensity. Four different intensities of 20%, 40%, 60%, and 80% were utilized to investigate the robustness of the five models. The models' robustness was evaluated through the accuracy of the coefficient of determination R^2 by studying the random distributed Gaussian white noise on the training dataset. Table 4 shows the variance of R^2 affected by different noise intensities.

Table 4. The accuracy reduction in coefficient of determination for different models under various noise intensities.

Noise Intensity	PSR	PMR	HWSS	HWDS	HWTS
0%	0.9709	0.9743	0.9641	0.9893	0.9899
20%	0.9697	0.9710	0.9619	0.9853	0.9872
40%	0.9671	0.9705	0.9592	0.9847	0.9867
60%	0.9670	0.9684	0.9587	0.9820	0.9858
80%	0.9667	0.9682	0.9552	0.9798	0.9816

The effects of different noise intensities are also plotted in Figure 5 to show the effects of noise on the five models' overall trends. The general trends showed an association between the increase in noise intensity and a reduction in the determination coefficient's value as expected. High robustness is noticed by the low variance of R^2 of the triple seasonality of the Holt–Winters model with the least value of 0.9816 at 80% noise intensity. The Holt–Winters model's single seasonality showed the least robustness among the other models with a minimum value of 0.9552. The other models showed excellent robustness across the different noise intensities. These results drive to the same previous conclusion that the triple seasonality then double seasonality of the Holt–Winters model outperformed the other models in terms of accuracy, generalization, and robustness.

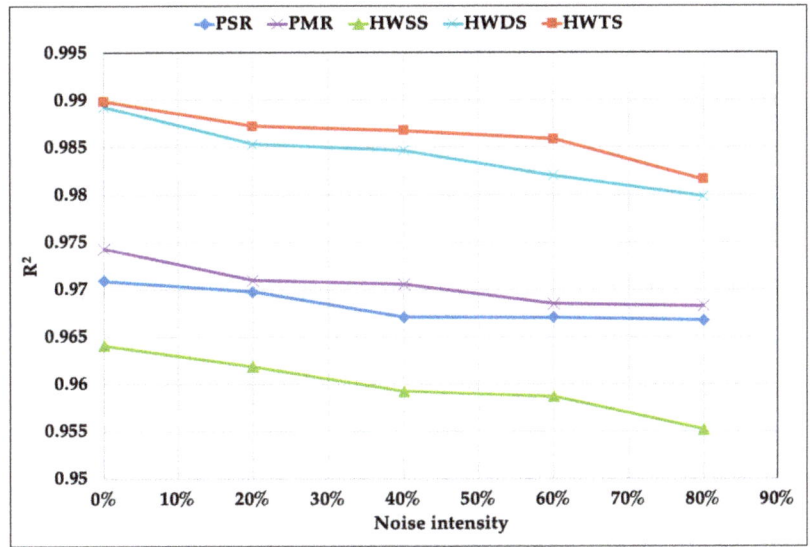

Figure 5. Variations of the coefficient of determination at different noise intensities for the five models.

3.2. Future Generation Forecasting

Long-term electricity forecasting studies can include the peak load forecasting as well as electricity generation forecasting as in the current study [18]. Each of the two forecasting approaches contributes to providing different information for the experts and reveals a comprehensive overview of the electricity grid. One of the common misconceptions is that the generated electricity's annual peak occurs on the same day as the annual peak load. However, this may not be true for all datasets and case studies due to several factors. These factors can be attributed to the nature of the annual peak load date, resulting from the high consumer consumption at a specific time due to temperature, the time during the day, and consumption pattern. The annual peak generation is associated with these factors during the whole day and not at a specific time. As a result, the annual peak load dates are not identical with the annual peak generation dates. Table 5 provides a comparison between the peak load dates, from [18], and the peak generation of this study in Kuwait between 2015–2020. It is evident that forecasting the peak load and the peak generation would be advantageous to policymakers to prepare for the expected loads in terms of logistics needed for the electrical generation. Moreover, it would help in making decisions for expanding the electricity grid and to assess the need for boosting from the current interconnected GCC power grid.

Table 5. The annual peak load and the matching generation and the annual peak generation and date.

Year	Date	Peak Load	Generation of the Same Date	Peak Generation	Date
2015	30 August 2015	12,810	279,228	279,228	30 August 2015
2016	15 August 2016	13,390	288,058	290,304	2 August 2016
2017	26 July 2017	13,800	290,288	299,694	14 August 2017
2018	10 July 2018	13,910	284,718	300,231	12 July 2018
2019	27 June 2019	14,420	318,531	318,531	27 June 2019
2020	30 July 2020	14,960	317,677	326,437	31 July 2020

The long-term electric generation forecasting for the year 2020–2030 of the five models, and the actual data are tabulated in Table A1. The forecasted data of the annual electrical generation of the five models are plotted in Figure 6.

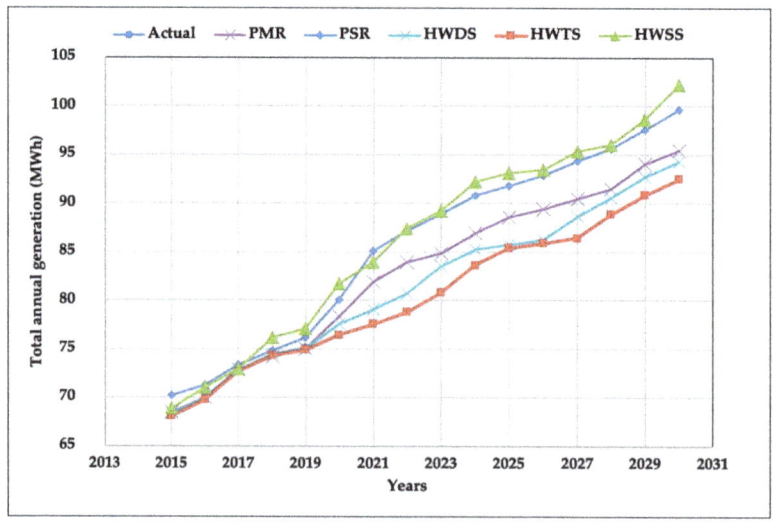

Figure 6. The long-term annual electrical generation forecasting of the five models.

According to the forecast of the triple seasonality of the Holt–Winters model, the annual electric generation in Kuwait will reach about 92,535,555 kWh by the year 2030. This forecasted value is around 23% higher than the actual generation in 2019. The other models are higher in the forecasted annual electrical generation, which reaches up to 102,262,507 kWh in single seasonality of Holt–Winters models, which is higher by 36% than the generation of 2019. The management needs to assess the needed facility or equipment needed for such a generation to be established and prepared.

The forecasted monthly consumptions of the coming two years for different models are depicted in Table A2 and Figure 7. In addition to the study's primary aim, analyzing the monthly electrical generation can provide mid-term information for the logistics needed for this generation. The highest generation is clearly in two months, July and August, where Kuwait has its harshest weather temperature and humidity. Moreover, the higher electrical generation period of each year is between May and September. The maximum monthly electrical generation in 2021 is July for all the models, whereas August is the maximum in 2022 for the PSR, PMR, and HWSS models, and July 2022 is the maximum for the HWDS and HWTS models. Such information provides management and policymakers with vital tools to reach the right decision for the proper generation of electricity and planning for major maintenance or shutdowns.

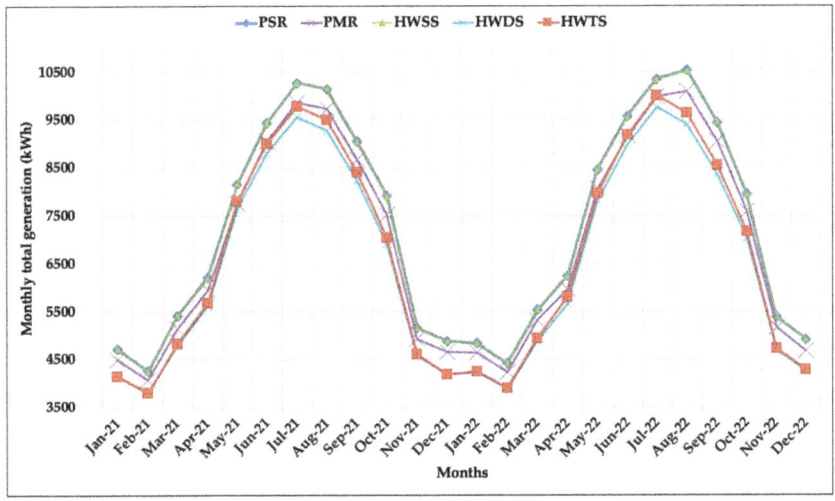

Figure 7. Monthly total generation of electricity for Kuwait between 2021 and 2022.

The monthly electrical generation introduces useful information to determine a map of electrical demand and associated maintenance program. In contrast, the long-term annual electrical generation forecasting help in estimating the fossil fuel power plants' fuel budget. Therefore, addressing fuel costs evaluation constitutes a positive addition in the current research and reflects the primary goal of electrical generation prediction for all-electric power entities.

3.3. Implications of Elecrical Generation on Fuels Cost

The long-term annual electrical generation forecasting can be used to estimate the fuel cost of the future till 2030. Since Kuwait is dependent on oil export as the primary source for the country's revenue, the electricity generation directly relates to the country's economy, especially with the depletion of oil due to burning fossil fuel as a fuel in electricity generation. Kuwait's power plants use four different types of fossil fuel: natural gas, gas oil, crude oil, and heavy fuel oil (HFO). The rate of increase in electricity consumption has significant effects on the stability of the country's economy. Therefore, the long-term forecasting of electrical generation is essential for policymakers to keep

Kuwait's prosperous future. The sharp increase in electrical generation can deplete the oil resources capacity and is critical to Kuwait's economic future. The total cost of fuel consumed in the electrical generation between 2012 and 2019 is tabulated in Table 6 to illustrate the fuel cost change.

Table 6. The consumption of fuels and the total cost of fuel consumption between years 2012–2019 [21–24].

Year	Natural Gas (KSCF) Standard Cubic Feet	Gas Oil (Barrels)	Crude Oil (Barrels)	Heavy Oil (Barrels)	Total Cost (KD)
2012	264,080,165	11,913,629	16,566,894	38,557,558	2,423,012,351
2013	253,461,108	9,237,306	11,323,855	46,967,101	2,327,992,356
2014	313,936,191	11,153,661	14,409,093	37,954,682	2,435,107,934
2015	350,979,921	8,570,450	4,849,437	46,722,496	1,288,525,905
2016	378,535,102	5,731,758	4,057,944	48,460,342	1,010,903,300
2017	374,964,177	5,196,552	9,194,665	41,591,383	1,297,642,956
2018	403,438,524	3,623,846	6,236,988	42,956,365	1,694,031,251
2019	433,605,520	5,376,675	3,439,839	39,107,701	1,442,738,912

It is clear from Table 6 that the total cost of fuel is fluctuating and associated with world fuel prices. Assessment of the power and desalination plants' fuel future requirements is vital to secure power generation and water supply stability. However, this may require thorough investigations to address all the parameters and be examined in the future. Instead, the analysis of possible simplified estimation of the total cost of fuel associated with the long-term electrical generation forecasting is introduced to address the uncertainties of fuel prices. The fuel cost represents the first source of expenses based on the life cycle assessment for the whole plant lifespan, which exceeds the capital investment cost. Fossil fuel constitutes about 99.6% of the total energy supply sources to the Kuwait power sector [21–24], and the high percentage level of dependency is typical in most oil countries.

There are two natural gas sources in Kuwait, local and imported liquefied natural gas (LNG). However, each type of fossil fuel has its own chemical and physical characteristics, and the price fluctuates according to several factors such as source, quality of the fuel, and demand-supply bases. The percentage of fuel consumptions map are varied year per year in power generation sectors and mainly governed by the strategies of Kuwait Petroleum Corporation (KPC), which is oriented economically. The fixed baseline of fuel price was selected throughout this work, as illustrated in Table 7, based on the average values extracted from the past five years data to evaluate the fuel budget for the next ten years using the five models' extracted outcomes.

Table 7. Average prices of the different fossil fuels used in power generation in Kuwait.

Fuel	Price			Unit
	Low	Average	High	
Natural Gas	0.294	0.375	0.456	KD/MSCF
Gas Oil	11.846	18.904	25.963	KD/bbl
Crude Oil	8.084	14.085	20.085	KD/bbl
H.F.O.	6.496	13.398	20.300	KD/bbl
LNG	1.265	2.626	3.987	KD/MSCF

Single and triple seasonality Holt–Winters models are the two models that cover the upper and lower band of the estimated cost of the forecasted annual electricity generation for Kuwait from 2020–2030 as it can be observed in Figure 8. Estimating the fuel budget is not limited only to the economic criteria but also to technical factors, such as type of unit, heat rate, degradation, and fuel quality. For the sake of simplicity, the average degradation value for the unit heat rate was assumed 1% as per registered and proposed by the manufacturers at standard conditions. Figure 8 shows the forecasted fuel budget for the Kuwait power and desalination plants in millions of Kuwaiti Dinars up to 2030 using all proposed models.

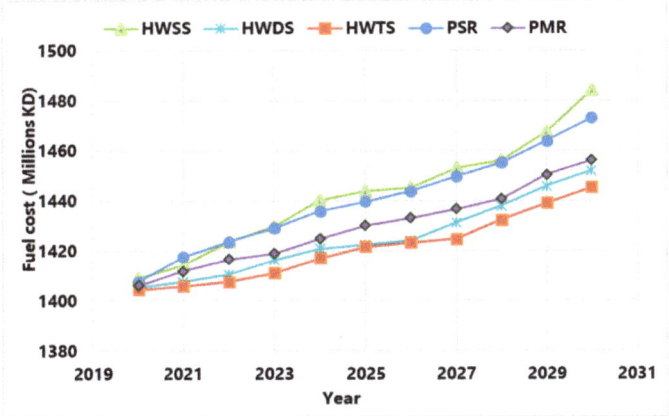

Figure 8. Forecasted fuel budget in millions of Kuwaiti Dinars for the upcoming ten years based on the power generation prediction of all proposed models.

All models elucidate consistent trend through the gradual increase in fuel cost due to increasing power generation. The gap between the upper model (HWSS) and lower model (HWTS) outcomes, as it can be noticed in Figure 8, increases at the end of the tested period compared to the beginning because of the rise in expected power generation difference, which exceeds 9 million kWh total annual production. The moderate growth of the fuel budget might be attributed to the rising dependency on natural gas on other liquid fossil fuels. Relying more on natural gas as a significant fuel source is evident in the electricity value between them.

The primary contribution of fuel to the total fossil fuel budget comes from natural gas with LNG, followed by Heavy fuel oil, gas oil, and crude oil for the year 2020, while gas oil and crude oil have the same contribution by 5% in the year 2030 as illustrated in Figure 9.

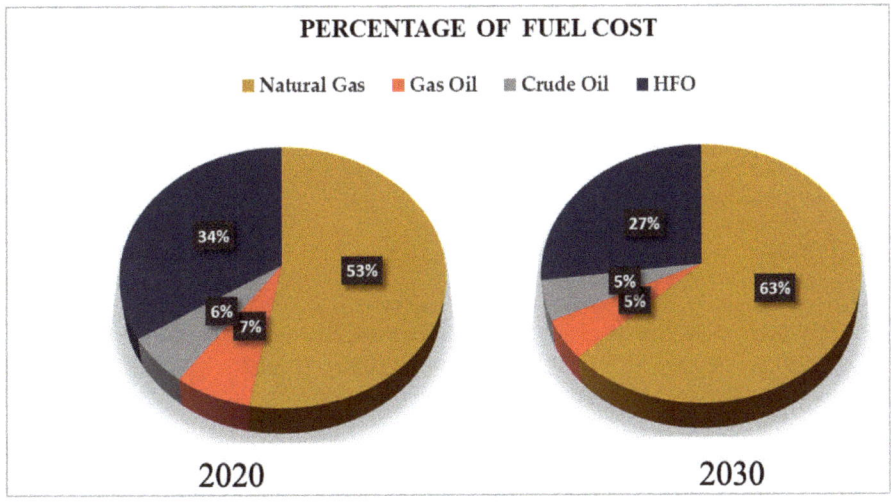

Figure 9. Fuel contribution cost as a percentage of total fossil fuel cost for the years 2020 and 2030.

The fuel distribution estimation was determined based on the actual fuel scenarios over the last five years, which do not depend on fuel price only but govern by fuel availability and type of available units. The distribution pattern shows that the natural gas share increases over the examined period by 10.9%, whereas the liquid fossil fuel reduces by 8.1%. The present study has confirmed the advantage of securing more natural gas on fuel future map by cost-effectively selecting new energy systems. The MEW's future fuel budget can be reduced by securing more local natural gas and implementing large-capacity renewable energy projects.

4. Conclusions

Long-term forecasting of electrical generation in Kuwait was investigated using five models to predict the electrical generation until 2030. Different statistical performance metrics were employed to assess the accuracy, generalization, and robustness of the models. The Holt–Winters model's triple seasonality outperformed the other models in terms of the MAPE, RMSE, CVRMSE, MAE, and R^2. According to the different performance indicators, the double seasonality of the Holt–Winters model was the second-best performing model with superior accuracy. The Prophet model, with multiple regressors, has shown comparable performance to the Holt–Winters double seasonality model. In contrast, the least performing models were the single regressor Prophet model followed by the single seasonality Holt–Winters model. The estimated annual electrical generation for the year 2030 of the Holt–Winters models' triple and single seasonality models were 92,535,555 and 102,262,507 kWh, respectively. The generation of electricity in Kuwait during the upcoming ten years was then presented and discussed. The results reveal that the higher electrical generation period occurs between May and September of the upcoming two years. The five models' long-term electrical generation forecast was then used to estimate the fuel's total cost to provide an overview for policymakers to support the execution of planning decisions.

Author Contributions: Conceptualization, A.I.A., A.M.A., and A.S.A.; methodology, A.M.A. and A.I.A.; software, A.M.A.; validation, A.M.A., A.I.A., A.S.A., M.R.A., and S.N.A.; formal analysis, A.M.A., A.I.A., A.S.A., and F.M.A.; investigation, A.M.A., A.I.A., and A.S.A.; resources, A.M.A., A.I.A., A.S.A., M.R.A., S.N.A., and F.M.A.; data curation, A.I.A., A.M.A., A.S.A., and F.M.A.; writing—original draft preparation, A.I.A., A.M.A., and A.S.A.; writing—review and editing, A.I.A., A.M.A., A.S.A., M.R.A., and S.N.A.; visualization, A.I.A., A.M.A., and A.S.A. All authors have read and agreed to the published version of the manuscript.

Funding: This research received no external funding.

Conflicts of Interest: The authors declare no conflict of interest.

Nomenclature

GDP	Gross domestic product
AI	Artificial intelligence
ML	Machine learning
DL	Deep learning
GA	Genetic algorithm
ANN	Artificial neural networks
SVR	Support vector regression
IPSO	Improved particle swarm optimization
PCA-FFNN	Principal component analysis and fuzzy feed-forward neural network
PCFI-RBF	Partial-consensus fuzzy intersection and radial basis function network
RMSE	Root mean square error
MAPE	Mean absolute percentage error
R^2	Coefficient of determination
MAE	Mean absolute error
CVRMSE	Coefficient of variation of root mean square error
PSR	Single regressor for Prophet Model
PMR	Multiple regressors for Prophet Model
HWSS	Single seasonality Holt-Winters model

HWDS	Double seasonality Holt-Winters model
HWTS	Triple seasonality Holt-Winters model
HFO	Heavy fuel oil
LNG	Liquefied natural gas
KPC	Kuwait Petroleum Corporation

Appendix A

Table A1. The real data and the forecasted annual generation of electricity for Kuwait from 2015–2030.

	Annual Total Electrical Generation (kWh)					
	Actual	PSR	PMR	HWSS	HWDS	HWTS
2015	68,286,350	70,208,828	68,449,290	68,935,381	68,299,370	68,047,664
2016	70,084,727	71,309,681	69,977,535	71,082,353	70,008,887	69,798,293
2017	72,787,590	73,359,898	72,903,860	72,910,975	72,810,502	72,665,778
2018	74,430,304	74,872,001	74,156,996	76,173,631	74,432,331	74,326,541
2019	75,069,410	76,179,317	75,040,336	77,113,949	75,008,034	74,916,365
2020		80,036,707	78,329,573	81,683,193	77,607,284	76,441,652
2021		85,131,998	81,893,161	83,971,685	79,070,098	77,576,721
2022		87,184,615	83,945,450	87,453,223	80,757,167	78,803,803
2023		88,888,944	84,818,623	89,208,193	83,518,864	80,801,914
2024		90,819,983	86,916,798	92,262,607	85,265,977	83,624,082
2025		91,833,231	88,556,264	93,165,837	85,770,309	85,417,389
2026		92,878,920	89,406,883	93,465,256	86,293,807	85,933,949
2027		94,350,541	90,451,648	95,353,865	88,667,276	86,469,671
2028		95,636,495	91,515,320	96,037,295	90,582,478	88,899,766
2029		97,623,149	94,049,623	98,668,062	92,751,443	90,860,715
2030		99,677,375	95,421,752	102,262,507	94,313,533	92,535,555

Table A2. The forecasted monthly generation of electricity for Kuwait between 2021 and 2022.

	Monthly Total Generation (kWh)				
	PSR	PMR	HWSS	HWDS	HWTS
21 January	4,719,195	4,506,418	4,723,899	4,154,973	4,160,775
21 February	4,265,083	4,085,284	4,253,269	3,812,010	3,819,632
21 March	5,407,054	5,148,962	5,413,977	4,797,070	4,828,850
21 April	6,207,547	5,940,924	6,196,026	5,609,673	5,679,516
21 May	8,150,344	7,765,217	8,169,369	7,655,697	7,802,910
21 June	9,445,881	9,051,420	9,446,366	8,798,820	8,997,350
21 July	10,276,964	9,856,725	10,275,340	9,567,496	9,791,745
21 August	10,152,294	9,738,065	10,157,051	9,287,612	9,500,731
21 September	9,048,569	8,676,132	9,050,778	8,229,272	8,404,845
21 October	7,912,560	7,534,398	7,904,534	6,922,840	7,040,503
21 November	5,160,468	4,926,339	5,163,376	4,584,972	4,613,376
21 December	4,884,369	4,663,277	4,878,559	4,186,849	4,194,054
22 January	4,841,008	4,639,763	4,849,182	4,240,582	4,251,986
22 February	4,423,749	4,236,537	4,423,660	3,890,423	3,903,769
22 March	5,532,091	5,310,500	5,534,806	4,884,470	4,934,148
22 April	6,248,921	5,960,376	6,239,217	5,639,118	5,802,449
22 May	8,455,250	8,067,020	8,473,173	7,812,368	7,970,160
22 June	9,582,494	9,164,224	9,567,936	8,978,583	9,189,225
22 July	10,355,563	9,995,653	10,348,046	9,762,630	10,000,339
22 August	10,534,098	10,092,835	10,528,398	9,414,655	9,637,299
22 September	9,431,675	9,043,116	9,461,242	8,355,913	8,540,640
22 October	7,942,639	7,593,484	7,936,245	7,039,516	7,165,731
22 November	5,376,527	5,160,420	5,371,959	4,683,238	4,718,244
22 December	4,912,699	4,681,523	4,909,340	4,271,941	4,285,130

References

1. Weron, R. *Modeling and Forecasting Electricity Loads and Prices: A Statistical Approach*; John Wiley & Sons: Chicester, UK, 2007; Volume 403.
2. Wei, N.; Li, C.; Peng, X.; Zeng, F.; Lu, X. Conventional models and artificial intelligence-based models for energy consumption forecasting: A review. *J. Pet. Sci. Eng.* **2019**, *181*, 106187. [CrossRef]
3. Lindberg, K.B.; Seljom, P.; Madsen, H.; Fischer, D.; Korpås, M. Long-term electricity load forecasting: Current and future trends. *Util. Policy* **2019**, *58*, 102–119. [CrossRef]
4. Kuster, C.; Rezgui, Y.; Mourshed, M. Electrical load forecasting models: A critical systematic review. *Sustain. Cities Soc.* **2017**, *35*, 257–270. [CrossRef]
5. Scheidt, F.v.; Medinová, H.; Ludwig, N.; Richter, B.; Staudt, P.; Weinhardt, C. Data analytics in the electricity sector—A quantitative and qualitative literature review. *Energy AI* **2020**, *1*, 100009. [CrossRef]
6. Amasyali, K.; El-Gohary, N.M. A review of data-driven building energy consumption prediction studies. *Renew. Sustain. Energy Rev.* **2018**, *81*, 1192–1205. [CrossRef]
7. Khuntia, S.R.; Rueda, J.L.; van der Meijden, M.A. Forecasting the load of electrical power systems in mid-and long-term horizons: A review. *IET Gener. Transm. Distrib.* **2016**, *10*, 3971–3977. [CrossRef]
8. Alfares, H.K.; Nazeeruddin, M. Electric load forecasting: Literature survey and classification of methods. *Int. J. Syst. Sci.* **2002**, *33*, 23–34. [CrossRef]
9. Pérez-García, J.; Moral-Carcedo, J. Analysis and long term forecasting of electricity demand trough a decomposition model: A case study for Spain. *Energy* **2016**, *97*, 127–143. [CrossRef]
10. Torrini, F.C.; Souza, R.C.; Cyrino Oliveira, F.L.; Moreira Pessanha, J.F. Long term electricity consumption forecast in Brazil: A fuzzy logic approach. *Socio-Econ. Plan. Sci.* **2016**, *54*, 18–27. [CrossRef]
11. Pessanha, J.F.M.; Leon, N. Forecasting Long-term Electricity Demand in the Residential Sector. *Procedia Comput. Sci.* **2015**, *55*, 529–538. [CrossRef]
12. Mohamed, Z.; Bodger, P. Forecasting electricity consumption in New Zealand using economic and demographic variables. *Energy* **2005**, *30*, 1833–1843. [CrossRef]
13. Ardakani, F.J.; Ardehali, M.M. Long-term electrical energy consumption forecasting for developing and developed economies based on different optimized models and historical data types. *Energy* **2014**, *65*, 452–461. [CrossRef]
14. Bianco, V.; Manca, O.; Nardini, S. Electricity consumption forecasting in Italy using linear regression models. *Energy* **2009**, *34*, 1413–1421. [CrossRef]
15. Chen, T.; Wang, Y.-C. Long-term load forecasting by a collaborative fuzzy-neural approach. *Int. J. Electr. Power Energy Syst.* **2012**, *43*, 454–464. [CrossRef]
16. da Silva, F.L.C.; Cyrino Oliveira, F.L.; Souza, R.C. A bottom-up bayesian extension for long term electricity consumption forecasting. *Energy* **2019**, *167*, 198–210. [CrossRef]
17. Taylor, S.J.; Letham, B. Forecasting at Scale. *Am. Stat.* **2018**, *72*, 37–45. [CrossRef]
18. Almazrouee, A.I.; Almeshal, A.M.; Almutairi, A.S.; Alenezi, M.R.; Alhajeri, S.N. Long-Term Forecasting of Electrical Loads in Kuwait Using Prophet and Holt–Winters Models. *Appl. Sci.* **2020**, *10*, 5627. [CrossRef]
19. Trull, O.; García-Díaz, J.C.; Troncoso, A. Initialization Methods for Multiple Seasonal Holt–Winters Forecasting Models. *Mathematics* **2020**, *8*, 268. [CrossRef]
20. Jiang, W.; Wu, X.; Gong, Y.; Yu, W.; Zhong, X. Holt–Winters smoothing enhanced by fruit fly optimization algorithm to forecast monthly electricity consumption. *Energy* **2020**, *193*, 116779. [CrossRef]
21. MEW. *Statistical Year Book, State of Kuwait Ministry of Electricity and Water*; MEW: Kuwait City, Kuwait, 2020.
22. MEW. *Statistical Year Book, State of Kuwait Ministry of Electricity and Water*; MEW: Kuwait City, Kuwait, 2019.
23. MEW. *Statistical Year Book, State of Kuwait Ministry of Electricity and Water*; MEW: Kuwait City, Kuwait, 2018.
24. MEW. *Statistical Year Book, State of Kuwait Ministry of Electricity and Water*; MEW: Kuwait City, Kuwait, 2017.
25. Ali, H.; Alsabbagh, M. Residential Electricity Consumption in the State of Kuwait. *Envrion. Pollut Clim. Chang.* **2018**, *2*. [CrossRef]
26. Soares, N.; Reinhart, C.F.; Hajiah, A. Simulation-based analysis of the use of PCM-wallboards to reduce cooling energy demand and peak-loads in low-rise residential heavyweight buildings in Kuwait. *Build. Simul.* **2017**, *10*, 481–495. [CrossRef]
27. Matar, W.; Anwer, M. Jointly reforming the prices of industrial fuels and residential electricity in Saudi Arabia. *Energy Policy* **2017**, *109*, 747–756. [CrossRef]

28. Shehabi, M. *Assessing Kuwaiti Energy Pricing Reforms*; Oxford Institute for Energy Studies: Oxford, UK, 2017.
29. Santosa, B. Dynamic Pricing in Electricity: Research Potential in Indonesia. *Procedia Manuf.* **2015**, *4*, 300–306.
30. Alajmi, A. Energy audit of an educational building in a hot summer climate. *Energy Build.* **2012**, *47*, 122–130. [CrossRef]
31. Gaete-Morales, C.; Gallego-Schmid, A.; Stamford, L.; Azapagic, A. A novel framework for development and optimisation of future electricity scenarios with high penetration of renewables and storage. *Appl. Energy* **2019**, *250*, 1657–1672. [CrossRef]
32. Alajmi, T.; Phelan, P. Modeling and Forecasting End-Use Energy Consumption for Residential Buildings in Kuwait Using a Bottom-Up Approach. *Energies* **2020**, *13*, 1981. [CrossRef]
33. AlHajri, M.; AlRashidi, M.; EL-Naggar, K. Long-term electric load forecast in Kuwaiti and Egyptian power systems. *J. Eng. Res.* **2018**, *6*, 116–135.
34. Almeshaiei, E.; Soltan, H. A methodology for Electric Power Load Forecasting. *Alex. Eng. J.* **2011**, *50*, 137–144. [CrossRef]
35. Alhajeri, H.M.; Almutairi, A.; Alenezi, A.; Alshammari, F. Energy Demand in the State of Kuwait During the Covid-19 Pandemic: Technical, Economic, and Environmental Perspectives. *Energies* **2020**, *13*, 4370. [CrossRef]
36. AlRashidi, M.R.; El-Naggar, K.M. Long term electric load forecasting based on particle swarm optimization. *Appl. Energy* **2010**, *87*, 320–326. [CrossRef]
37. Atalla, T.N.; Hunt, L.C. Modelling residential electricity demand in the GCC countries. *Energy Econ.* **2016**, *59*, 149–158. [CrossRef]
38. Bianchi, F.; Castellini, A.; Tarocco, P.; Farinelli, A. Load Forecasting in District Heating Networks: Model Comparison on a Real-World Case Study. In Proceedings of the International Conference on Machine Learning, Optimization, and Data Science, Siena, Italy, 10–13 September 2019; Springer: Cham, Switzerland, 2019; pp. 553–565.
39. Rehman, S.A.U.; Cai, Y.; Fazal, R.; Das Walasai, G.; Mirjat, N.H. An integrated modeling approach for forecasting long-term energy demand in Pakistan. *Energies* **2017**, *10*, 1868. [CrossRef]
40. Hussain, A.; Rahman, M.; Memon, J.A. Forecasting electricity consumption in Pakistan: The way forward. *Energy Policy* **2016**, *90*, 73–80. [CrossRef]
41. García-Díaz, J.C.; Trull, Ó. Competitive Models for the Spanish Short-Term Electricity Demand Forecasting. In *Time Series Analysis and Forecasting*; Springer: Cham, Switzerland, 2016; pp. 217–231.
42. Brockwell, P.J.; Davis, R.A.; Calder, M.V. *Introduction to Time Series and Forecasting*; Springer: Cham, Switzerland, 2002; Volume 2.
43. Trull, Ó.; García-Díaz, J.C.; Troncoso, A. Stability of Multiple Seasonal Holt-Winters Models Applied to Hourly Electricity Demand in Spain. *Appl. Sci.* **2020**, *10*, 2630. [CrossRef]
44. Lewis, C.D. *Industrial and Business Forecasting Methods: A Practical Guide to Exponential Smoothing and Curve Fitting*; Butterworth-Heinemann: London, UK, 1982.
45. Wang, R.; Lu, S.; Feng, W. A novel improved model for building energy consumption prediction based on model integration. *Appl. Energy* **2020**, *262*, 114561. [CrossRef]
46. Cai, M.; Pipattanasomporn, M.; Rahman, S. Day-ahead building-level load forecasts using deep learning vs. traditional time-series techniques. *Appl. Energy* **2019**, *236*, 1078–1088. [CrossRef]

Publisher's Note: MDPI stays neutral with regard to jurisdictional claims in published maps and institutional affiliations.

© 2020 by the authors. Licensee MDPI, Basel, Switzerland. This article is an open access article distributed under the terms and conditions of the Creative Commons Attribution (CC BY) license (http://creativecommons.org/licenses/by/4.0/).

Article

Short Term Electric Load Forecasting Based on Data Transformation and Statistical Machine Learning

Nikos Andriopoulos [1,2], Aristeidis Magklaras [1], Alexios Birbas [1,*], Alex Papalexopoulos [3], Christos Valouxis [1], Sophia Daskalaki [1], Michael Birbas [1], Efthymios Housos [1] and George P. Papaioannou [2]

1. Department of Electrical and Computer Engineering, University of Patras, 265 00 Patras, Greece; nandriopoulos@ece.upatras.gr (N.A.); ece8115@upnet.gr (A.M.); cvalouxis@upatras.gr (C.V.); sdask@upatras.gr (S.D.); mbirbas@ece.upatras.gr (M.B.); housos@upatras.gr (E.H.)
2. Research, Technology & Development Department, Independent Power Transmission Operator (IPTO) S.A., 89 Dyrrachiou & Kifisou Str. Gr, 104 43 Athens, Greece; g.papaioannou@admie.gr
3. Ecco International Inc., San Francisco, CA 94104, USA; alexp@eccointl.com
* Correspondence: birbas@ece.upatras.gr; Tel.: +30-261-099-6426; Fax: +30-261-099-6818

Abstract: The continuous penetration of renewable energy resources (RES) into the energy mix and the transition of the traditional electric grid towards a more intelligent, flexible and interactive system, has brought electrical load forecasting to the foreground of smart grid planning and operation. Predicting the electric load is a challenging task due to its high volatility and uncertainty, either when it refers to the distribution system or to a single household. In this paper, a novel methodology is introduced which leverages the advantages of the state-of-the-art deep learning algorithms and specifically the Convolution Neural Nets (CNN). The main feature of the proposed methodology is the exploitation of the statistical properties of each time series dataset, so as to optimize the hyperparameters of the neural network and in addition transform the given dataset into a form that allows maximum exploitation of the CNN algorithm's advantages. The proposed algorithm is compared with the LSTM (Long Short Term Memory) technique which is the state of the art solution for electric load forecasting. The evaluation of the algorithms was conducted by employing three open-source, publicly available datasets. The experimental results show strong evidence of the effectiveness of the proposed methodology.

Keywords: short-term electrical load forecasting; machine learning; deep learning; statistical analysis; parameters tuning; CNN; LSTM

1. Introduction

Load forecasting has always been a challenging task that triggers the interest of both academia and the industrial sector. Since the 1960s, auto-regressive (AR) models have been widely used for designing and implementing predictive load forecasting models. These were based on the assumption that the system/substation load at any given time can be satisfactorily described as a linear combination of past load values and other values of a set of exogenous variables. Therefore, they were either plain AR models or AR models with exogenous variables (ARX) and/or AR models with moving average components (ARMA and ARMAX). Such models and variants thereof were used extensively for electric load forecasting [1,2].

The linearity assumption was relaxed with the development of machine learning-based models such as neural networks [3,4] and kernel-based methods (e.g., support vector machines [5]). Neural networks are nowadays the most widely used machine learning tool for nonlinear regression in electrical load forecasting. At the same time, support vector regression is gaining popularity in this area [6].

In this paper we focus on the state-of-the-art Artificial Neural Network (ANN) deep learning algorithms, namely the Convolution Neural Nets (CNNs) in order to perform load prediction. Currently the most successful and popular algorithm in literature for addressing this issue is the use of Long Short Term Memory (LSTM) [7] method, which belongs to the Recurrent Neural Network (RNN) architectural type and exploits the short and long term relationships that exist in a data series in order to build a predictive model. LSTM algorithms are considered to be the most suitable choice for electric load forecasting compared to other neural network architectures. CNNs, on the other hand, are considered to be the preferred choice for image processing related tasks, like image recognition, due to their ability to take advantage of the inherent stationarity usually observed in the pixel data, thus resulting in more accurate models. Nevertheless, it will be shown that CNN-based models can also provide efficient solutions for the electric load forecasting problem and under certain conditions, such as applying proper data preprocessing and analysis, they could even outperform the LSTM-based models.

Despite the black box nature of ANN solutions, there is considerable freedom for differentiating model selection choices and parameter tuning, such as the number of epochs, batch size or hidden dimensions and filters (i.e., the number of output filters in the convolution) for the CNN-based models. The proposed approach offers a comprehensive methodology for model selection and parameter tuning resulting in significantly lower forecasting errors compared to the LSTM model. Furthermore, the data transformation which was performed after extensive statistical analysis allows optimal input selection for our models. The most common input in such cases is the previous state (t-1) of the forecasted variable. This leads to higher accuracy for uni-step forecasting applications, but at the same time it lowers the performance of the multi-step ones by introducing several defects. In our case, the input value is derived directly from the results of statistical analysis. It is important to mention that this paper does not focus on the CNN algorithm itself, but rather on the proper statistical analysis (pre-processing) which facilitates the data transformation based on data features (i.e., stationarity) and achieve best possible performance of the algorithm. The methodology and the different techniques employed will be thoroughly described in Section 2.

According to the time horizon used for prediction, load forecasting can be classified into very short-term load forecasting (VSTLF), short-term load forecasting (STLF), medium-term load forecasting (MTLF), and long-term load forecasting (LTLF). The forecasting horizon varies from 5 min, to one day, to two weeks or to three or more years; depending on the planning or operational function it supports [8].

Across literature a wide range of methodologies and models have been proposed to improve the accuracy of load forecasting, yet most of them are based upon aggregated power consumption data at the system (top) level with little to no information regarding power consumption profiles at the customer class level. This approach was acceptable till now, since the operational focus until recently had been on the bulk transmission system and the wholesale energy markets. Since the interest now is shifted towards the distribution system and the efficient integration of Distributed Energy Resources (DERs) connected close to the edge of the grid, this approach is not sufficient anymore. Hence, distribution substation load forecasting becomes a necessity for the Distribution System Operators (DSOs). Forecasting on distribution feeder has not been widely examined across literature. Low Voltage (LV) distribution feeders are more volatile compared to the high voltage (HV) ones, since they consist of low aggregations of consumers [9]. One approach is to adopt the forecasting techniques and models that are currently employed at higher voltage levels. The main forecasting research in these areas has been presented in [10,11], that apply both ARIMAX and ANN methods to a single LV transformer (consisting of 128 customers) for forecasting the total energy and peak demand. In their method they take into account historical weather data and they achieve MAPEs of 6–12%. In [12] a three-stage methodology, which consists of pre-processing, forecasting, and post-processing, was applied to forecast loads of three datasets ranging from distribution level to transmission level. A semi-parametric additive model was proposed in [13] to forecast the load of Australian National Electricity Market. The same technique was also applied to forecast more than 2200 substation loads of the French distribution network in [14]. Another load forecasting study on seven substations from the French network was performed in [15], where a conventional time series forecasting methodology was utilized. In [16], the authors proposed a neural network model to forecast the load of two French distribution substations, which outperformed a time series model. It is focused on developing a methodology for neural network design in order to obtain a model that has the best achievable predictive ability given the available data. Variable selection and model selection was applied to electrical load forecasts to ensure an optimal generalization capacity of the neural network model.

Exponential smoothing model and its variations, such as double and triple seasonal exponential smoothing ones, have also showcased good results [17] but are less popular in real-life applications due to their inability to accommodate exogenous variables. Another popular approach, denoted as hybrid, is to combine different models as in [1] where Principal Component Analysis (PCA) and Multiple Linear Regression (MLR) are combined for daily load predictions.

For LV networks accurate load forecasting can be employed to support a number of operations, including demand side response [18], storage control [19,20] and energy management systems [21,22]. Load forecasting for low scale consumers, such as residential loads, is valuable for home energy management systems (HEMS) [23] while house level load forecasting can play a significant role in the future Local Energy Markets (LEM) which will facilitate the energy transactions among participants [24]. Load forecasting has been implemented for either the HV or system level and typically consists of the aggregated demand of hundreds of thousands or millions of consumers. Such demand is much less volatile than the LV demand, and hence, is easier to predict. Load forecasting at this level is very mature research-wise and there is a great volume of literature describing and testing a number of methods and algorithms, including ANNs, Support Vector Machine (SVM), ARIMA, exponential smoothing, fuzzy systems, and linear regression. Recent methods upon load forecasting can be found in [25].

However, the loads of a house, a factory, and a feeder are more volatile than HV level loads. Therefore, developing a highly accurate forecast at lower consumption levels is nontrivial. Although the majority of the load forecasting literature has been dedicated to forecasting at the top (high voltage) level, the information from medium/low voltage levels offers a promising field of research. The highly volatile nature of house load time series makes it particularly difficult to achieve very accurate predictions. In [26] the authors showed that the "double peak" error for spiky data sets means that it is difficult to measure the accuracy of household-level point forecasts objectively introducing traditional pointwise errors. Similar methods have been applied at the household level as at the HV level, including ANNs [27,28] ARIMAs, wavelets [29], Kalman filters [30] and Holt-Winters exponential smoothing [31]. The prediction errors of these methods are much higher compared to those reported at the HV level, with MAPEs ranging from 7% up to 85% in some cases.

Regardless the voltage level and the load scale, load forecasting problems share certain common factors that may affect the prediction accuracy of energy consumption. These are the energy markets, the variables affected by the weather and the hierarchical topology of the grid. In competitive energy retail markets, the electricity consumption is largely driven by the number of customers. Since the number of customers is uncertain, the load profile is consequently characterized by high stochasticity. In [32] the authors propose a two-stage long-term retail load forecasting method to take customer reduction into consideration. The first stage forecasts each customer's load using multiple linear regression with a variable selection method. The second stage forecasts customer attrition using survival analysis. Then, the final forecast results from the product of the two forecasts. Another issue regarding the energy market is the demand response programs which pose another challenge in load forecasting, since some consumers are willing to alter their consumption patterns according to price signals, while others are not. In [33] the authors detect the price-driven customers by applying a non-parametric test so that they can be forecasted separately. Across literature, many papers have shown strong correlations between weather effects and demand. A weather variable investigated in literature is humidity [34], where the authors discovered that the temperature-humidity index (THI) may not be optimal for load forecasting models. Instead, more accurate load forecasts than the THI-based models were performed when the authors separated relative humidity, temperature and their higher order terms and interactions in the model, with the corresponding parameters being estimated by the training data. In [35] the load of a root node of any sub-tree was forecasted first. The child nodes were then treated separately based on their similarities. The forecast of a "regular" node was proportional to that of the parent node, while the "irregular" nodes were forecasted individually using neural networks. In [36] the authors exploit the hierarchical structure of electricity grid for load forecasting. Two case studies were investigated, one based on New York City and its substations, and the other one based on Pennsylvania-New Jersey-Maryland (PJM) and its substations. The authors demonstrated the effectiveness of aggregation in improving the higher level load forecast accuracy.

The availability of data from Advanced Metering Infrastructure (AMI) systems enables the use of novel approaches to the way load forecasting is performed, ranging from the distribution level to even the residential scale. In existing literature, researchers have focused on: (1) longitudinal and (2) cross-sectional grouping methods trying to handle efficiently load data. Longitudinal grouping refers to identifying time periods with similar load patterns, which are derived from statistical analysis based on historical data. On the other hand, cross-sectional grouping refers to the aggregation of customers with similar consumption characteristics. In [37] the authors examined six methods which are usually employed in large-scale energy systems to predict a load similar to that of a single transformer. The models that were investigated were ANNs, AR, ARMA, autoregressive integrated moving average, fuzzy logic, and wavelet NNs for day-ahead and week-ahead electric load forecasting in two scenarios with different number of houses. In [38] a clustering based on AMI data is performed among customers to identify groups with similar load patterns prior to performing load forecasting, in favor of forecasting accuracy. In [39], the authors implemented a neural network (NN)-based method for the construction of prediction intervals (PIs) to quantify potential uncertainties associated with forecasts. A newly introduced method, called lower upper bound estimation (LUBE), is applied and extended to develop PIs using NN models. In [40] a new hybrid model is proposed. This model is a combination of the manifold learning Principal Components (PC) technique and the traditional multiple regression (PC-regression), for short and medium-term forecasting of daily, aggregated, day-ahead, electricity system-wide load in the Greek Electricity Market for the period 2004–2014. PC-regression is compared with a number of classical statistical approaches as well as with the more sophisticated artificial intelligence models, ANN and SVM. The authors have concluded that the forecasts of the developed hybrid model outperforms the ones generated by the other models, with the SARIMAX model being the next best performing approach, giving comparable result.

The advantages that smart meters bring to load forecasting are two-fold. Firstly, smart meters offer the opportunity to distribution companies and electricity retailers to better understand and forecast the load of small scale consumers. Secondly, the high granularity and volume of load data provided by smart meters may improve the forecast accuracy of the models on the grounds that the training dataset will be more representative and will capture the highly volatile demand patterns that describe the load behavior of households or buildings. Therefore, the traditional techniques and methods developed for load forecasting at an aggregate level may not be well suited. Many different approaches are currently examined, all attempting to leverage the large volume of data derived from the numerous operating smart meters so as to improve the forecasting accuracy. In [41] seven existing techniques, including linear regression, ANN, SVM and their variants were examined. The case study was conducted on two datasets, one comprising of two commercial buildings and the other of three residential homes. The study demonstrated that these techniques could produce forecasts with high accuracy for the two commercial loads, but did not perform well for the residential ones. In [29] a self-recurrent wavelet neural network (SRWNN) was proposed to forecast the load for a building within a microgrid. The proposed SRWNN was shown to be more accurate than its ancestor wavelet neural network (WNN) for both building level and higher level load cases. Deep learning techniques for the household and building-level load forecasting are also employed across literature. In [42] a pooling-based deep RNN was proposed to learn spatial information shared between interconnected customers and to address the over-fitting problems. The proposed method outperformed ARIMA, SVR, and classical deep RNN on the Irish CER residential dataset. In [43] a spatio-temporal forecasting approach was proposed to leverage the sparsity which is a valuable element in small scale load forecasting. The proposed method combined ideas from compressive sensing and data decomposition to exploit the low-dimensional structures governing the interactions among the nearby houses. The dataset upon which the method was examined was the Pecan Street dataset.

Additional categorization among the different load forecasting methods in the literature can be summarized as follows: (1) Physics principles-based models and (2) Statistical/Machine learning-based models. In [44] ANNs were used to perform load forecasting in buildings. Finally, in [45] a short-term residential load forecasting based on resident behavior learning was examined. RNNs, such as LSTM, seem as a reasonable selection for time series applications since they are developed explicitly to handle sequential data. In [46] a custom Deep Learning model that combines multiple layers of CNNs for feature extraction is presented, where both LSTM layers (prediction) and parallel dense layers (transforming exogenous variables) are proposed. Finally in [47] a novel method to forecast the electricity loads of single residential households is proposed based on CNNs (combined with a data-augmentation technique), which can artificially enlarge the training data in order to face the lack of sufficient data.

This work focuses on a statistical learning-based approach by examining and leveraging the special statistical features of each given dataset [48] and thereafter transforming the dataset into a form according to the statistical analysis performed for that purpose. Our framework is based on the employment of a CNN architecture. CNNs are among the most popular techniques for deep learning, mainly for image processing tasks [49], where they leverage the spatial locality of pixels. There have been recently presented remarkable efforts of using CNN models for electrical load forecasting [50]. CNNs choice is based on the fact that in load time series, two neighboring points do not exhibit significant deviation. Therefore, load time series are characterized by temporal locality which can be exploited by CNNs. In this paper, we demonstrate that LSTMs for load forecasting under certain conditions can be outperformed; this finding is supported by experimental evidence. To prove our point, we furthermore compare our CNN model with three other machine learning techniques, namely LSTM, ANN and Multilayer Perceptron (MLP). The main contributions of the paper can be summarized in the following:

1. We introduce a method for properly tuning the model's parameters by taking into account the time series statistical properties and especially its auto correlation.
2. We offer a valid alternative to the load forecasting problem in the case of low scale energy deployments where it is derived that our CNN based approach is more efficient than other methods.
3. We identify the conditions under which the CNN outperforms the other widely used forecasting solutions such as high temporal relationship between time series observations, lack of historical data and low scale load consumption.
4. We offer a solution to times series forecasting in cases where there is shortage of training data, since in our experiments the historical data available for training were limited.

The rest of the paper is organized as follows: In Section 2 the proposed methodology is analyzed in detail, in Section 3 the results of our investigation is given and in Section 4 we present the discussion and the conclusions of our work and suggest possible future research extensions.

2. Proposed Methodology

2.1. Convolutional Neural Networks (CNN)

CNN is a class of deep neural networks, most commonly applied to analyzing visual imagery. They are also known as shift invariant or space invariant artificial neural networks (SIANN), based on their shared-weights architecture and translation invariance characteristics [51,52]. CNNs are regularized versions of multi-layer perceptron but they take a different approach towards regularization, since they take advantage of the hierarchical form in data and assemble more complex patterns using smaller and simpler patterns. Therefore, on the scale of connectivity and complexity, CNNs are functioning on the lower extreme. CNNs use relatively little pre-processing compared to other image classification algorithms. This means that the network trains the filters that in traditional algorithms were hand-engineered. This independence from prior knowledge and human effort in feature design is a major advantage.

As presented in Figure 1, a CNN consists of an input and an output layer, as well as multiple hidden layers. These layers perform operations that alter data with the intent of extracting features specific to the data. Three of the most common layers are: convolution, activation or ReLU, and pooling. The hidden layers of a CNN typically consist of a series of convolutional layers that convolve through multiplication or other dot product each of which activates certain image features.

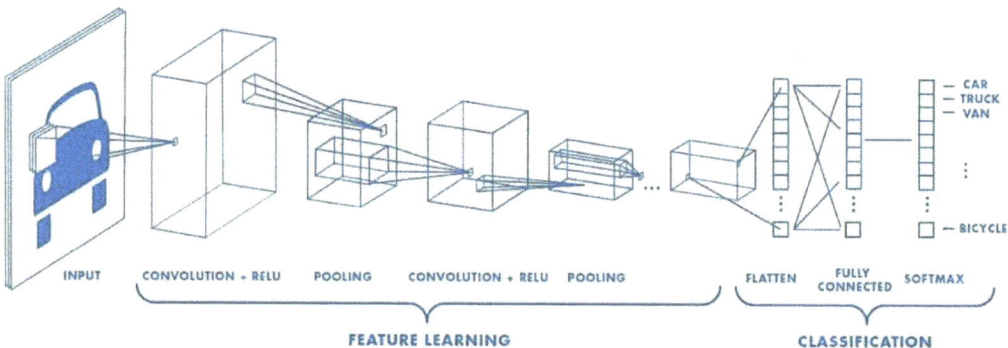

Figure 1. CNN architecture [53].

The input layer reads an input image into the CNN. It consists of various low-level image-processing functions to pre-process the input image as an appropriate data type for the minimal CNN. Practically, the size of the input image is preferably on the order of power of 2 so that to ensure computation efficiency for a CNN. However, input images with uneven row-column dimensions can also be used. The convolution layer extracts pixel-wise visual features from an input image [54–56]. The trainable convolution kernels in this layer adjust their (kernel) weights automatically through back-propagation to learn the input image features [56,57]. Image features learned by the convolution layer allow the successive algorithmic layers to process the extracted image features for other computational operations. The convolution layer is the dot product of the input image I and the kernel used, K. The result is a convolved feature map, f_c which is derived by the Equation (1).

$$f_c = conv(i,j) = (I \otimes K)(i,j) = \sum_m \sum_n I(m,n) K(i-m, j-n) \tag{1}$$

Here $\otimes$ denotes a two-dimensional discrete convolution operator. Equation (1) shows that the convolution kernel K spatially slides over the input image I to compute the element-wise multiplication and sum to produce an output, a convolved feature map f_c. Convolution provides weights sharing, sparse interaction (and local connectivity), and equivariant representation for unsupervised feature learning. More in depth technical details on these convolution properties can be found in [54,55,57–60]. The activation function is commonly a Rectified Linear Unit (*ReLU*) layer. *ReLU* allows for faster and more effective training by mapping negative values to zero and maintaining positive values. This is sometimes referred to as activation, because only the activated features are carried forward to the next layer. The objective of the *ReLU* layers is to introduce a point-wise nonlinearity to a CNN, which allows it to learn through a nonlinear input function. *ReLU* has also proven to be an effective solution to resolve vanishing gradient problems when training a CNN using the backpropagation algorithm [55,56]. The mathematical structure of the ReLU function is a piecewise nonlinear operator with a max output indicative function [54,58]. The output of a *ReLU* is a rectified feature map, f_r that can be obtained by Equation (2).

$$f_r = ReLU(x_i) = max(0, x_i) \qquad (2)$$

Equation (2) produces zero for negative inputs and linearly conveys the input for positive inputs. The activation layer is followed by pooling layers which simplify the output by performing nonlinear down-sampling, thus reducing the number of parameters that the network needs to learn, controlling the overfitting by progressively reducing the spatial size of the network and reducing the computational burden in the network. Those layers are referred to as hidden layers because their inputs and outputs are masked by the activation function and final convolution. The final convolution, in turn, often involves backpropagation in order to more accurately weight the end product.

Though the layers are colloquially referred to as convolutions, this is only by convention. Mathematically or technically, it is a sliding dot product or cross-correlation. This is significant for the indices in the matrix, in the sense that it affects how the weight is determined at a specific index point.

This special design of CNNs renders them capable to successfully capture the spatial and temporal dependencies in an image through the application of the relevant aforedescribed filters. The architecture shows a better fitting to the image dataset due to the reduction in the number of parameters involved and reusability of weights. In other words, the network can be trained to understand the sophistication of the image better. In this context, a CNN-based methodology is analyzed to evaluate its performance for forecasting applications with short period datasets with the motivation behind the CNN-based approach being its wide usage for image recognition applications. More specifically, the CNN models exploit the spatial locality of the pixel data in order to recognize an image. Similarly, in load time series, time locality, expressed by data stationarity and autocorrelation, forms the main motivation for utilizing CNN-based models in load forecasting applications. In our approach we transform the time series data into image-like data, taking advantage of the autocorrelation excibited by time series. Therefore, the first step is to perform statistical analysis and test the data for stationarity. If the data are not stationary then a second step of stationarity analysis is conducted by deploying a Unit Root Test, in order to capture more complex forms of stationarity, which is the case in most datasets.

2.2. Load Time Series Formulation and Statistical Analysis

The time-varying nature of both residential and community electrical load datasets is modeled by deploying smaller auto-regressive data models. An autoregressive model depicts that the output variable depends linearly on its own previous values and on a stochastic term, therefore the model is in the form of a stochastic difference equation. Specifically, an autoregressive model of order p is defined as in Equation (3):

$$X_t = c + \sum_{i=1}^{p} \phi_i + X_{t-1} + e_t \qquad (3)$$

Here ϕ_i are the parameters of the model, c is a constant, and e_t is the error, where $E(e_t) = 0$ and $Var(e_t) = \sigma^2$.

The stationarity of the load time series is explored by deploying the unit root test [61]. A linear stochastic process has a unit root, if 1 is a root of the process' characteristic equation. Such a process is non-stationary but does not always have a trend. If the other roots of the characteristic equation lie inside the unit circle—that is, have a modulus (absolute value) less than one—then the first difference of the process will be stationary; otherwise, the process will need to be differentiated multiple times to become stationary. Due to this characteristic, unit root processes are also called difference stationary. Unit root processes may sometimes be confused with trend-stationary processes; while they share many properties, they are different in many aspects. It is possible for a time series to be non-stationary, yet to have no unit root and be trend-stationary. In both unit root and trend-stationary processes, their mean average may be increasing or decreasing over time; however, in the presence of a shock, trend-stationary processes are mean-reverting. The previous discrete-time stochastic process can be rewritten as an autoregressive process of order p:

$$X_t = \alpha_1 x_{t-1} + \alpha_2 x_{t-2} + \ldots + \alpha_p x_{t-p} + e_t \qquad (4)$$

and

$$E(X_t | X_{t-1}, \ldots, X_p) = \sum_{i=1}^{p} \alpha_i X_{t-i} \qquad (5)$$

The time series is a serially uncorrelated, zero-mean stochastic process with constant variance σ^2. If $m = 1$ is a root of the characteristic Equation (6) then the stochastic process has a unit root.

$$m^p - m^{p-1} \alpha_1 - m^{p-2} \alpha_2 - \ldots - \alpha_p = 0 \qquad (6)$$

The stochastic process has a unit root or, alternatively, is 1st order integrated. If $m = 1$ with a root of multiplicity r, then the stochastic process is r_{th} integrated, denoted $I(r)$. There are various tests to check the existence of a unit root. In this paper we use the Augmented Dickey Fuller (ADF) [62] test which is widely used in statistics and econometrics. This analysis tests the null hypothesis that a unit root is present in a time series sample. If the unit root is not present then we cannot determine whether the time series is stationary. The ADF test is suitable for a large and more complicated set of time series models. The ADF index (γ) is a negative number; the more negative it is, the stronger the rejection of the hypothesis of non-stationarity for the observed level of significance is. As can be seen from Table 1, for all datasets the null hypothesis for non-stationarity has been rejected at the 0.01 significance level. Therefore it is quite likely that the electric load measured in all these cases displays the characteristic of trend or differential stationarity. The testing process of the ADF test is similar to the Dickey Fuller test but it is applied to the following model Equation (7).

$$\Delta x_t = \alpha + \beta_t + \gamma_{t-1} + \delta \Delta x_{t-1} + \cdots + \delta_{p-1} \Delta x_{t-p+1} + e_t \qquad (7)$$

2.3. Stationarity Analysis

The CNN structure is based on image as an input and for this reason the first step of our methodology is to transform the time series-sequential data into an appropriate, image-like form in order to be processed by the CNN. Image data can be more efficiently processed by CNNs because of their ability to handle the local stationarity of the respective pixels. Image data, namely pixels are characterized as highly stationary and this is the feature that our investigation will leverage. By detecting such behavior in our data we will accordingly transform our time series into "image" like structures. Electrical load data, as mentioned before, appear to have time stationarity.

In order to determine the stationarity of each dataset we calculate their sample means (Mean in Table 1) and standard deviations (STD in Table 1). In a stationary process the unconditional joint probability distribution (and consequently its mean and standard deviations) does not change when shifted in time, so we split each dataset into two sets of equal size and we check how close their corresponding mean and standard deviations values are. Table 1 contains the results of this analysis.

Table 1. Stationarity analysis results.

Dataset	Trento	Household	Office
Mean 1	44.58	235.73	1.25
Mean 2	61.43	215.45	1.15
STD 1	18.97	298.70	1.30
STD 2	17.14	218.62	1.07
Stationary	NO	NO	YES

As it can be seen, only the office dataset display a clearly stationary behavior, while the Trento and Household data need further investigation. For these two datasets the second step of the stationary analysis, the Unit Root ADF test is performed. Those results are presented in Table 2.

Table 2. ADF Test results.

Dataset	p-Value (ADF Test)	ADF	Stationary
Trento	0.01	-3.40	YES
Household	$\ll 0.01$	-18.4	YES

Apparently, the results of the ADF test indicate that both datasets can be assumed to be stationary, based on their corresponding p-values. Therefore the CNN model can now be further exploited.

2.4. Time Interval Selection

After examining stationarity, the next step would be to partition the dataset and transform it into an image-like matrix. For this step a deep statistical analysis is necessary, in order to determine the autocorrelation coefficients of the given datasets by applying the Auto-Correlation Function (ACF) test. The majority of multi-step forecasting strategies introduce errors, which are directly dependent on the forecasting horizon; the longer the forecasting horizon, the higher the errors. Consequently, reduced precision is inevitable as the horizon grows. To alleviate the absence of data stationarity, a novel technique is proposed that leads to a performance closer to uni-step forecasting methods. Specifically, we introduce a technique that manages to shorten the forecasting horizon so as to mimic a uni-step forecasting method. This is achieved by choosing the inputs of our model in an alternative way, which is explained below.

Despite that the method of determining the inputs of NN for STLF still remains an open question. The most common technique is to use as input the immediately preceded value. So, if we want to predict n we will have as input the $n-1$ value. This achieves great results in uni-step forecasting but for multi-step it introduces some errors, since the forecasted errors are accumulated and the final predicted value will not be accurate. In our case, the inputs are determined based on the experience or an-priori knowledge about the behavior of the system. A rather intuitive guess in load forecasting is that there must be instants in the past homologous to the current period, either during the same period on the previous day (24 h ago) or during the same period on the previous week, or previous two weeks, and so on.

In this paper, the inputs for the neural networks are determined after examining the ACF; the assumption regarding homologous instants is analyzed in the second part of our proposed methodology. Based on this analysis it was derived that the most recent 24-h data exhibit the highest correlation with the forecasts and as such they form the basic input of the proposed methodology. In this way, the day ahead forecast problem is transformed into a uni-step problem. The first part of the analysis deals with the development of the auto-correlation plot of observations starting at time t and for two days duration. Figures 2–4 present the correlation analysis and auto-correlation plots for Trento, household and office datasets. The vertical axis shows the ACF value, which ranges from −1 to 1. The horizontal axis of the plot shows the size of the lag between the elements of the time series. For instance, the autocorrelation with lag 4 is the correlation between the time series elements and the corresponding elements observed four periods earlier.

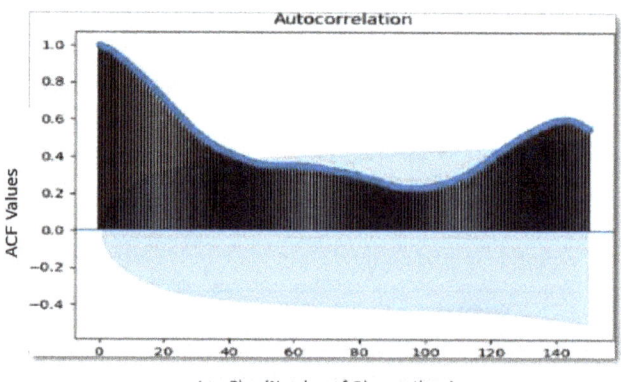

Figure 2. Autocorrelation plot for Trento data . The vertical axis shows the ACF value. The horizontal axis of the plot shows the size of the lag between the elements of the time series.

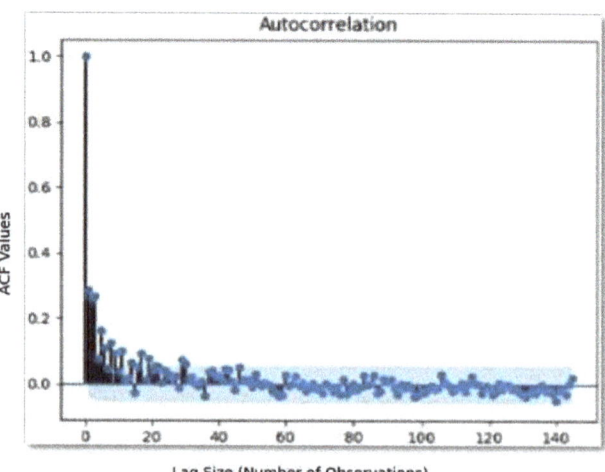

Figure 3. Autocorrelation plot for the single household data. The vertical axis shows the ACF value. The horizontal axis of the plot shows the size of the lag between the elements of the time series.

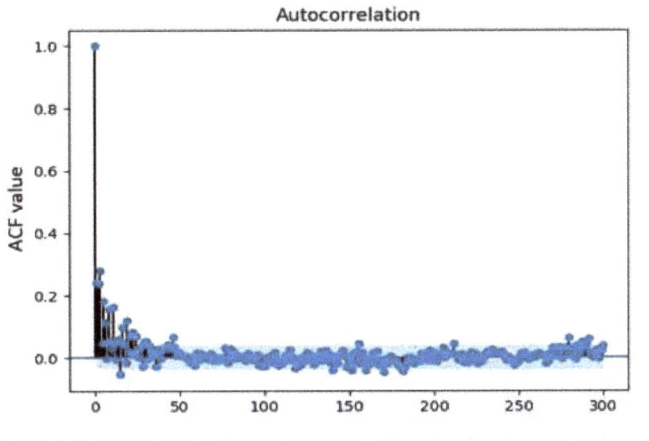

Figure 4. Autocorrelation plot for the office data. The vertical axis shows the ACF value. The horizontal axis of the plot shows the size of the lag between the elements of the time series.

As it can be seen, the highest correlation values are derived at the same time the previous or next day (every 24 h), which confirms the assumption of stationarity of Table 1. According to these results, the highest correlated value, always for after one day, is the:

1. t-144 for Trento
2. t-144 for Household dataset
3. t-288 for the Office dataset

The first step of data transformation is then performed, since these results determine the one of the two dimension of our matrix, namely the columns. The following step is linked with the examination of the datasets in terms of these columns; more precisely we are trying to define a B (batch size) $\times I$ (highest correlated value) matrix. Additionally, it is evident that the highest correlated value, determined above will be the input for out model.

3. Results

Batch Size (Hyper-Parameters Tuning) and Data Transformation

Hyper-parameters tuning can enhance the effectiveness of the ANN-based models. The most common method for tuning the model parameters is trial and error. Regarding the number of epochs, there is no general rule or special procedure, since this parameter expresses only the times the dataset is parsed.

On the other hand, the batch size is a much more complex parameter. It determines the number of samples that will be propagated through the network, while the model updates the weights after each propagation instance. The batch size is a very important parameter because it can accelerate or slow down the training process of the model. In this paper, we study the effects that batch size has on the accuracy of the proposed model and an optimal batch size tuning method is proposed. After the correlation analysis is concluded, a time interval is selected which is used as input for our models. Our method ensures that the optimal batch size must correspond to the chosen time interval. When the batch size is randomly selected or the classic trial and error method is employed, the weights are updated in randomly chosen time periods, considering groups of observations that do not match the statistical analysis of the dataset. As a result, the updated weights are incorrect. On the contrary, if the batch size is determined consistently with the chosen time interval, the model reviews a specific time period with proven inclusion of the relevant observations.

In this way, the proposed methodology leads to a more efficient tuning process and in most cases to better performances.

Regarding the CNN architecture it comprises of three elements involved in the convolution operation: the input pattern (image), the feature detector (kernel or filter) and the feature map. The feature detector (filter) takes into consideration the parameter that is expressed through its length. In image recognition applications the CNN parses the image into groups determined by the filter length. For example an image of 256 pixels determines a filter length of 256. In our case, as mentioned before, the full time series dataset is separated into smaller groups which express a specific time period with high correlation. Those smaller groups are handled as different images, of different pixel size and the filter length is chosen accordingly. If the statistical analysis concludes that the highest correlated interval is that corresponding to the same time the day before, we have an 1-D image or if it corresponds to that of the same time two days ago, we have a 2-D image of n (observations per day) $\times$ 2 (days ago). The $n \times 2$ multiplication implies the resulting filter length following the same reasoning as with the batch size tuning (filter length should be equal to batch size or a derivative of that).

The proposed algorithm was tested on metering data from three different publicly available datasets. For the household use case the measurement site refers to a single family housing with four family members. The sampling period is 10 min. spanning from 12 July 2012 to 26 July 2012. For the office use case the sampling period is 50 min. spanning from 2 July 2014 to 17 July 2014. The energy consumption dataset for Trento is provided by the local energy company, SET, that manages almost the entire electrical network over the Trentino territory [63]. SET uses around 180 primary (medium voltage) distribution lines to bring energy from the national grid (high voltage) to Trentino's consumers. The dataset was collected from 1 November 2013 to 10 November 2013 over a territory of 6000 km^2 in Northern Italy, the province of Trento. The dataset comprises 50 thousand records for energy consumption and the sampling period consists of 10 min. intervals. The main criterion for the use cases selection was the diversity of the examined datasets. Hence, we test our methodology with different time periods, level/magnitude of demand, consumption patterns and specific characteristics such as demand volatility. By doing so, its applicability is expanded and its advantages are verified. The size of the examined datasets is summarized in Table 3.

Table 3. Datasets Results.

Dataset	Trento	Household	Office
Size (days)	9	14	15
Dataset size (observations)	1296	2016	4320

For each dataset, the results of the proposed method are compared with the corresponding results from algorithms which are among the most employed methods across literature. To evaluate the forecasting accuracy, we estimate the Mean Absolute Error (MAE) and the Root Mean Square Error (RMSE) [64] as follows:

$$MAE = \frac{\sum_{i=1}^{n}|A_t - F_t|}{n}, \quad RMSE = \sqrt{\frac{1}{T}\sum_{t=1}^{T}|A_t - F_t|} \quad (8)$$

where A_t are the actuals and F_t the corresponding forecasted values. Another metric that is also very popular across literature is the Mean Absolute Percentage Error (MAPE) [65] which is defined as:

$$MAPE = \frac{100}{n}\frac{\sum_{i=1}^{n}|A_t - F_t|}{A_t}\% \quad (9)$$

MAPE gives a percentage, so it is useful for comparison purposes. Moreover, percentages are in general, more understandable to people and thus MAPE provides initial information regarding the accuracy of the forecasted time series. Like all percentage errors, MAPE has the advantage of being scale-independent hence it is often employed when we need to compare different time series. On the other hand, MAPE as a percentage, has the disadvantage of being undefined or infinite in case of $A_t = 0$, or having extreme values when A_t is close to zero. Some software tools ignore actual values that are equal to zero, however this aggravates the aforementioned issue since MAPE cannot take into account the forecasts when the actual value is zero. Another issue with percentage metrics is the assumption that A_t has a scale based on quantity. However, this is not the case with time series like temperature or energy demand since they are not measuring quantity. Moreover, MAPE value can be over 100% or even negative. A MAPE over 100% means that the errors are "much greater" than the actual values. Based on the above limitations, MAPE, which is a very common accuracy metric, should be used in conjunction with other metrics in order to have a clear indication and better understanding of the examined forecasting models. Because of the nature of load time series and the shortcomings of MAPE, in order to evaluate the performance of our proposed method, we employed only metrics that are related to the absolute values or squared differences of the examined time series, namely Mean Absolute Error (MAE) and Root Mean Square Error (RMSE).

In order to determine the optimal batch sizes for our model, we need to examine the results of the trial and error method applied. The batch sizes examined were multiples of the highest correlated values above. For example for the Trento dataset we experimented with batch sizes of 144, 288 (144 × 2), 432 (144 × 3), but also with a number of randomly chosen ones like 231 or 216 for the office dataset in order to strengthen our assumption. In Figures 5–7 the achieved values of MAE and RMSE are presented for different batch sizes for the Trento, household and office datasets respectively. Each dataset is split in two parts, namely the training (80%) and the testing (20%) datasets. Those three datasets present the most interesting scenarios, because the availability of data is very limited and the investigated datasets present higher volatility on their consumption patterns, since they are small scale examples. Therefore, the proposed method offers a solution to the forecasting problem, when data shortage is present and small scale cases are employed.

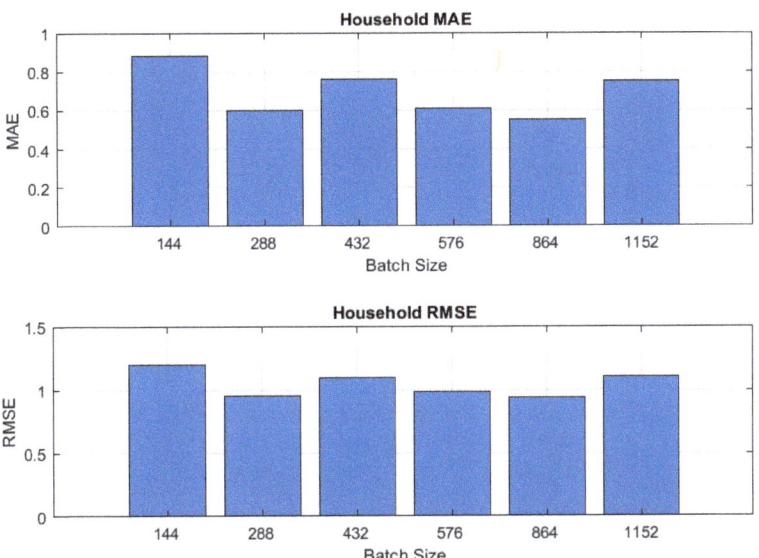

Figure 5. Metrics for the Household case: Household MAE and Household RMSE.

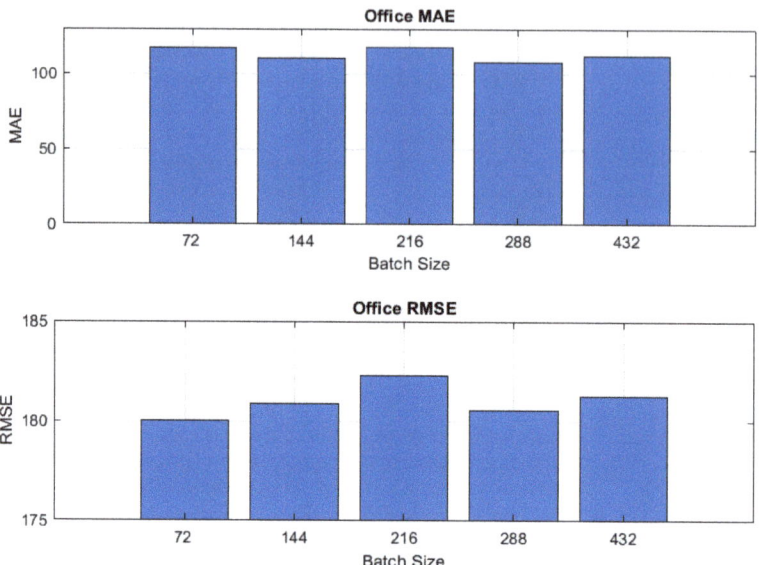

Figure 6. Metrics for the Office case: Office MAE and Office RMSE.

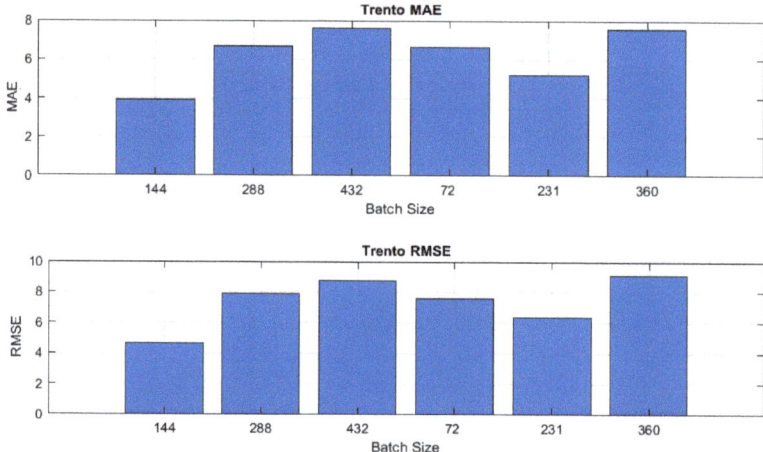

Figure 7. Metrics for Trento case: Trento MAE and Trento RMSE.

The household and office datasets are the most challenging ones, since they exhibit low auto-correlation and higher volatility/stochasticity compared to the rest. In the household case, the minimum MAE corresponds to batch sizes (144 observations/day) of 288 and 864 observations respectively (both multiples of 144). Since the minimum RMSE corresponds to a forecasting period of 864 observations, experimental data with different batch sizes indicated that the batch size should be chosen to be 864. Similarly, for the Trento dataset the batch size is chosen at 144 (144 observations per day). The batch size for the office dataset is chosen accordingly. The selected batch sizes for each dataset are summarized in Table 4. The best RMSE and MAE values are derived as a multiple of the number of the batch observations for each dataset. This is derived as a result of the ACF analysis. In Table 5–7, the summarized results of MAE and RMSE for all models and for every dataset are presented.

Table 4. Parameters Selection.

Dataset	Trento	Household	Office
Batch size	144 (144 × 1)	864 (144 × 6)	288 (288 × 1)
Input	t-144	t-144	t-288

At this point we have a clear picture of the dataset transformation. As shown in Figure 8, we started from a sequential time series dataset and transformed it accordingly into a matrix. The transformed data are then ready to be fed into the CNN model. If the statistical analysis concludes that the interval with the highest correlation is that corresponding to the same time the day before, we have an 1D image. If it corresponds to that of the same time two days ago, we have a 2D image n (observations per day) × 2 (days ago) image. The $n \times 2$ multiplication implies the resulting filter length following the same reasoning as with the batch size tuning (the filter length should be equal to batch size or to a derivative of that).

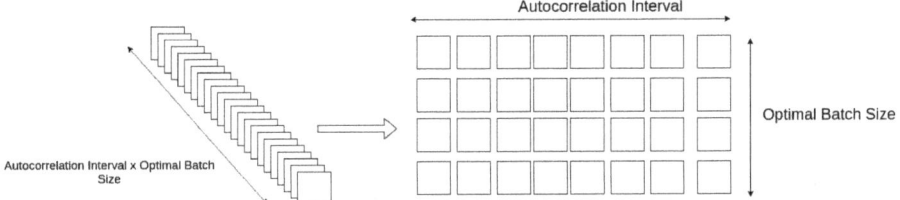

Figure 8. Data transformation.

The proposed methodology was developed and tested in Python with Keras library the backend of which is Tensorflow. Based on the experimental results shown in Tables 5–7 the methodology appears to have good performance and the model selection approach, works satisfactorily even for datasets that exhibit high variability. Our approach was compared against a number of other well reputed AI algorithms such as LSTM, ANN and MLP. These models were chosen due to the fact that are widely accepted in literature and are considered to be suitable for time series forecasting applications, like load forecasting, thus forming a valid candidate for the problem under examination. Regarding ANN we have chosen one hidden layer while for MLP, CNN and LSTM the hidden layers were 5. Such choices were made by trial and error, i.e., adding more hidden layers did not enhance the prediction accuracy. The activation function used was ReLU and the number of epochs was 150 for all models; the optimizer was RMS-Prop and the additional parameters for CNN were the following: size of filter 3 × 3, number of input filters 24, maximum pooling size 3 × 3, and size of strides 1. The batch size was settled based on the methodology explained earlier for all models.

The forecast chosen is the "Day ahead" one as defined by the electricity market. The "Day ahead" market is essential for the operation of the power system since a better forecasting tool means that a market participant (i.e., an aggregator, balance responsible party, local energy market operator etc) will make better choices for the next day operation and will minimize the costs that low-accuracy forecasts would bring (high deviations from the forecasted load would mean higher cost in order to balance the system). In our case study the forecast horizon was restricted by the limited availability of historical data.

Table 5. Results (Trento).

Models	LSTM	CNN	MLP	ANN
MAE	4.58	3.93	5.27	7.58
RMSE	5.3	4.67	4.56	6.63

Table 6. Results (Household).

Models	LSTM	CNN	MLP	ANN
MAE	0.66	0.55	0.58	0.78
RMSE	1.1	0.93	0.96	1.25

Table 7. Results (Office).

Models	LSTM	CNN	MLP	ANN
MAE	114.8	108.29	140.55	172.38
RMSE	189.38	180.54	224.96	236

In Tables 5–7 the results of the investigated models (LSTM, CNN, MLP and ANN) for each one of the datasets are presented. The metrics utilized are the Mean Absolute Error (MAE) and Root Mean Squared Error (RMSE) which are shown in the left column of each table. The CNN-based model outperforms the other ones for all three datasets. CNN achieves better results both in terms of MAE and RMSE, with the only exception being the Trento's dataset where the RMSE result of MLP is slightly better than that of CNN. The performance of CNN regarding MAE is better than that of MLP and this fact can compensate the RMSE difference while CNN also outperforms the rest of the models. The relatively small RMSE and MAE values justify the claim that the proposed batch size tuning method and the time interval input selection strategy substantially improve the performance of our methodology.

Figures 9–11 present the plots of the best forecasts for Trento, household and office datasets. We have chosen to present only the last 20% of all observations from each examined load time series. This was due to two main reasons. Firstly, this part of the dataset is used for testing the algorithm and measuring accuracy of each methodology. Secondly, if we presented all observations and load time series it would be difficult for the reader to drive any conclusions. Also, we present graphically only the CNN algorithm performance since it outperforms all other solutions tested with respect to forecasting accuracy. In Figures 9–11 the actual load is depicted with red color line while the blue line represents the forecast for specific observation numbers (X axis). Y corresponds to the total load either actual or forecasted. As shown in Figures 9 and 10 the proposed model follows the actual load successfully with the exception of one spike for each dataset (where our forecast could not predict it successfully). In the household dataset, (in Figure 9) for 1900 observations our model provides a much higher value of the electric load compared to the real one. We observe the same behaviour for the office dataset (Figure 10). For the Trento dataset (Figure 11), the CNN model performs adequately well and follows quite precisely the value of real, expected load. In general, the results indicate that our model was accurate for all datasets.

Apparently, our model in all three forecasted time series exposes sufficiently good accuracy and follows satisfactorily the actual load time series. Of course, CNN cannot predict the spikes that occur randomly and are the results of sudden disturbances without any pattern and thus very difficult to be predicted. As explained earlier, CNN exploits the temporal stationarity of the load time series, hence it is not possible to predict future observations with high variability. In case of load spikes the temporal stationarity is distorted, therefore CNN cannot provide an accurate prediction.

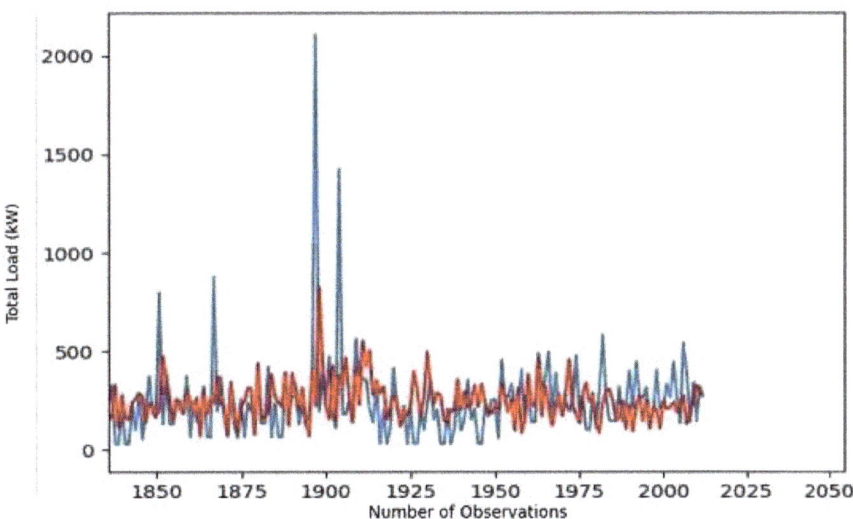

Figure 9. Actual and forecasted load (household). The actual load is depicted with red color and the forecasted time series with blue color.

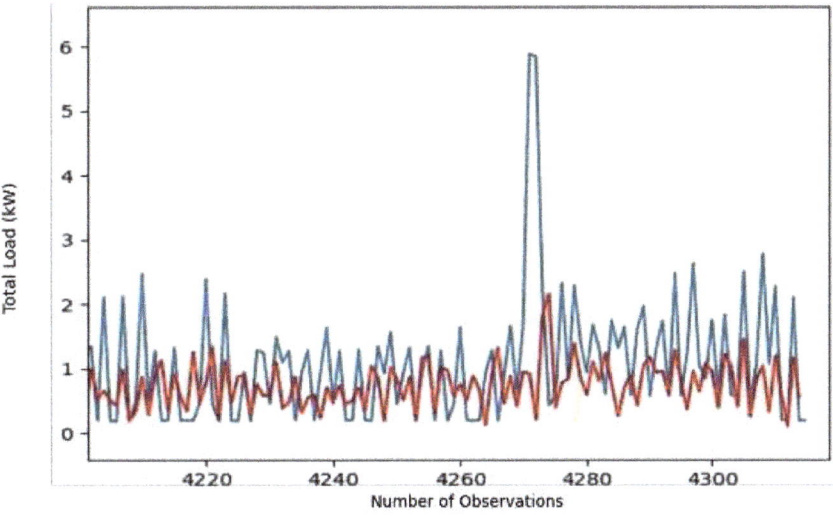

Figure 10. Actual and forecasted load (office). The actual load is depicted with red color and the forecasted time series with blue color.

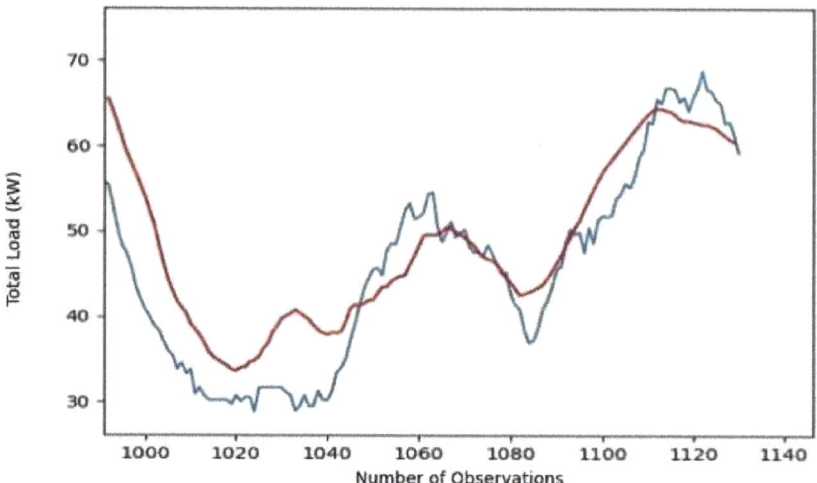

Figure 11. Actual and forecasted load (Trento). The actual load is depicted with red color and the forecasted time series with blue color.

4. Discussion

In this work we present a methodology that is based on statistical analysis and involves the preprocessing of the time series data before addressing the problem of short term electric load forecasting. The methodology employs statistical learning and proper data transformation in an image-like format in order to benefit from the CNN-based models, which exploit stationarity and time locality. While the superiority and the efficiency of LSTM (based on the importance of the inherent memory in load time series) are widely accepted, we showed that CNN-based models present a credible alternative for short term forecasting problems when compared to LSTM algorithms (leveraging the temporal locality of load time series by analogy with image processing where space locality is exploited). The achieved accuracy, based on MAE and RMSE, indicates that the proposed CNN algorithm's performance was improved compared to the LSTM model. CNNs seem to achieve better accuracy when we lack of historical data, the scale of the energy entities is small and the forecast horizon is short (day -ahead forecast). Since the efficiency of the LSTM for long term dependencies is unquestionable, a hybrid LSTM-CNN model is worth examining in future research work, especially for multi-step method considerations. The presented methodology performs demand forecasting at low scale level and thus the forecasted time series can be used as input to various energy management algorithms at microgrid or house level, providing a useful tool for optimizing the operation of the energy entities at the grid edge. Even though LSTM is the most common model to tackle the load forecasting problem, we have proven here that CNN can outperform LSTM in cases where the number of the observations and the energy deployment are limited (loads in a household or in a small energy community) and the load patterns change dynamically. We conclude that if AMI and the relevant communications infrastructure exist, the CNN model is more suitable for forecasting loads of a house, office, building or even of an energy community.

Author Contributions: This paper was a collaborative effort among the authors. N.A. and A.M., designed and performed experiments, analysed data, validated the results and co-wrote the paper; A.B., M.B., C.V. and S.D. supervised the research and co-wrote the paper; E.H., A.P. and G.P.P. reviewed the paper. All authors have read and agreed to the published version of the manuscript.

Funding: This research was funded by the EU H2020 research and innovation program under project CROSSBOW—CROSS BOrder management of variable renewable energies and storage units enabling a transnational Wholesale market (Grant No. 773430).

Institutional Review Board Statement: Not applicable.

Informed Consent Statement: Not applicable.

Conflicts of Interest: The authors declare no conflict of interest.

Abbreviations

The following abbreviations are used in this manuscript:

RES	Renewable Energy Systems
CNN	Convolution Neural Network
LSTM	Long Short Term Memory
AR	Autoregressive
ARX	Autoregressive with Exogenous Variables
ARMA	Autoregressive Moving Average
ANN	Artificial Neural Network
RNN	Recurrent Neural Network
VSTLF	Very Short Term Load Forecasting
STLF	Short Term Load Forecasting
MTLF	Medium Term Load Forecasting
LTLF	Long Term Load Forecasting
DER	Distributed Energy Resources
DSO	Distribution System Operator
LV	Low Voltage
HV	High Voltage
PCA	Principal Component Analysis
MLR	Multiple Linear Regression
HEMS	Home Energy Management Systems
LEM	Local Energy Markets
THI	Temperature-Humidity Index
PJM	Pennsylvania-New Jersey-Maryland
AMI	Advanced Metering Infrastructure
PI	Prediction Intervals
LUBE	Lower Upper Bound Estimation
SSA	Singular Spectrum Analysis
PC	Principal Components
SVM	Support Vector Machine
WNN	Wavelet Neural Network
SRWNN	Self-Recurrent Wavelet Neural Network
CRBM	Conditional Restricted Boltzmann Machine
FCRBM	Factored Conditional Restricted Boltzmann Machine
CKD	Conditional Kernel Density
MLP	Multilayer Perceptron
SIANN	Space Invariant Artificial Neural Networks
ReLU	Rectified Linear Unit
ADF	Augmented Dickey Fuller
STD	standard deviation
ACF	Auto-Correlation Function
MAE	Mean Absolute Error
RMSE	Root Mean Square Error
MAPE	Mean Absolute Percentage Error

References

1. Zhang, G.P. Time series forecasting using a hybrid ARIMA and neural network model. *Neurocomputing* **2003**, *50*, 159–175. [CrossRef]
2. Papalexopoulos, A.D.; Hesterberg, T.C. A regression-based approach to short-term system load forecasting. *IEEE Trans. Power Syst.* **1990**, *5*, 1535–1547. [CrossRef]
3. Papalexopoulos, A.D.; Hao, S.; Peng, T.M. An implementation of a neural network based load forecasting model for the EMS. *IEEE Trans. Power Syst.* **1994**, *9*, 1956–1962. [CrossRef]
4. Papalexopoulos, A.D.; Hao, S.; Peng, T.M. Application of neural network technology to short-term system load forecasting. In Proceedings of the Joint International Power Conference Athens Power Tech, Athens, Greece, 5–8 September 1993; Volume 2, pp. 796–800.
5. Chen, B.J.; Chang, M.W. Load forecasting using support vector machines: A study on EUNITE competition 2001. *IEEE Trans. Power Syst.* **2004**, *19*, 1821–1830. [CrossRef]
6. Ghelardoni, L.; Ghio, A.; Anguita, D. Energy load forecasting using empirical mode decomposition and support vector regression. *IEEE Trans. Smart Grid* **2013**, *4*, 549–556. [CrossRef]
7. Hochreiter, S.; Schmidhuber, J. Long short-term memory. *Neural Comput.* **1997**, *9*, 1735–1780. [CrossRef]
8. Zheng, J.; Xu, C.; Zhang, Z.; Li, X. Electric load forecasting in smart grids using long-short-term-memory based recurrent neural network. In Proceedings of the 2017 51st Annual Conference on Information Sciences and Systems (CISS), Baltimore, MD, USA, 22–24 March 2017; pp. 1–6.
9. Giasemidis, G.; Haben, S.; Lee, T.; Singleton, C.; Grindrod, P. A genetic algorithm approach for modelling low voltage network demands. *Appl. Energy* **2017**, *203*, 463–473. [CrossRef]
10. Bennett, C.; Stewart, R.A.; Lu, J. Autoregressive with exogenous variables and neural network short-term load forecast models for residential low voltage distribution networks. *Energies* **2014**, *7*, 2938–2960. [CrossRef]
11. Bennett, C.J.; Stewart, R.A.; Lu, J.W. Forecasting low voltage distribution network demand profiles using a pattern recognition based expert system. *Energy* **2014**, *67*, 200–212. [CrossRef]
12. Høverstad, B.A.; Tidemann, A.; Langseth, H.; Öztürk, P. Short-term load forecasting with seasonal decomposition using evolution for parameter tuning. *IEEE Trans. Smart Grid* **2015**, *6*, 1904–1913. [CrossRef]
13. Fan, S.; Hyndman, R.J. Short-term load forecasting based on a semi-parametric additive model. *IEEE Trans. Power Syst.* **2011**, *27*, 134–141. [CrossRef]
14. Goude, Y.; Nedellec, R.; Kong, N. Local short and middle term electricity load forecasting with semi-parametric additive models. *IEEE Trans. Smart Grid* **2013**, *5*, 440–446. [CrossRef]
15. Ding, N.; Bésanger, Y.; Wurtz, F. Next-day MV/LV substation load forecaster using time series method. *Electr. Power Syst. Res.* **2015**, *119*, 345–354. [CrossRef]
16. Ding, N.; Benoit, C.; Foggia, G.; Bésanger, Y.; Wurtz, F. Neural network-based model design for short-term load forecast in distribution systems. *IEEE Trans. Power Syst.* **2015**, *31*, 72–81. [CrossRef]
17. Cecati, C.; Citro, C.; Siano, P. Combined operations of renewable energy systems and responsive demand in a smart grid. *IEEE Trans. Sustain. Energy* **2011**, *2*, 468–476. [CrossRef]
18. Liu, Y. Continuous dependence for a thermal convection model with temperature-dependent solubility. *Appl. Math. Comput.* **2017**, *308*, 18–30. [CrossRef]
19. Rowe, M.; Yunusov, T.; Haben, S.; Holderbaum, W.; Potter, B. The real-time optimisation of DNO owned storage devices on the LV network for peak reduction. *Energies* **2014**, *7*, 3537–3560. [CrossRef]
20. Rowe, M.; Yunusov, T.; Haben, S.; Singleton, C.; Holderbaum, W.; Potter, B. A peak reduction scheduling algorithm for storage devices on the low voltage network. *IEEE Trans. Smart Grid* **2014**, *5*, 2115–2124. [CrossRef]
21. El-Baz, W.; Tzscheutschler, P. Short-term smart learning electrical load prediction algorithm for home energy management systems. *Appl. Energy* **2015**, *147*, 10–19. [CrossRef]
22. Keerthisinghe, C.; Verbič, G.; Chapman, A.C. A fast technique for smart home management: ADP with temporal difference learning. *IEEE Trans. Smart Grid* **2016**, *9*, 3291–3303. [CrossRef]
23. Pratt, A.; Krishnamurthy, D.; Ruth, M.; Wu, H.; Lunacek, M.; Vaynshenk, P. Transactive home energy management systems: The impact of their proliferation on the electric grid. *IEEE Electrif. Mag.* **2016**, *4*, 8–14. [CrossRef]
24. Morstyn, T.; Farrell, N.; Darby, S.J.; McCulloch, M.D. Using peer-to-peer energy-trading platforms to incentivize prosumers to form federated power plants. *Nat. Energy* **2018**, *3*, 94–101. [CrossRef]
25. Hong, T.; Xie, J.; Black, J. Global energy forecasting competition 2017: Hierarchical probabilistic load forecasting. *Int. J. Forecast.* **2019**, *35*, 1389–1399. [CrossRef]
26. Haben, S.; Ward, J.; Greetham, D.V.; Singleton, C.; Grindrod, P. A new error measure for forecasts of household-level, high resolution electrical energy consumption. *Int. J. Forecast.* **2014**, *30*, 246–256. [CrossRef]
27. Sousa, J.M.; Neves, L.M.; Jorge, H.M. Short-term load forecasting using information obtained from low voltage load profiles. In Proceedings of the 2009 International Conference on Power Engineering, Energy and Electrical Drives, Lisbon, Portugal, 18–20 March 2009; pp. 655–660.

28. Veit, A.; Goebel, C.; Tidke, R.; Doblander, C.; Jacobsen, H.A. Household electricity demand forecasting: Benchmarking state-of-the-art methods. In Proceedings of the 5th International Conference on Future Energy Systems, Cambridge, UK, 11–13 June 2014; pp. 233–234.
29. Chitsaz, H.; Shaker, H.; Zareipour, H.; Wood, D.; Amjady, N. Short-term electricity load forecasting of buildings in microgrids. *Energy Build.* **2015**, *99*, 50–60. [CrossRef]
30. Ghofrani, M.; Hassanzadeh, M.; Etezadi-Amoli, M.; Fadali, M.S. Smart meter based short-term load forecasting for residential customers. In Proceedings of the 2011 North American Power Symposium, Boston, MA, USA, 4–6 August 2011; pp. 1–5.
31. Yu, C.N.; Mirowski, P.; Ho, T.K. A sparse coding approach to household electricity demand forecasting in smart grids. *IEEE Trans. Smart Grid* **2016**, *8*, 738–748. [CrossRef]
32. Xie, J.; Hong, T.; Stroud, J. Long-term retail energy forecasting with consideration of residential customer attrition. *IEEE Trans. Smart Grid* **2015**, *6*, 2245–2252. [CrossRef]
33. Vercamer, D.; Steurtewagen, B.; Van den Poel, D.; Vermeulen, F. Predicting consumer load profiles using commercial and open data. *IEEE Trans. Power Syst.* **2015**, *31*, 3693–3701. [CrossRef]
34. Xie, J.; Chen, Y.; Hong, T.; Laing, T.D. Relative humidity for load forecasting models. *IEEE Trans. Smart Grid* **2016**, *9*, 191–198. [CrossRef]
35. Sun, X.; Luh, P.B.; Cheung, K.W.; Guan, W.; Michel, L.D.; Venkata, S.; Miller, M.T. An efficient approach to short-term load forecasting at the distribution level. *IEEE Trans. Power Syst.* **2015**, *31*, 2526–2537. [CrossRef]
36. Borges, C.E.; Penya, Y.K.; Fernandez, I. Evaluating combined load forecasting in large power systems and smart grids. *IEEE Trans. Ind. Inform.* **2012**, *9*, 1570–1577. [CrossRef]
37. Marinescu, A.; Harris, C.; Dusparic, I.; Clarke, S.; Cahill, V. Residential electrical demand forecasting in very small scale: An evaluation of forecasting methods. In Proceedings of the 2013 2nd International Workshop on Software Engineering Challenges for the Smart Grid (SE4SG), San Francisco, CA, USA, 18 May 2013; pp. 25–32.
38. Quilumba, F.L.; Lee, W.J.; Huang, H.; Wang, D.Y.; Szabados, R.L. Using smart meter data to improve the accuracy of intraday load forecasting considering customer behavior similarities. *IEEE Trans. Smart Grid* **2014**, *6*, 911–918. [CrossRef]
39. Quan, H.; Srinivasan, D.; Khosravi, A. Short-term load and wind power forecasting using neural network-based prediction intervals. *IEEE Trans. Neural Netw. Learn. Syst.* **2013**, *25*, 303–315. [CrossRef] [PubMed]
40. Papaioannou, G.P.; Dikaiakos, C.; Dramountanis, A.; Papaioannou, P.G. Analysis and modeling for short-to medium-term load forecasting using a hybrid manifold learning principal component model and comparison with classical statistical models (SARIMAX, Exponential Smoothing) and artificial intelligence models (ANN, SVM): The case of Greek electricity market. *Energies* **2016**, *9*, 635.
41. Edwards, R.E.; New, J.; Parker, L.E. Predicting future hourly residential electrical consumption: A machine learning case study. *Energy Build.* **2012**, *49*, 591–603. [CrossRef]
42. Shi, H.; Xu, M.; Li, R. Deep learning for household load forecasting—A novel pooling deep RNN. *IEEE Trans. Smart Grid* **2017**, *9*, 5271–5280. [CrossRef]
43. Tascikaraoglu, A.; Sanandaji, B.M. Short-term residential electric load forecasting: A compressive spatio-temporal approach. *Energy Build.* **2016**, *111*, 380–392. [CrossRef]
44. Kumar, R.; Aggarwal, R.; Sharma, J. Energy analysis of a building using artificial neural network: A review. *Energy Build.* **2013**, *65*, 352–358. [CrossRef]
45. Kong, W.; Dong, Z.Y.; Hill, D.J.; Luo, F.; Xu, Y. Short-term residential load forecasting based on resident behaviour learning. *IEEE Trans. Power Syst.* **2017**, *33*, 1087–1088. [CrossRef]
46. Keren, G.; Schuller, B. Convolutional RNN: An enhanced model for extracting features from sequential data. In Proceedings of the 2016 International Joint Conference on Neural Networks (IJCNN), Vancouver, BC, Canada, 24–29 July 2016; pp. 3412–3419.
47. Acharya, S.K.; Wi, Y.M.; Lee, J. Short-Term Load Forecasting for a Single Household Based on Convolution Neural Networks Using Data Augmentation. *Energies* **2019**, *12*, 3560. [CrossRef]
48. Canizes, B.; Silva, M.; Faria, P.; Ramos, S.; Vale, Z. Resource scheduling in residential microgrids considering energy selling to external players. In Proceedings of the 2015 Clemson University Power Systems Conference (PSC), Clemson, SC, USA, 10–13 March 2015; pp. 1–7.
49. Almabdy, S.; Elrefaei, L. Deep convolutional neural network-based approaches for face recognition. *Appl. Sci.* **2019**, *9*, 4397. [CrossRef]
50. Li, L.; Ota, K.; Dong, M. Everything is image: CNN-based short-term electrical load forecasting for smart grid. In Proceedings of the 2017 14th International Symposium on Pervasive Systems, Algorithms and Networks & 2017 11th International Conference on Frontier of Computer Science and Technology & 2017 Third International Symposium of Creative Computing (ISPAN-FCST-ISCC), Exeter, UK, 21–23 June 2017; pp. 344–351.
51. Zhang, W. Shift-invariant pattern recognition neural network and its optical architecture. In Proceedings of the Annual Conference of the Japan Society of Applied Physics, Keio Plaza Hotel, Tokyo, Japan, 24–26 August 1988.
52. Zhang, W.; Itoh, K.; Tanida, J.; Ichioka, Y. Parallel distributed processing model with local space-invariant interconnections and its optical architecture. *Appl. Opt.* **1990**, *29*, 4790–4797. [CrossRef] [PubMed]

53. Saha, S. A Comprehensive Guide to Convolutional Neural Networks—the ELI5 Way. 2018. Available online: https://towardsdatascience.com/a-comprehensive-guide-to-convolutional-neural-networks-the-eli5-way-3bd2b1164a53 (accessed on 16 Decmber 2016).
54. LeCun, Y.; Bengio, Y.; Hinton, G. Deep learning. *Nature* **2015**, *521*, 436–444. [CrossRef] [PubMed]
55. LeCun, Y.; Kavukcuoglu, K.; Farabet, C. Convolutional networks and applications in vision. In Proceedings of the 2010 IEEE International Symposium on Circuits and Systems, Paris, France, 30 May–2 June 2010, pp. 253–256.
56. LeCun, Y.; Boser, B.; Denker, J.S.; Henderson, D.; Howard, R.E.; Hubbard, W.; Jackel, L.D. Backpropagation applied to handwritten zip code recognition. *Neural Comput.* **1989**, *1*, 541–551. [CrossRef]
57. Fukushima, K.; Miyake, S.; Ito, T. Neocognitron: A neural network model for a mechanism of visual pattern recognition. *IEEE Trans. Syst. Man. Cybern.* **1983**, *5*, 826–834. [CrossRef]
58. Krizhevsky, A.; Sutskever, I.; Hinton, G.E. Imagenet classification with deep convolutional neural networks. In *(NIPS'12), Proceedings of the 25th International Conference on Neural Information Processing Systems—Volume 1, Lake Tahoe, Nevada, 3–8 December 2012*; Curran Associates Inc.: Red Hook, NY, USA, 2012; pp. 1097–1105.
59. Simonyan, K.; Zisserman, A. Very deep convolutional networks for large-scale image recognition. *arXiv* **2014**, arXiv:1409.1556.
60. Deng, L.; Yu, D. Deep learning: Methods and applications. *Found. Trends Signal Process.* **2014**, *7*, 197–387. [CrossRef]
61. Mills, T.C.; Mills, T.C. *Time Series Techniques for Economists*; Cambridge University Press: Cambridge, UK, 1991.
62. Greene, W.H. *LIMDEP. New York: Econometric Software.* _. 1990. *Econometric Analysis*; MacMillan: New York, NY, USA, 1989.
63. Barlacchi, G.; De Nadai, M.; Larcher, R.; Casella, A.; Chitic, C.; Torrisi, G.; Antonelli, F.; Vespignani, A.; Pentland, A.; Lepri, B. A multi-source dataset of urban life in the city of Milan and the Province of Trentino. *Sci. Data* **2015**, *2*, 1–15. [CrossRef]
64. Willmott, C.J.; Matsuura, K. Advantages of the mean absolute error (MAE) over the root mean square error (RMSE) in assessing average model performance. *Clim. Res.* **2005**, *30*, 79–82. [CrossRef]
65. De Myttenaere, A.; Golden, B.; Le Grand, B.; Rossi, F. Mean absolute percentage error for regression models. *Neurocomputing* **2016**, *192*, 38–48. [CrossRef]

Article

Forecasting Irregular Seasonal Power Consumption. An Application to a Hot-Dip Galvanizing Process

Oscar Trull [1,*], Juan Carlos García-Díaz [1] and Angel Peiró-Signes [2]

1. Department of Applied Statistics, Operational Research and Quality, Universitat Politècnica de València, E-46022 Valencia, Spain; juagardi@eio.upv.es
2. Management Department, Universitat Politècnica de València, E-46022 Valencia, Spain; anpeisig@omp.upv.es
* Correspondence: otrull@eio.upv.es

Featured Application: The method described in this document makes it possible to use the techniques usually applied to load prediction efficiently in those situations in which the series clearly presents seasonality but does not maintain a regular pattern.

Abstract: Distribution companies use time series to predict electricity consumption. Forecasting techniques based on statistical models or artificial intelligence are used. Reliable forecasts are required for efficient grid management in terms of both supply and capacity. One common underlying feature of most demand–related time series is a strong seasonality component. However, in some cases, the electricity demanded by a process presents an irregular seasonal component, which prevents any type of forecast. In this article, we evaluated forecasting methods based on the use of multiple seasonal models: ARIMA, Holt-Winters models with discrete interval moving seasonality, and neural networks. The models are explained and applied to a real situation, for a node that feeds a galvanizing factory. The zinc hot-dip galvanizing process is widely used in the automotive sector for the protection of steel against corrosion. It requires enormous energy consumption, and this has a direct impact on companies' income statements. In addition, it significantly affects energy distribution companies, as these companies must provide for instant consumption in their supply lines to ensure sufficient energy is distributed both for the process and for all the other consumers. The results show a substantial increase in the accuracy of predictions, which contributes to a better management of the electrical distribution.

Keywords: time series; demand; load; forecast; DIMS; irregular; galvanizing

Citation: Trull, O.; García-Díaz, J.C.; Peiró-Signes, A. Forecasting Irregular Seasonal Power Consumption. An Application to a Hot-Dip Galvanizing Process. *Appl. Sci.* **2021**, *11*, 75. https://dx.doi.org/10.3390/app11010075

Received: 1 November 2020
Accepted: 22 December 2020
Published: 23 December 2020

Publisher's Note: MDPI stays neutral with regard to jurisdictional claims in published maps and institutional affiliations.

Copyright: © 2020 by the authors. Licensee MDPI, Basel, Switzerland. This article is an open access article distributed under the terms and conditions of the Creative Commons Attribution (CC BY) license (https://creativecommons.org/licenses/by/4.0/).

1. Introduction

Demand management is a primary process in the development of industrial activity. Distribution companies must ensure a supply is provided at a reasonable cost, and for this reason, they need to manage resources efficiently. The use of electrical prediction models contributes to their management of the distribution lines by offering tools to estimate future demand with great precision. The techniques allow for forecasting based on time series using statistical models or artificial intelligence (AI).

The most widely used univariate forecasting tools for electricity demand can be classified into three broad groups [1]: fundamental models, statistical models, and computational models. There is growing interest in the use of computational models, although the most widely used models are statistical models, both exponential smoothing models and autoregressive integrated moving average (ARIMA) models.

The fundamental models are made up of hybrid models that introduce all the possible physical variables, adopting a complex relationship between them and also using the techniques of statistical models.

Computational models are based on AI and emulate natural behaviors through the use of mathematical models. These are algorithms whose learning is automatic and are part of the science of Machine Learning [2]. At present, deep learning techniques represent an evolution and have found applications in demand forecasting, especially in areas where prediction is difficult, such as renewable energies [3]. The most widely used techniques for electricity demand are artificial neural networks (ANN) [4], particularly non-linear autoregressive neural networks with exogenous variables (NARX) [5,6]. Support vector machines (SVM) [7] and bagged regression trees (BRT) [8] also stand out, and these occasionally apply fuzzy logic [9].

Electricity demand series show stochastic behavior, and they have traditionally been modeled using statistical methods. The ARIMA models are considered to be the econometric models par excellence. The Box–Jenkins methodology [10] is used to determine which ARIMA model to use, although some authors [11] state that simpler methods are better than this methodology at providing forecasts. The application of ARIMA models to demand is usually carried out in a general way in Seasonal Autoregressive Integrated Moving Average Exogenous (SARIMAX) models [12–14] in which exogenous variables are included to improve demand. The introduction of two seasonalities allows substantial improvement in the predictions of these models [15].

State-space models (SSM) are a form of exponential smoothing representation. They are commonly applied to demand [16], especially since the introduction of the Kalman filter (see [17]). They also allow the introduction of various seasonalities in a complex way [18] and with covariates [19]. De Livera and Hyndman include modifications that include adjustment of the error using autoregressive moving average (ARMA) models and with Box-Cox transformations (BATS [20]) and trigonometric seasonality (TBATS [18]).

Other very common smoothing techniques are the Holt-Winters models [20]. These models are excellent predictors for time series with marked seasonality [1,21]. The inclusion of more seasonality [22–24] improves their forecasts, leading to the development of multiple seasonal Holt-Winters models (nHWT). Trull et al. [25] introduce discrete seasonality that takes into account seasonalities whose occurrences are not regular (nHWT-DIMS models).

The current trend is to create hybrid models in which traditional techniques are combined with machine learning [26,27]. An example can be found in [28], which applies an exponential smoothing method and neural networks to divide the forecasting process between a linear part and a non-linear part.

The use of wavelets for irregular series has been combined with ARIMA models [29], Holt-Winters models [30], or ANN [31].

Regularization techniques have also been applied to prevent over- and under-fitting issues, based on a Least Absolute Shrinkage and Selection Operator (LASSO) [32], and have been applied to short-term load forecasting models based on multiple linear regression [33]. Banded regularization is also used to estimate parameters without overfitting in autoregressive models [34].

Newer methods use an anti-leakage least-squares spectral analysis (ALLSSA) to simultaneously estimate the trend and seasonal components before making a regularization and make forecasts [35]. The ALLSSA method determines the statistically significance of the components preventing under- and over-fitting issues. The least-squares wavelet analysis (LSWA) is a natural extension of the least-squares spectral analysis and allows the forecaster to obtain spectrograms for equally and unequally spaced time series and identify statistically significant peaks in the time series [36].

One common feature of most demand-related time series is their strong seasonality components [37]. In some cases, the electricity demanded by a process could present an irregular seasonal component that seriously distorts the behavior of the series in a way that the models cannot deal with.

The zinc hot-dip galvanizing process is a process that is widely used in the automotive sector to protect steel against corrosion [38,39]. It requires an enormous consumption of energy, and this has a direct impact on companies' income statements. However, the process also significantly affects energy distribution companies, since they must foresee the instantaneous consumption in their lines in order to ensure the distribution of energy both for the process and for the other consumers. A characteristic of the demand in this process is the presence of seasonal patterns that resemble seasonality but, because of their irregular behavior, are difficult to assimilate to seasonality.

The structure shown by the series in this study means that it is more suitable to work with time series models rather than frequency or signal analysis. We have therefore considered it convenient to preferably use traditional time series models with seasonality.

In this article, we present several solutions to this problem based on the use of ARIMA models, multiple seasonal Holt-Winters models with and without discrete interval moving seasonalities (DIMS), state space models, and neural network models. To verify the effectiveness of the techniques described, they are applied to the industrial process of hot-dip galvanizing.

The article is organized as follows: Section 2 conducts a review of the forecasting methods as well as an explanation of the production process; Section 3 demonstrates the results and their analysis; Section 4 discusses the results; and finally, in Section 5, the conclusions are summarized.

2. Materials and Methods

2.1. Study Area

The study has been applied to the consumption node of a hot-dip galvanizing company. The process is carried out by coating extruded steel strips with a zinc foil that forms an alloy with the steel and gives the desired properties. This process is continuous and produces high-quality products [40].

Figure 1 shows a general scheme for the galvanizing process, where the greatest consumption is in the zinc bath. In the annealing furnace, the steel strip is preheated, and then it is immersed in a bath of molten zinc at 460 °C. Subsequently, the galvanized steel strip goes through the skin-pass process [41–43] after it has cooled down.

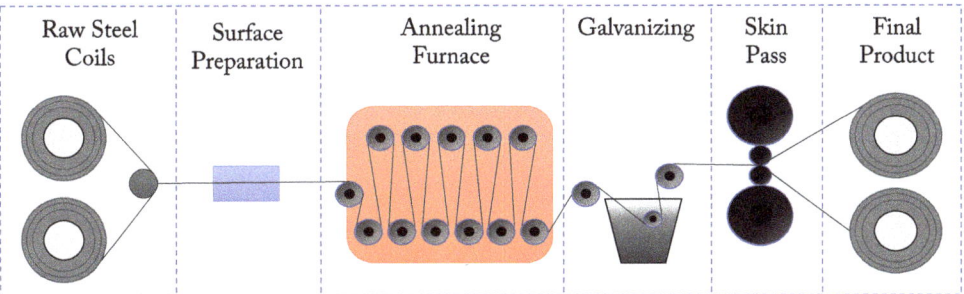

Figure 1. Representation of a hot dip galvanizing process.

The zinc bath consists of a molten alloy of Zn in a bath, which is kept at 460 °C by the action of two heating inductors located at the bottom of the bath. Figure 2 schematically shows the operation of the zinc bath. The bath temperature is measured as an average of the local temperatures provided by the thermocouples Ta, Tb and Tc. The inductors heat from the bottom of the bath and a natural flow inside the bath is produced so that the bath achieves the targeted temperature.

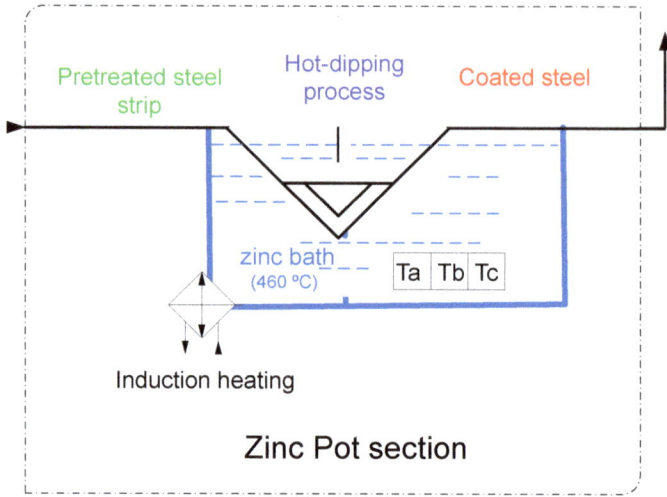

Figure 2. Galvanizing section (hot dip zinc bath). Pretreated steel goes into the zinc pot, which is filled with an Al–Zn solution at 460 °C. Thermocouples Ta, Tb and Tc measure the local temperatures in the bath. Induction heaters located at the base of the bath keep the temperature as targeted. After the bath, the steel is coated with Zn.

The electrical consumption associated with the process can be seen in Figure 3. This graph shows the consumption for eight working days, measured every six minutes. It begins on 14th November, 2009 at 00:00 am and ends on 22nd November, 2009 at 08:00 am. There are in total 2000 measurements. The oscillations shown in the time series are produced by the action of induction heaters that keep the bath at the targeted temperature. The big peaks in consumption are produced when the bath needs to be recharged, and new Zn (dropped in ingots) is added into the bath. At this moment, the heaters must be put into full operation. From this dataset, the first 1800 observed values are used for training purposes, and the last 200 ones are used for validation.

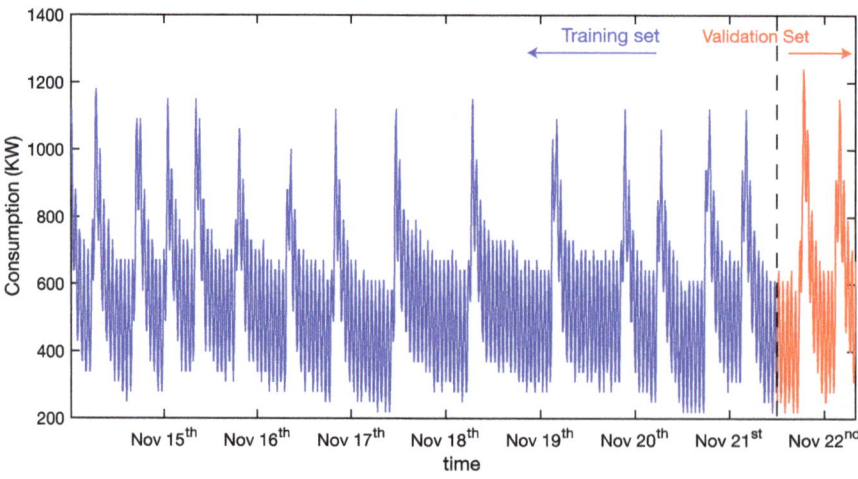

Figure 3. Electricity demand for the hot-dip galvanizing. The ticks represent the beginning of each day. The blue dataset designates the data used for training, whereas the red one represents the data used for testing and validation.

A series of cyclical patterns can be observed (oscillations) that are repeated throughout the series, with a short–length pattern that is repeated continuously throughout the series clearly standing out. There are other patterns that are repeated irregularly, with differentiated behaviors. A closer view of the series is shown in Figure 4. In graph (a) and graph (b), a common underlying pattern can be identified, with a length of around ten time units (which means an hour, as the temperature is measured every six minutes). This first pattern is repeated regularly over the whole time period, and it is considered as a seasonality.

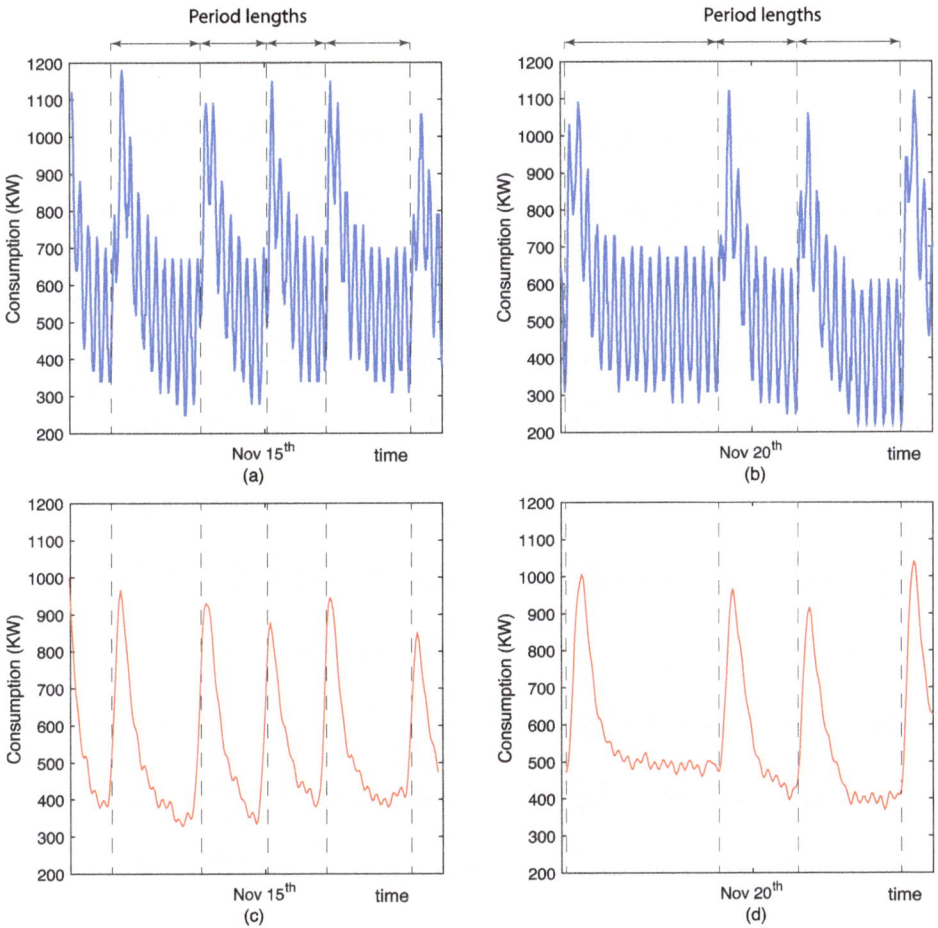

Figure 4. Close-up version of Figure 3, where different seasonal patterns can be located: a first pattern along the whole series, with sort oscillations as shown in (**a**,**b**); and a second pattern covering the consumption peaks, as shown in (**c**,**d**). This second pattern has a different length on every appearance.

Figure 4, graph (c) and (d) show the time series after removing the first seasonal pattern. It can also be seen that other patterns develop throughout the series in such a way that the time of their appearance or their length are not constant. Technically, this non-regular behavior cannot be considered as a seasonality, since it is not possible to predict the fluctuation pattern that will develop in the future. To make consumption predictions, it is necessary to take into account this seasonal behavior, even though it is not regular.

2.2. Forecasting Methods

In this section, we describe the forecasting methods applied to the time series under study. The most common methods applied to short-term electricity demand forecasting, using both AI and statistical methods, have been chosen. First, the methods used with regular seasonal behavior are described, and then we describe the models with discrete seasonality.

2.2.1. Artificial Neural Networks

Neural networks are computational models structured in the form of layers with nodes interconnected as a network. They are named because of their resemblance to the human brain structure. The nodes, called neurons, perform simple operations in parallel and are located in each of the layers of the network. The layers are of three different types: the input layer, where neurons receive direct information from the inputs; hidden layer (s), whose neurons use the information from the neurons of previous layers and feed the next layers; and the output layer, where neurons use the information from the hidden layers to produce an output. Thus, there is an input layer, one or more hidden layers, and an output layer. The connections between the different layers are made through the connection of their neurons, which are called synapses. The strength of the connection between neurons is determined by a weighting established at the synapse.

The most suitable structure for forecasting time series is the NARX type structure [44,45]. It is a recurrent dynamic neural network, with feedback connections. Figure 5 shows a close-loop representation of the NARX structure [46]. Neurons receive information from exogenous input variables in addition to the target series itself and the feedbacks. In order to improve forecasts, it can be used the past predicted and observed values delayed through a tapped delay line (TDL) memory. The circles after the input layers denote the TPL delay (e.g., one to two delays in the figure).

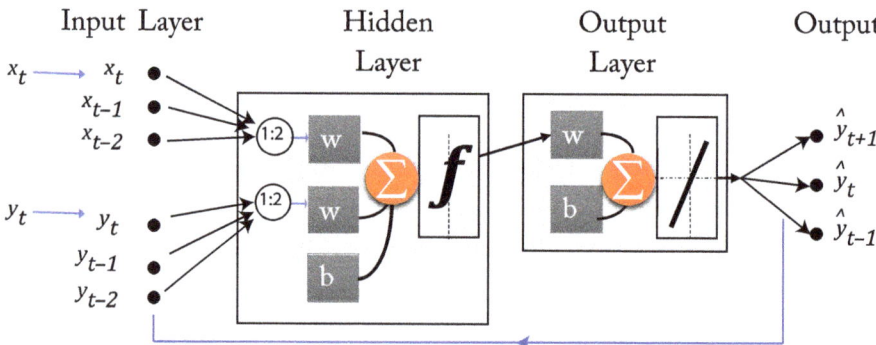

Figure 5. NARX neural network schema. There is an input layer with variables, one hidden layer and one output layers. Circles represent tapped delay line (TDL).

The input variables x_t are exogenous variables used in the model. Both x_i and y_t are connected by axioms to which weights w_i are assigned, and with an activation function f that is integrated with an aggregation function Σ. The output $\hat{y}_{t+1}$ provides future forecasts after the network has been trained. b stands for the bias whose presence increases or decreases the neuron's processing capacity.

The mathematical and non-linear representation that governs the network is shown in (1), where x_t represents the inputs and y_t the objective function, while $\hat{y}_{t+1}$ represents the prediction. D_x and D_y are the time delays applied in the network.

$$\hat{y}_{t+1} = f\left[x_t, x_{t-1}, \ldots, x_{t-D_x+1}, y_t, y_{t-1}, \ldots, y_{t-D_y+1}\right]. \tag{1}$$

The NARX neural network maps the function through the multilayer perceptron, using the time delays for both the input variables and the output feedback [47].

An alternative to this neural network is a function fitting neural network. This is a type of shallow neural network based on multilayer perceptron (MLP) with which we can make adjustments to non-linear functions (non-linear regression, NLR). The use and application of such a network for the prediction of electricity demand has been discussed previously [48]. The mathematical representation that governs this network is shown in (2).

$$\hat{y}_{t+1} = f[x_t, x_{t-1}, \ldots, x_{t-D_x+1}]. \tag{2}$$

Here x_t are the predictors, which are several variables (including the observed values of the time series) used to feed the model. A representative schema for this neural network is shown in Figure 6.

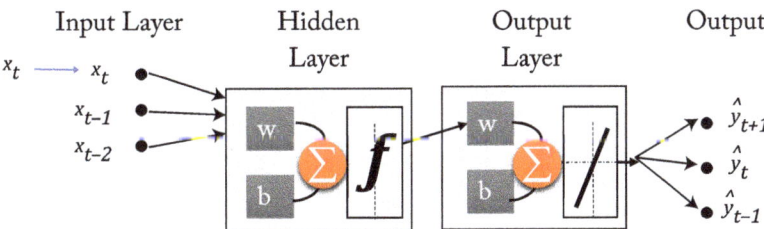

Figure 6. Function fitting neural network schema.

By training the network, weights are assigned to the synaptic connections, minimizing an error criterion. The ANNs used in this work are trained using the Levenberg-Marquardt algorithm [49], and minimizing the mean squared error (MSE). After the training process, to give the predictions, a closed loop network is performed, and forecasts are provided.

2.2.2. ARIMA Models

ARIMA models were introduced by Box and Jenkins [50] to model non–stationary series and allow predictions to be made. A description and in-depth analysis can be found in [51] and in the book by Brockwell and Davis [52]. Seasonal ARIMA models are usually denoted by $ARIMA(p, d, q) \times (P, D, Q)_S$. S indicates the length of the seasonal pattern under consideration. The compact representation of the ARIMA model is usually, as shown in (3), a function of autoregressive polynomials and polynomials of moving means, and of the difference operators.

$$\phi_p(B)\Phi_P(B^S)\nabla^d\nabla_S^D\left(y_t^{(\lambda)} - c\right) = \theta_q(B)\Theta_Q(B^S)\varepsilon_t, \\ \{\varepsilon_t\} \sim N(0, \sigma^2). \tag{3}$$

$\{y_t, t = 0, \pm 1, \pm 2, \ldots\}$ are the observed data of the univariate series. If the variability in the data grows with time, it is necessary to transform the data to stabilize the variance. The Box-Cox power transformation family is a general class of variance-stabilizing transformations. The Box-Cox transformation of y_t with power parameter λ to the transformed data $y_t^{(\lambda)}$ is defined by (4).

$$y_t^{(\lambda)} = \begin{cases} \frac{y_t^\lambda - 1}{\lambda}; & \text{if } \lambda \neq 0, \\ \ln y_t; & \text{if } \lambda = 0. \end{cases} \qquad (4)$$

The power parameter λ is estimated by the maximum–likelihood method. The polynomials $\phi_p(B) = 1 - \phi_1 B - \phi_2 B^2 - \cdots - \phi_p B^p$ and $\theta_q(B) = 1 - \theta_1 B - \theta_2 B^2 - \cdots - \theta_q B^q$ represent the regular or non–seasonal autoregressive and the moving averages components, respectively, and the polynomials $\Phi_P(B^S) = 1 - \Phi_1 B^S - \Phi_2 B^{2S} - \cdots - \Phi_P B^{PS}$ and $\Theta_Q(B^S) = 1 - \Theta_1 B^S - \Theta_2 B^{2S} - \cdots - \Theta_Q B^{QS}$ represent the seasonal autoregressive and the moving averages components, respectively, with B as the lag operator. ∇ is the is the backward difference operator, $[By_t = y_{t-1}; B^S y_t = y_{t-S}; \nabla = (1-B); \nabla^d = (1-B)^d; \nabla_S^D = (1-B^S)^D]$. d and D are the number of differencings required to make the time series stationary ($d, D \leq 2$). $\{\varepsilon_t\}$ is a Gaussian white noise process, $[\{\varepsilon_t\} \sim N(0, \sigma^2)]$. c is the model constant.

The orders of the polynomials $\{p, d; P, Q\}$ are selected using the Akaike's Information Criterion (AIC, AICc) or Schwarz's or the Bayesian Information Criterion (SIC or BIC). The model coefficients $\{\phi_1, \phi_2, \ldots, \phi_p; \theta_1, \theta_2, \ldots, \theta_q; \Phi_1, \Phi_2, \ldots, \Phi_P; \Theta_1, \Theta_2, \ldots, \Theta_Q\}$ and σ^2 are estimated by the maximum likelihood method.

ARIMA models can present more than one seasonality, as indicated in (5). To do this, the models are expressed as ARIMA $(p, d, q) \times (P_1, D_1, Q_1)_{S_1} \times (P_2, D_2, Q_2)_{S_2}$ where S_1 and S_2 indicate the two seasonalities to which they refer.

$$\phi_p(B)\Phi_{P_1}\left(B^{S_1}\right)\Omega_{P_2}\left(B^{S_2}\right)\nabla^d \nabla_{S_1}^{D_1} \nabla_{S_2}^{D_2}\left(y_t^{(\lambda)} - c\right) = \theta_q(B)\Theta_{Q_1}\left(B^{S_1}\right)\Psi_{Q_2}\left(B^{S_2}\right)\varepsilon_t. \qquad (5)$$

The polynomials $\Omega_{P_2}(B^{S_2})$ and $\Psi_{Q_2}(B^{S_2})$ represent the second seasonal autoregressive and the moving averages components, respectively.

2.2.3. Multiple Seasonal Holt-Winters Models

Exponential smoothing uses information from the past through weighted averages to make predictions. The weight decreases as newer values are entered into the time series, giving more importance to newer data over older. A smoothing parameter determines this weight. The introduction of these models dates back to the 1960s with the work of Holt [53] and Brown [54]. Winters [20] presented the Holt-Winters models, in which exponential smoothing techniques are performed on the three components of the series: level (l_t), trend (b_t) and seasonality (s_t). The model includes a series of structured equations, called smoothing equations, the information from which is compiled by a forecast equation to provide forecasts. The equations can be combined with additive or multiplicative trends and seasonality.

Gardner and McKenzie [55] introduced a damping factor for the trend, and their model outperforms the previous models when the trend shows high variations [56]. Taylor broke down seasonality into two or three nested components so that the models can capture the series that present more than one seasonality, such as series for short-term demand [22,23]. Taylor also included in the model an adjustment using the one-step-ahead error as proposed by Chatfield [57]. This adjustment adds an AR(1) model for the residuals, obtaining the parameter at the same time as the smoothing parameters are obtained. In the same way, García-Díaz and Trull [24] generalized the model including the way the initial values are obtained, to n seasonalities. The nHWT models are shown in Equations (6)–(9).

$$l_t = \alpha \left(\frac{y_t}{\prod s_{t-s_i}^{(i)}} \right) + (1-\alpha)(l_{t-1} + \varrho b_{t-1}), \qquad (6)$$

$$b_t = \gamma(l_t - l_{t-1}) + (1-\gamma)\varrho b_{t-1}, \tag{7}$$

$$s_t^{(i)} = \delta^{(i)}\left(\frac{y_t}{l_t \prod_{j \neq i} s_{t-s_j}^{(j)}}\right) + \left(1 - \delta^{(i)}\right) s_{t-s_i}^{(i)}, \tag{8}$$

$$\hat{y}_{t+k} = \left(l_t + \sum_{j=1}^{k} \varrho^j b_t\right) \prod_i s_{-s_i+k}^{(i)} + \varphi_{AR}^k \varepsilon_t. \tag{9}$$

The smoothing equations include the smoothing parameters α, γ and $\delta^{(i)}$ for smoothing the level, the trend and the different seasonal indices (i) of length s_i. The equation $\hat{y}_{t+k}$ provides the k–future prediction values from the observed values of the series y_t. Here, ε_t is the one–step–ahead error, and the parameter φ_{AR} is the parameter for the AR(1) adjustment. The damping parameter for the trend is denoted by ϱ [58].

The equations of the model are recursive, and therefore they need initial values so that they can fit the model. Several methodologies for initialization have been documented [56,57]. To be able to use the models, it is necessary to estimate the smoothing parameters by minimizing the error using non-linear algorithms [59,60]. The Nelder-Mead [61,62] simplex method has been used, which minimizes the root of mean squared error (RMSE).

2.2.4. State Space Models

The SSM refers to a form of graphical–probabilistic representation [63] to describe the dependence between an observed measurement and a series of latent state variables through equations called state equations that describe its evolution. Taking into account the fact that a time series can be decomposed into components of level, seasonality and trend, this terminology applied to time series would be understood as the model that interprets the evolution of the relationship of the observed variables (y_t) with the latent unobservable variables (level, trend, and seasonality).

SSMs have a great variety of formulations. In this paper, the formulation indicated by Durbin and Koopman [64] and Hyndman et al. [16] applied to univariate stochastic time series is used. These models are structured through a formulation of two matrix equations, as shown in (10)–(11):

$$y_t = \mu_t + rx_{t-1} + \varepsilon_t, \tag{10}$$

$$x_t = fx_{t-1} + g\varepsilon_t. \tag{11}$$

Equation (11) is known as the state transition equation, and Equation (10) is known as the observation equation. Here x_{t-1} is known as the vector of states, y_t is the vector of observations, while ε_t is a vector of Gaussian white noise and is known as the innovation process. r, f and g are matrices and vectors of coefficients with appropriate dimensions. f explains the evolution of x_t and g provides the innovation correction of ε_t. The term μ_t is the one step ahead forecast, and r is a term to include the error additively.

De Livera [18] introduced modified models, based on the exponential smoothing methods, in which a Box-Cox transformation is applied to the data, and the residuals are modeled using an ARMA process and include the damping factor for trend and multiple seasonalities. The acronym for this method is BATS (Box-Cox transform ARMA errors Trend and Seasonal Components). This model is described in (12)–(16).

$$y_t^{(\lambda)} = l_{t-1} + \varrho b_{t-1} + \sum_{i=1}^{n_s} s_{t-s_i}^{(i)} + d_t, \tag{12}$$

$$l_t = l_{t-1} + \varrho b_{t-1} + \alpha d_t, \tag{13}$$

$$b_t = (1-\varrho)b + b_{t-1} + \gamma d_t, \tag{14}$$

$$s_t^{(i)} = s_{t-s_i}^{(i)} + \delta_i d_t, \tag{15}$$

$$d_t = \sum_{i=1}^{p} \varphi_i d_{t-i} + \sum_{i=1}^{q} \theta_i \varepsilon_{t-i} + \varepsilon_t. \tag{16}$$

In these equations, $y_t^{(\lambda)}$ indicates the value of the observed data after the Box-Cox transformation with the value λ, described in (4). l_t, b_t and $s_t^{(i)}$ are the values of the level, trend and seasonalities with smoothing parameters α, γ and δ_i. The subscript i denotes the seasonality under consideration, of seasonal length s_i, and n_s is the number of seasonalities. d_t is an ARMA (p, q) process with residuals whose coefficients are determined by φ_i and θ_i. ϱ is the damping factor for trend. The term b_t stands for a long–run trend term. ε_t is a Gaussian white noise process $N(0, \sigma^2)$. The nomenclature for BATS includes the following arguments $(\lambda, \varrho, p, q, s_1, \ldots, s_{n_s})$.

Additionally, De Livera et al. [18] presented the same model but with seasonality based on trigonometric models. The seasonality Equation (16) is replaced by the set of Equations (17)–(20), a seasonal component based on Fourier series. These are known as TBATS (Trigonometric seasonal BATS).

$$s_t^{(i)} = \sum_{j=1}^{(k_i)} s_{j,t}^{(i)}, \tag{17}$$

$$s_{j,t}^{(i)} = s_{j,t-1}^{(i)} \cos(\omega_{j,i}) + s_{j,t-1}^{*(i)} \sin(\omega_{j,i}) + \delta_1^{(i)} d_t, \tag{18}$$

$$s_{j,t}^{*(i)} = -s_{j,t-1}^{(i)} \sin(\omega_{j,i}) + s_{j,t-1}^{*(i)} \cos(\omega_{j,i}) + \delta_2^{(i)} d_t, \tag{19}$$

$$\omega_{j,i} = 2\pi j / s_i. \tag{20}$$

Every seasonal component of the model $s_t^{(i)}$ results from the sum of the k_i stochastic levels $s_{j,t}^{(i)}$ of period i. $s_{j,t}^{*(i)}$ is the stochastic growth for each period. $\delta_1^{(i)}$ and $\delta_2^{(i)}$ are the smoothing parameters. The nomenclature for TBATS includes the following arguments $(\lambda, \varrho, p, q, \{s_1, k_1\}, \ldots, \{s_i, k_i\})$.

Obtaining the values of the previous matrices and vectors requires the application of an algorithm based on the Kalman filter and the maximum likelihood function using the sum of squared errors (SSE) as the minimization criterion. This algorithm carries a high computational load and manages to obtain these parameters iteratively. The reference [18] explains in detail the process to be carried out in order to use the BATS and TBATS methods.

2.2.5. Multiple Seasonal Holt-Winters Models with Discrete Interval Moving Seasonalities

nHWT models are robust to variations in the series, but sometimes special situations occur in which it is interesting to take these anomalies into account. One of the clearest examples is the influence of the calendar effect on electricity demand [65]. These anomalous and specific situations can sometimes be modeled as a discrete seasonality, if they follow a repetitive pattern. Despite being seasonal, since they are discrete, they have the particular quality that they are not located at fixed moments in the time series; therefore, they are not linked to a deterministic appearance, as would be the case for regular seasonality. These seasonalities are called discrete interval moving seasonality (DIMS).

Trull et al. [25] include the use of discrete seasonality in their model, so that the model seen in (6)–(9) now results in (21)–(25), which is named nHWT–DIMS:

$$l_t = \alpha \left(\frac{y_t}{\prod s_{t-s_i}^{(i)} \prod D_{t_h^* - s_m^*}^{(m)}} \right) + (1 - \alpha)(l_{t-1} + \varrho b_{t-1}), \tag{21}$$

$$b_t = \gamma(l_t - l_{t-1}) + (1 - \gamma)\varrho b_{t-1}, \tag{22}$$

$$s_t^{(i)} = \delta^{(i)} \left(\frac{y_t}{l_t \prod_{j \neq i} s_{t-s_j}^{(j)} \prod_m D_{t_h^* - s_m^*}^{(m)}} \right) + \left(1 - \delta^{(i)}\right) s_{t-s_i}^{(i)}, \tag{23}$$

$$D_{t_h^*}^{(h)} = \delta_D^{(h)} \left(\frac{y_t}{l_t \prod_j s_{t-s_j}^{(j)} \prod_{m \neq h} D_{t_h^* - s_m^*}^{(m)}} \right) + \left(1 - \delta_D^{(h)}\right) D_{t_h^* - s_h^*}^{(h)}, \tag{24}$$

$$\hat{y}_{t+k} = \left(l_t + \sum_{v=1}^{k} \varrho^v b_t \right) \prod_i s_{t-s_i+k}^{(i)} \prod_j D_{t_h^* - s_h^* + k}^{(h)} + \varphi_{AR}^k \varepsilon_t. \tag{25}$$

Here the term $D_{t_h^*}^{(h)}$ is included, which represents the discrete seasonal indices, for each DIMS (h) considered up to n_{DIMS}. DIMS are only defined in the time intervals in which the special event takes place. These time intervals are designated using t_h^* for each DIMS (h). This nomenclature is chosen in order to distinguish this from the continuous time interval t.

The great difference between this model and other methods of modeling special situations is that the effect produced by the anomaly in the series is modeled as an internal part of the model, as one more seasonality, and is smoothed with each new appearance, unlike the use of models with dummy variables and/or modifications of the original series.

In the nHWT models, the seasonality equation shows a fixed recurrence for each seasonal pattern (s_i) being considered. With DIMS, this is not possible, since the occurrences of special events are not subjected to a deterministic pattern in the series. Therefore, the use of the variable s_h^* indicates, for each DIMS and each occurrence, which is the recurrence to consider.

One possible situation with special events is the simultaneous occurrence of two events. In such a case, the forecaster should consider the option of using only one of the DIMS that occur at that time, or using both, if the effects produced by the two special events add up.

An important aspect to consider is the initialization of the DIMS. A DIMS may have few occurrences in the time series and, therefore, its seasonal indexes must be calculated in such a way that it converges rapidly to the desired effect.

The initialization method consists in first obtaining the initial values of the level, the trend, and the seasonal indices for the regular seasonality. Subsequently, a decomposition of the series is carried out using trend and multiple seasonality. It is common to use the multiple STL method (Seasonal–Trend decomposition procedure using Loess [66], where Loess is a method to estimate linear relationships).

From the decomposition, the series can be reconstructed without including the irregular part, which is where the information necessary to obtain the desired indices is found. The initial values are obtained by weighting the time series against the reconstructed series.

The adjustment of the parameters is carried out following the same procedure as for the nHWT, with the exception that, if necessary, this adjustment can be carried out in two steps—first adjusting the parameters of the regular model and then adjusting the parameters associated with the DIMS. Adjusting all the parameters simultaneously obtains models with more reliable predictions, while the second option is faster. Thus, the first option is chosen for this work.

3. Results

The approach proposed for the work described below has the following scheme. First, a study of the series is carried out to determine the seasonal periods. The study is carried out using continuous seasonality models and discrete seasonality models, all as described in the previous section. Although it is preferable to use an error minimization criterion for each technique when fitting the models, the RMSE—defined in (26)—is used to standardize and compare the fitted results.

$$\text{RMSE} = \sqrt{\frac{1}{N}\sum_{t=1}^{N}(y_t - \hat{y}_t)^2}. \tag{26}$$

Here N stands for length of the dataset used for the training. The final comparison will be made according to the forecasts made in the validation set.

3.1. Analysis of the Seasonality of the Series

The series shown in Figure 3 clearly presents a seasonality with periodicity of one hour. However, to study the following seasonal patterns it is necessary to perform an analysis on the frequency domain. To investigate the appreciable frequencies in the time series, a spectral density analysis is carried out, the result of which is shown in Figure 7 in the form of a smoothed periodogram. A smoothed periodogram is the preferred tool here as the periodic cycles do not show a regular periodicity [67].

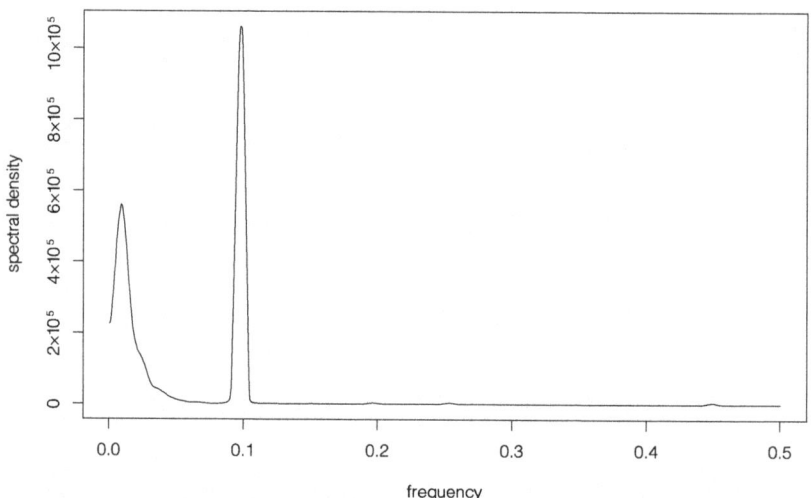

Figure 7. Smoothed periodogram obtained from the time series shown in Figure 3.

Analyzing the figure, the presence of a clearly dominant frequency is observed, which corresponds to the periodicity of ten units of time (one hour). Also, the presence of another dominant frequency can be observed. This corresponds to a second seasonality with a period of 106 time-units. However, this is the second seasonality and is associated with a greater variability around its value, which confirms what is seen in Figure 3.

To confirm these hypotheses, an ALLSSA analysis is performed. This method is robust against unequally spaced time series, estimating trend and seasonal components simultaneously, and providing statistically significant components in the time series [35]. The analysis shows three main and significant frequencies at periodicities of 10, 118, and 203 time-units. This disagreement between the two methods suggests that, despite various seasonalities clearly coexisting, non-dominant seasonalities do not occur continuously and may influence the analysis.

In contrast to this result, an analysis based on the use of wavelets is also carried out. The advantage of using wavelets to analyze the spectral content of the series is that we obtain a map in the time-scale plane. The concept of frequency in spectral analysis is now replaced by the scale factor, and therefore, instead of using a periodogram, we use a scalogram. The scale measures the stretching of the wavelets, being directly related to frequency, as the greater the scale is, the higher the frequency of the series, which is related to the inverse of a frequency, that is, to a period [68]. This map allows the non–stationary characteristics of the signal, including changes in periodicity, to be studied, which is the objective.

Figure 8 shows the average wavelet power graph. This graph shows the means of the powers developed over time for each period or frequency. Although the results are similar to those shown in the previous graph, a greater variability is observed in the longer periods. Three main periods are located at 10, 94, and 196 time units. The results are very close to the previous one.

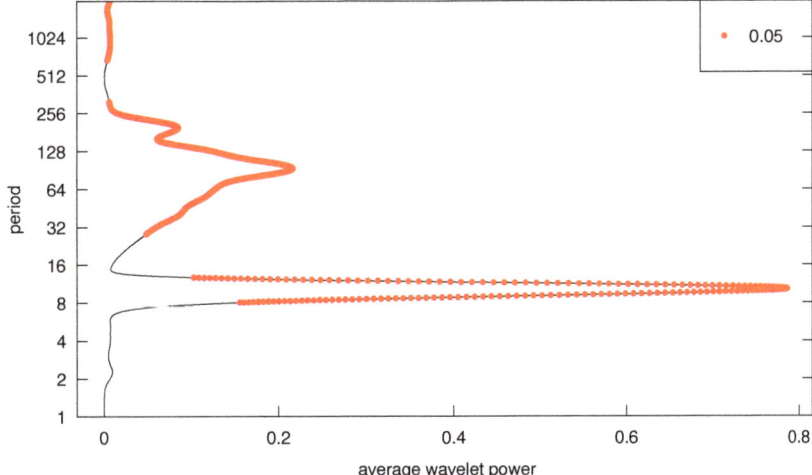

Figure 8. Plot of wavelet power averages across time. The red bullets show the significance level (0.05).

The need for a robust analysis using the time and frequency domain motivates the use of LSWA [35,69]. The software LSWAVE [70] in MATLAB® is an easy and intuitive tool for performing this analysis. This software computes the least square wavelet spectrum (LSWS) for the series, with no need for preprocessing, transforming, or detrending. LSWA considers the correlations of the sinusoidal functions and constituents and the noise at the same time. We apply LSWA to the training set, with the results shown in Figure 9.

The abscissa axis indicates the time scale used, while the ordinate axis shows the cyclical frequencies (as 1/period). The level of variance explained is reflected by colors, according to the scale to the right of the graph.

The first conclusion is clear from the graph: the one–hour seasonality remains practically throughout the series as the predominant seasonality (with a percentage of variance greater than 90%), but discontinuously. In the sections where this does not occur, a series of sawtooth-shaped formations stand out from the rest, although the percentage of variance that it reflects does not exceed 30%. Some areas are shaded with more than 40% of the variation within high frequencies areas. This graph is shown in closer detail of in Figure 10.

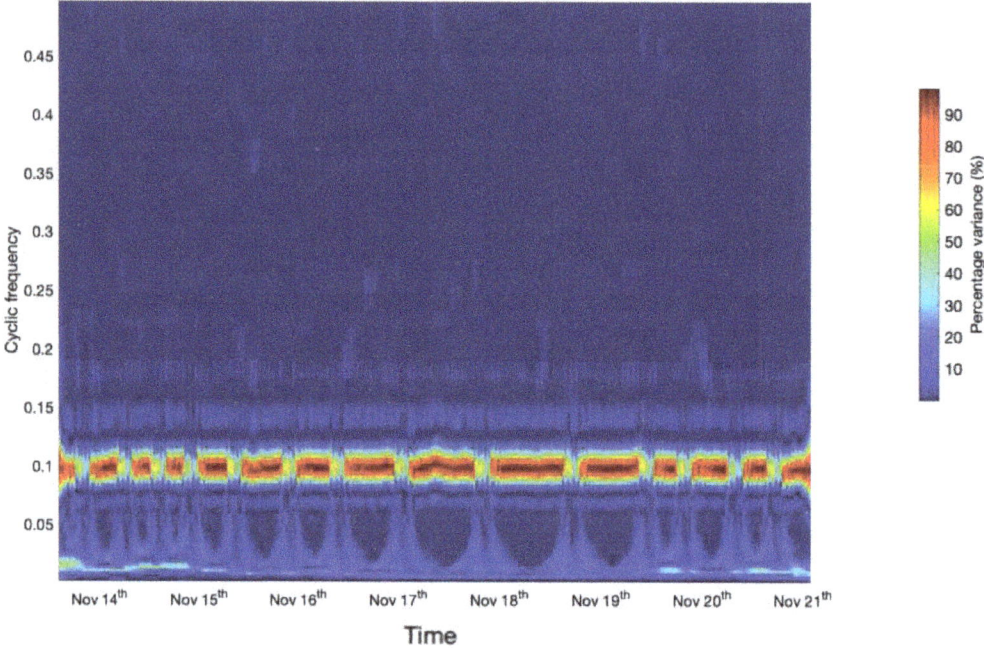

Figure 9. Least-squares wavelet analysis (LSWA) applied to the training set of electricity consumption.

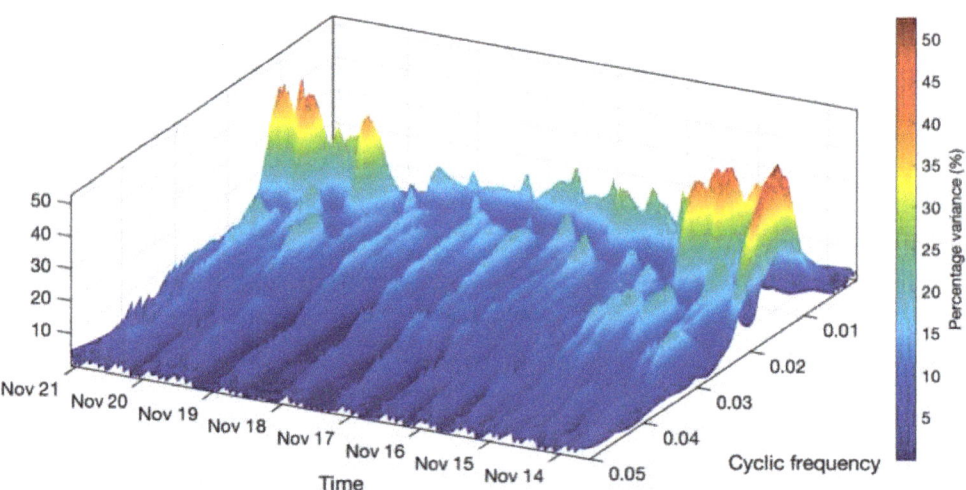

Figure 10. Detail in 3D for the lowest cyclic frequencies in the LSWA analysis.

We decided to use a 3D representation because it is then easier to appreciate the lowest cyclic frequencies. Between 14 November and 15 November and later between 19 November and 21 November, two frequencies with a percentage of variance of over 40% appear. This corresponds to a period of 100 time-units. In the middle, between the two intervals, some peaks with 30% of the variance are also located. This corresponds to a periodicity of 200-time units.

The conclusion from this analysis is that there is clearly one seasonality that occurs every hour (ten-time units), and a second pattern with unregular behavior over time and a periodic length that has been established at between 94 and 118 units. Although it is not strictly a seasonality, it can be modeled as a second seasonality. A marginal seasonality can be obtained for long cycles but will not be taken into account as it seems that its influence on the time series is very small compared to the previous one.

3.2. Application of Models with Regular Seasonality

Given this disparity of values for the determination of the length of the seasonal periods, we choose to carry out one analysis with the models using a single seasonality (ten-time units) and another using two seasonalities.

For the models with regular seasonality, the second seasonality to be tested will be for a range of periods of between 90 and 110 time-units.

3.2.1. Application of ANN

One of the most powerful tools for working with neural networks is the MATLAB® Deep Machine Learning toolbox. This toolbox includes a great variety of possibilities and different neural networks. From this range of possibilities, the NARX network and the NLR network are used. These two networks have been proven to be efficient in predicting future electricity demand values. The method of working with them is described in Figure 11. Here, it can be seen that it is first necessary to use the historical information about demand.

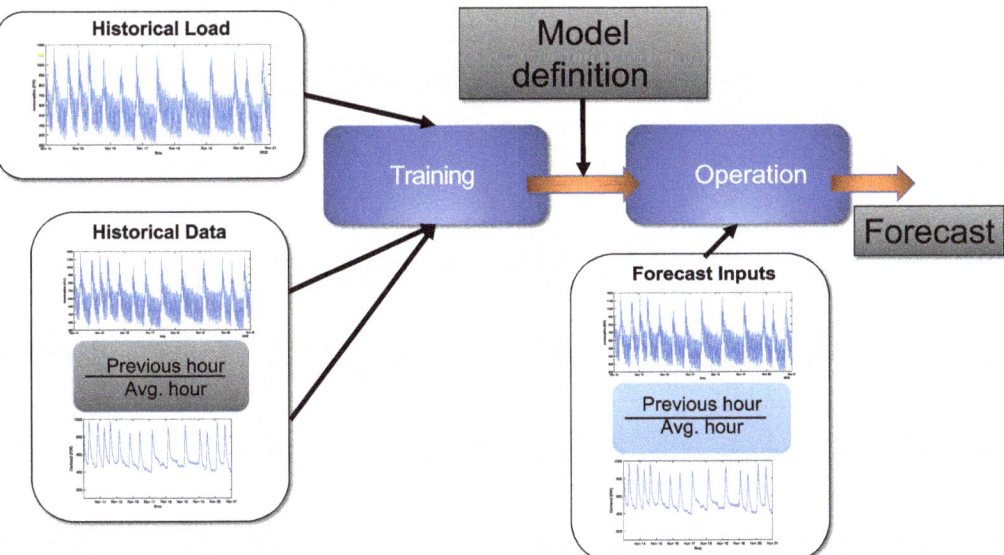

Figure 11. Working scheme with neural networks using the Deep learning machine tool from MATLAB.

To address the observed seasonality, the series is additionally given a delay, according to the seasonality. In this case, the seasonality of one hour corresponds to ten units of time of six minutes, so a delay of ten units is introduced to the series. Additional variables are added to the information provided by the time series. The exogenous information supplied to the model is:

- Previous hour's average electricity consumption.
- Consumption of electricity from the previous hour.
- Timestamp (only in NARX model).

The networks used are described in Table 1. The NARX model includes a single hidden layer and a TDL of three time units. It was checked that greater TDL did not improve the results. NLR model also include a single hidden layer.

Table 1. Neural network parameters and RMSE for fitted results.

Neural Network	Parameters	Fit RMSE
NARX	1 input layer 1 hidden layer with 20 neurons 1 output layer TDL = 3	33.95
NLR	1 input layer 1 hidden layer with 20 neurons 1 output layer	33.21

The training process is performed by minimizing the MSE and using the Levenberg-Marquardt algorithm. The training result is displayed as the RMSE in Table 1.

In the same way as the first seasonality was introduced, the second seasonality is added, following what we have seen in Section 3.2. The result of adding a new seasonality does not improve the result. The chosen model has only one seasonality.

3.2.2. Application of ARIMA Models

To apply the ARIMA models, MATLAB® is the chosen platform, using Econometrics Toolbox and SSMMATLAB [71] for double seasonal ARIMA. R is also tested with the 'forecast' package, but the MATLAB® results outperformed the R results. Like the previous models, models with one and two seasonalities according to Section 3.2 are tested. The best results are found using a single seasonality of one hour (ten-time units). The best model is ARIMA $(4,2,4) \times (4,1,4)_{10}$, for which the parameters are shown in Table 2.

Table 2. ARIMA parameters and RMSE for fitted results.

Parameters		Fit RMSE
AR	$\phi_1 = -0.145; \phi_2 = -0.472;$ $\phi_3 = -0.190; \phi_p = 0.170$	
MA	$\theta_1 = 0.861; \theta_2 = -0.601;$ $\theta_3 = 0.443; \theta_4 = 0.174$	50.42
SAR	$\Phi_1 = -0.487; \Phi_2 = 0.067;$ $\Phi_3 = -0.260; \Phi_4 = -0.067$	
SMA	$\Theta_1 = 0.142; \Theta_2 = 0.069;$ $\Theta_3 = -0.292; \Theta_4 = -0.065$	

3.2.3. Application of nHWT Models

To perform the analysis using the nHWT models, a proprietary tool developed in MATLAB® is used. This tool comes in the form of a toolbox, but it has not been published yet. Models with one and two seasonalities are tested.

The results show that the model that best adapts to this series presents a single seasonality, with the parameters $\alpha = 0.0001$, $\gamma = 0.0001$, $\delta_{10} = 0.4856$ and $\varphi_{AR} = 0.9286$. The damping factor ϱ is set to 0. Models including this parameter were tested, but results were not improved, thus it was removed from the model. The RMSE of the fit process is 54.93.

The result is not surprising since the nHWT models are structural and do not allow for a relaxation of seasonality. Once seasonality is established, the model will continue to develop the same pattern, even though this is not really reflected in the series. When using a single seasonality, the information provided by the second seasonal pattern is lost, but it has less influence than the error caused by a second seasonality that does not coincide with the real seasonality of the series.

3.2.4. Application of SSM Models

To work with the state spaces, the 'forecast' library is used in R [72]. Models with a single seasonality are tested, as well as models that include several seasonalities as indicated in Section 3.1. Here again, the use of the trend damping parameter did not provide better results and was removed from the model.

As in the previous cases, the models with several seasonalities do not show better results than the models with a single seasonality. Table 3 shows the models used—including their arguments—in the first column, the parameters obtained after the adjustment process in the second column, and the RMSE value of the adjustment in the third column.

Table 3. SSM models, their parameters, and fit RMSE for fitted results.

Model Arguments	Parameters	Fit RMSE
BATS (0.717,0, 5,2, 10)	$\lambda = 0.717, \alpha = 0.120, \gamma = 0.206,$ $\delta = -0.004,$ $\phi_1 = 0.945, \phi_2 = -0.625, \phi_3 = 0.022,$ $\phi_4 = 0.104, \phi_5 = -0.500,$ $\theta_1 = -0.153, \theta_2 = 0.515.$	46.77
TBATS (0.756,0, 5,2, {10,1})	$\lambda = 0.756, \alpha = 0.862, \gamma = 0.105, \delta_1 = -0.0004,$ $\delta_2 = 0.0001,$ $\phi_1 = 1.293, \phi_2 = -0.552, \phi_3 = -0.359, \phi_4 = 0.227,$ $\phi_5 = -0.1968,$ $\theta_1 = -1.358, \theta_2 = 0.783.$	45.44

3.3. Application of Discrete Seasonality Models (nHWT-DIMS)

The application of discrete seasonality carries with it a differentiated strategy. The use of nHWT-DIMS models makes it possible to model localized seasonality at specific instants of time, independently of other seasonality. In Figure 12, we show two different periods for the series. In addition to the seasonal pattern described at the beginning (of one hour), a new pattern can also be observed in Figure 12a, whose length is established at 27 time units (2 h and 42 min). This pattern is framed between two dashed lines including the demand peaks. Figure 12b shows another seasonal pattern that has the same length, but a different behavior. These two patterns will be called DIMS a and DIMS b.

The appearance of each discrete seasonality does not occur on a regular basis. This situation causes the recursion required in the Holt-Winters models to be variable. This is indicated in Figure 12 by the lines with arrows. The solid lines indicate the recursion for the DIMS a, and the dashed lines indicate it for the DIMS b. The information regarding the DIMS is organized in Table 4. This table includes the locations of the discrete seasonalities on every appearance (starting and ending time when the DIMS is defined, used in the variable t_h^*) and the associated recursivity in minutes, which corresponds to s_h^*. As an example, the time interval when the second appearance of DIMS a is defined starts at 04:00 pm on the 14th and ends at 06:42 pm on the 14th. The recursivity s_h^* during this interval is 618 min.

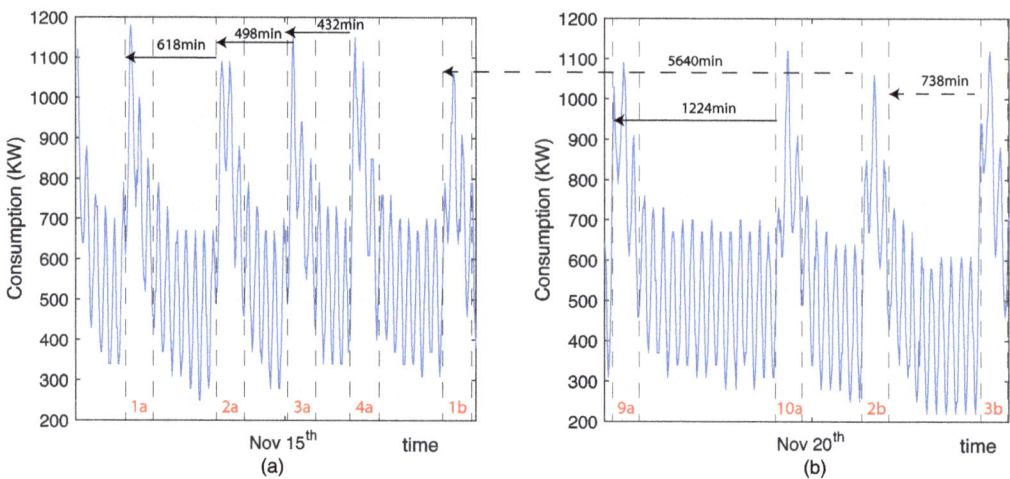

Figure 12. Discrete interval moving seasonality (DIMS) locations and recursion design. Two additional seasonal patterns are located, the first mostly appears in (**a**) while the second pattern appears in (**b**). Vertical dashed lines delimitate the DIMS period length. The appearance number of each DIMS is numbered at the bottom of the figure in red. Lines with arrows represent the recursivity of the DIMS, with full lines for the DIMS in (**a**) and dashed lines for the DIMS in (**b**). The time span of the previous appearance is shown in minutes over the line.

Table 4. Location in the time series of the discrete seasonalities (DIMS) and their recursivity. The column Nr. indicates the order of appearance of the corresponding DIMS. 'Time starts' and 'Time ends' reflect the moving interval in which DIMS is defined, and 'Recursivity' shows the length of time since the previous appearance.

DIMS	Nr.	Time Starts	Time Ends	Recursivity
DIMS a	1	14th November at 05:42 am	14th November at 08:24 am	
	2	14th at 04:00 pm	14th at 06:42 pm	618 min.
	3	15th at 00:18 am	15th at 03:00 am	498 min
	4	15th at 07:30 am	15th at 10:12 am	432 min
	5	15th at 06:42 pm	15th at 09:24 pm	672 min
	6	16th at 07:24 pm	16th at 10:06 pm	1482 min
	7	17th at 10:42 am	17th at 01:24 pm	918 min
	8	18th at 06:06 am	18th at 08:48 am	1164 min
	9	19th at 02:30 am	19th at 05:12 am	1224 min
	10	19th at 08:48 pm	19th at 23:30 pm	1098 min
	11	21th at 06:06 pm	21th at 20:48 pm	2718 min
DIMS b	1	16th November at 07:06 am	16th November at 09:48 am	
	2	20th at 05:06 am	20th at 07:48 am	5640 min
	3	20th at 05:24 pm	20th at 08:06 pm	738 min
	4	21th at 02:36 am	21th at 05:18 am	552 min
	5	22th at 02:24 am	22th at 05:06 am	1428 min

The general model described by Equations (21)–(25) now results in the Equations shown in (27)–(32), with one seasonality of length ten time units and two DIMS as described in Table 4.

$$l_t = \alpha \left(\frac{y_t}{I_{t-s_{10}}^{(10)} D_{t_a^*-s_a^*}^{(a)} D_{t_b^*-s_b^*}^{(b)}} \right) + (1-\alpha)(l_{t-1} + b_{t-1}), \qquad (27)$$

$$b_t = \gamma(l_t - l_{t-1}) + (1-\gamma)b_{t-1}, \qquad (28)$$

$$s_t^{(10)} = \delta^{(10)} \left(\frac{y_t}{l_t D_{t_a^*-s_a^*}^{(a)} D_{t_b^*-s_b^*}^{(b)}} \right) + \left(1 - \delta^{(10)}\right) s_{t-10}^{(10)}, \qquad (29)$$

$$D_{t_a^*}^{(a)} = \delta_D^{(a)} \left(\frac{y_t}{l_t s_{t-s_{10}}^{(10)} D_{t_b^*-s_b^*}^{(b)}} \right) + \left(1 - \delta_D^{(a)}\right) D_{t_a^*-s_a^*}^{(a)}, \qquad (30)$$

$$D_{t_b^*}^{(b)} = \delta_D^{(b)} \left(\frac{y_t}{l_t s_{t-s_{10}}^{(10)} D_{t_a^*-s_a^*}^{(a)}} \right) + \left(1 - \delta_D^{(b)}\right) D_{t_b^*-s_b^*}^{(b)}, \qquad (31)$$

$$\hat{y}_t(k) = (l_t + k b_t) s_{t-s_{10}+k}^{(10)} D_{t_a^*-s_a^*+k}^{(a)} D_{t_b^*-s_b^*+k}^{(b)} + \varphi_{AR}^k \varepsilon_t. \qquad (32)$$

Here, $s_t^{(10)}$ is the seasonal equation for the regular seasonality of ten-time units with smoothing parameter $\delta^{(10)}$. $D_{t_a^*}^{(a)}$ and $D_{t_b^*}^{(b)}$ are the DIMS as described in Table 4 with smoothing parameters $\delta_D^{(a)}$ and $\delta_D^{(b)}$ defined only in time t_a^* and t_b^*. The recursivity s_a^* and s_b^* is defined in Table 4.

To use the model, the procedure described in [25] is carried out. Initially, the initial values for the level are obtained as the moving average of the first period of one hour; for the trend as the slope between the first and second cycle of one hour; and for the seasonal indices, the weighting of the series in the first cycle on the moving average. Subsequently, the seasonal indices of the DIMS are obtained. The time series is decomposed into its trend, seasonality, and irregular components using STL decomposition with the period length of one hour. From these components, the series is rebuilt, but without the irregular component being included. The seasonal indices are obtained by weighting the original series over the reconstructed one.

Once the initial values of the model have been determined, the model is fitted by minimizing the RMSE, and the smoothing parameters are obtained. The tool for this analysis is software developed in MATLAB (R) for this purpose. The obtained RMSE is 58.65. The smoothing parameters of the model obtained are $\alpha = 0.0001$, $\gamma = 0.0001$, $\delta^{(10)} = 0.4853$ for the first regular seasonality, $\delta^{(a)} = 0.0005$ for DIMS type a (see Figure 12a), $\delta^{(b)} = 0.0652$ for DIMS type b (see Figure 12b) and $\varphi_{AR} = 0.9056$. Here again, it has is decided not to use the damping parameter for trend. The RMSE of the fitted model is 58.65.

3.4. Model Fit Comparison

A benchmark summary is reported in Table 5, where the RMSE in the fit process is summarized. The RMSE used to compare the models while fitting shows that the ANN fits better than the other models to the time series. The worst case seems to be nHWT-DIMS. The comparison shows that the state space models and the ARIMA models fit the observed data better than the nHWT and nHWT–DIMS models. Similar behavior is expected in the forecasts.

Table 5. Main benchmarking results. RMSE used to compare fitted results. MAPE used to compare forecasts accuracy.

	RMSE on Fit	Average MAPE for Forecasts
NARX	33.95	26.63%
NN-NLR	33.21	13.94%
ARIMA	50.42	24.03%
nHWT	54.93	18.55%
TBATS	46.77	37.60%
BATS	45.44	37.61%
nHWT-DIMS	58.65	16.00%

3.5. Forecasts Comparison

The greatest interest is in forecast reliability. To compare the results of the forecasts given by the different methods, the mean absolute percentage error (MAPE) as a percentage is used, as indicated in (33). This is a common indicator used to compare forecasts of demand [73].

$$\text{MAPE}(h) = \frac{1}{h} \sum_{t=1}^{h} \left| \frac{y_t - \hat{y}_t}{y_t} \right|. \tag{33}$$

Here, h is the forecast horizon to evaluate. As the forecasts are made one hour ahead (ten units) throughout the validation subset, h can take values from one to ten time units. From the forecasts of one hour ahead, the MAPE is obtained by comparing these with the real values of the validation set, using the procedure described in [74]. The benchmark summary in Table 5 includes the average of the MAPE. The average is obtained as the mean of the MAPE(h) with $h = 1, 2, \ldots, 10$. The best forecasts, on average, are produced by the NLR. The nHWT-DIMS models are revealed as a competitive method against the regular seasonal models, outperforming the other models.

Figure 13 shows the MAPE of the forecasts as a function of the forecasting horizon. It is clear from the results obtained that traditional models with one seasonality are not capable of working with this type of series. The BATS and TBATS models of state spaces do not drop below 30% MAPE. The ARIMA model starts by making very short-term forecasts that have MAPE of below 15%, but beyond three time units it is not capable of making good predictions. The nHWT models improve the forecasts with respect to the previous ones, although the use of the DIMS allows the level of the predictions to be always kept below 20%. However, the method that produces the best results is NN–NLR. These models give forecasts that remain almost constant with an accuracy of about 14% of MAPE.

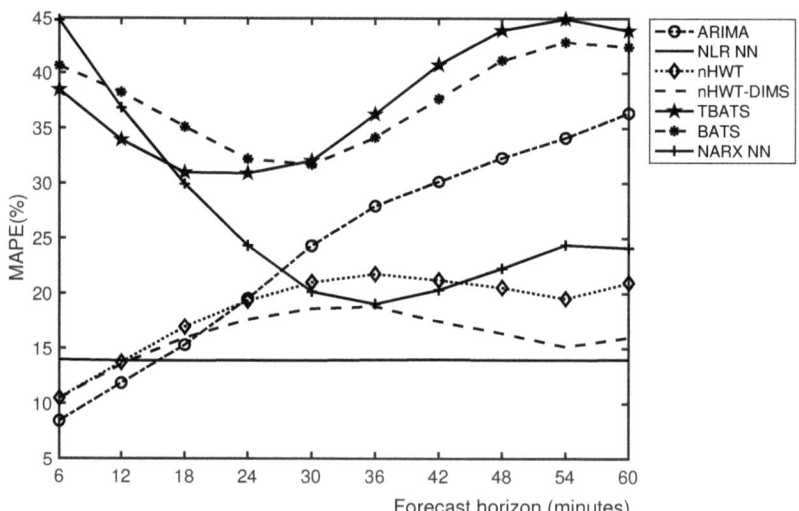

Figure 13. Mean absolute percentage error (MAPE) comparison of one hour-ahead forecasts.

4. Discussion

The results obtained in the previous exercise show that the fact that having irregularities in the series has an enormous influence on the result in statistical models used in this article. The models that use regular seasonalities require that they appear with a regular length, regardless of whether the pattern varies. When dealing with series whose seasonality is not completely defined, the models cannot overcome these variations.

The use of models with discrete seasonality allows for progress in this problem, since it is capable of introducing seasonality only where it occurs.

Though the periodicity of 200-time units did not show a consistent pattern over time in this data set, having a longer time series more than seven days (e.g., two-month record or more) may reveal discontinuous patterns repeating themselves at that low frequency, which may help to better train the model for forecasting such signals. This requires further investigation and research.

However, the best tool for this series is the use of AI to address these irregularities. Curiously, the NARX neural network does not offer good results, but the NLR neural network manages to improve the results. This situation responds to the fact that the previously described models require seasonal stability if they are to make predictions, since they are based on linear or structural models. The neural network model is not subject to these restrictions and uses these irregularities to make forecasts.

Future studies in this area should aim to ensure that the structural models are capable of introducing an ambiguity between their seasonal processes produced by the inconsistency of the series in terms of seasonality.

5. Conclusions

In this article, we have analyzed time series forecasting methods applied to a pattern of electricity demand that has an irregular periodicity, so that the seasonality is not well defined. We have analyzed models of neural networks, ARIMA, multiple seasonal Holt-Winters models and state spaces using regular seasonalities, and multiple seasonal Holt-Winters models with discrete interval moving seasonalities.

To compare the behavior of all the models discussed, they were applied to the situation of a connection node with a hot-dip galvanizing company, where the time series of electricity consumption due to the heating of the bath causes seasonalities. A frequency analysis using spectral density and least square wavelets with the series showed that a first seasonality of one hour could be easily located; some other seasonalities could be considered, but their period was not clear. The problem with irregular seasonality is that the models need to use patterns that constantly repeat themselves, so the pattern must be defined for the entire time series. Nevertheless, the use of Holt-Winters models with discrete seasonality (nHWT-DIMS) allows these seasonalities to be separated efficiently and reliable predictions to be made.

The results showed that the use of nHWT–DIMS models improves the results compared to the rest of the models. This is an interesting proposal for companies because of the simplicity of its application and good results—the MAPE obtained is around 16%. However, NLR (ANN) showed better predictions, with a MAPE of 14%.

Our study contributes to the improvement of forecasting systems with time series by including discrete seasonality in the model. This allows for an efficient method of prediction to be applied in situations of electrical demand with marked seasonality but non–regular periodic appearances.

Author Contributions: Conceptualization, O.T. and J.C.G.-D.; methodology, O.T. and J.C.G.-D.; software, O.T.; validation, J.C.G.-D. and A.P.-S.; formal analysis, A.P.-S.; investigation, O.T.; data curation, J.C.G.-D.; writing—original draft preparation, O.T.; writing—review and editing, J.C.G.-D. and A.P.-S.; supervision, J.C.G.-D. All authors have read and agreed to the published version of the manuscript.

Funding: This research received no external funding.

Acknowledgments: The authors would like to thank the editor and the anonymous referees for their thorough comments, deep analysis and suggestions.

Conflicts of Interest: The authors declare no conflict of interest.

Abbreviations

AI	Artificial intelligence
Al	Aluminum
AIC, AICc	Akaike's information criterion
ALLSSA	Anti-leakage least-squares spectral analysis
ANN	Artificial neural networks
AR(1)	Auto regressive model of order 1
ARIMA	Autoregressive integrated moving average
ARMA	Autoregressive moving average
BATS	Exponential smoothing state space model with Box-Cox transformation, ARMA errors, trend and seasonal components
BIC	Bayesian information criterion
BRT	Bagged regression trees
DIMS	Discrete interval moving seasonalities
LASSO	Least absolute shrinkage and selection operator
LSWA	Least-squares wavelet analysis
LSWS	Least square wavelet spectrum
MSE	Mean squared error
MAPE	Mean absolut percentage error
MLP	Multilayer perceptron
NARX	Non-linear autoregressive neural networks with exogenous variables
nHWT	Multiple seasonal Holt-Winters
nHWT-DIMS	Multiple seasonal Holt-Winters with discrete interval moving seasonalities
NLR	Non-linear regression
RMSE	Root of mean squared error
SARIMAX	Seasonal autoregressive integrated moving average exogenous model
SIC	Schwarz's information criterion
SSM	State-space models
STL	Seasonal–trend decomposition procedure using Loess
SVM	Support vector machines
TBATS	Exponential smoothing state space model with Box-Cox transformation, ARMA errors, trend and trigonometric seasonal components
TDL	Tapped delay line
Zn	Zinc

References

1. Weron, R. *Modeling and Forecasting Electricity Loads and Prices: A Statistical Approach*; John Wiley & Sons, Ltd.: Chichester, UK, 2006; ISBN 978-0-470-05753-7.
2. Michalski, R.S.; Carbonell, J.G.; Mitchell, T.M. (Eds.) *Machine Learning. An Artificial Intelligence Approach*; Morgan Kaufmann: San Francisco, CA, USA, 1983; ISBN 978-0-08-051054-5.
3. Wang, H.; Lei, Z.; Zhang, X.; Zhou, B.; Peng, J. A review of deep learning for renewable energy forecasting. *Energy Convers. Manag.* **2019**, *198*, 111799. [CrossRef]
4. Fallah, S.; Ganjkhani, M.; Shamshirband, S.; Chau, K.; Fallah, S.N.; Ganjkhani, M.; Shamshirband, S.; Chau, K. Computational Intelligence on Short–Term Load Forecasting: A Methodological Overview. *Energies* **2019**, *12*, 393. [CrossRef]
5. Buitrago, J.; Asfour, S. Short–term forecasting of electric loads using nonlinear autoregressive artificial neural networks with exogenous vector inputs. *Energies* **2017**, *10*, 40. [CrossRef]
6. López, M.; Valero, S.; Senabre, C. Short–term load forecasting of multiregion systems using mixed effects models. In Proceedings of the 2017 14th International Conference on the European Energy Market (EEM), Dresden, Germany, 6–9 June 2017; pp. 1–5.
7. Ahmad, W.; Ayub, N.; Ali, T.; Irfan, M.; Awais, M.; Shiraz, M.; Glowacz, A. Towards short term electricity load forecasting using improved support vector machine and extreme learning machine. *Energies* **2020**, *13*, 2907. [CrossRef]
8. Khan, A.R.; Razzaq, S.; Alquthami, T.; Moghal, M.R.; Amin, A.; Mahmood, A. Day ahead load forecasting for IESCO using Artificial Neural Network and Bagged Regression Tree. In Proceedings of the 2018 1st International Conference on Power, Energy and Smart Grid (ICPESG), Mirpur, Pakistan, 12–13 April 2018; pp. 1–6.
9. Zahedi, G.; Azizi, S.; Bahadori, A.; Elkamel, A.; Wan Alwi, S.R. Electricity demand estimation using an adaptive neuro–fuzzy network: A case study from the Ontario province—Canada. *Energy* **2013**, *49*, 323–328. [CrossRef]
10. Box, G.E.P.; Jenkins, G.M.; Reinsel, G.C.; Ljung, G.M. *Time Series Analysis: Forecasting and Control*, 5th ed.; John Wiley & Sons: Hoboken, NJ, USA, 2015; ISBN 978-1-118-67502-01.
11. Makridakis, S.; Hibon, M. ARMA models and the Box–Jenkins methodology. *J. Forecast.* **1997**, *16*, 147–163. [CrossRef]

12. Cancelo, J.R.; Espasa, A.; Grafe, R. Forecasting the electricity load from one day to one week ahead for the Spanish system operator. *Int. J. Forecast.* **2008**, *24*, 588–602. [CrossRef]
13. Elamin, N.; Fukushige, M. Modeling and forecasting hourly electricity demand by SARIMAX with interactions. *Energy* **2018**, *165*, 257–268. [CrossRef]
14. Bercu, S.; Proïa, F. A SARIMAX coupled modelling applied to individual load curves intraday forecasting. *J. Appl. Stat.* **2013**, *40*, 1333–1348. [CrossRef]
15. Taylor, J.W.; de Menezes, L.M.; McSharry, P.E. A comparison of univariate methods for forecasting electricity demand up to a day ahead. *Int. J. Forecast.* **2006**, *22*, 1–16. [CrossRef]
16. Hyndman, R.J.; Koehler, A.B.; Ord, J.K.; Snyder, R.D. *Forecasting with Exponential Smoothing: The State Space Approach*; Springer: Berlin/Heidelberg, Germany, 2008; ISBN 978-3-540-71916-8.
17. Welch, G.; Bishop, G. An Introduction to the Kalman Filter. *Proc. Siggraph Course* **2006**, *7*, 1–16.
18. De Livera, A.M.; Hyndman, R.J.; Snyder, R.D. Forecasting time series with complex seasonal patterns using exponential smoothing. *J. Am. Stat. Assoc.* **2011**, *106*, 1513–1527. [CrossRef]
19. Bermúdez, J.D. Exponential smoothing with covariates applied to electricity demand forecast. *Eur. J. Ind. Eng.* **2013**, *7*, 333–349. [CrossRef]
20. Winters, P.R. Forecasting sales by exponentially weighted moving averages. *Management* **1960**, *6*, 324–342.
21. Taylor, J.W.; McSharry, P.E. Short–term load forecasting methods: An evaluation based on European data. *Power Syst. IEEE Trans.* **2007**, *22*, 2213–2219. [CrossRef]
22. Taylor, J.W. Short–term electricity demand forecasting using double seasonal exponential smoothing. *J. Oper. Res. Soc.* **2003**, *54*, 799–805. [CrossRef]
23. Taylor, J.W. Triple seasonal methods for short–term electricity demand forecasting. *Eur. J. Oper. Res.* **2010**, *204*, 139–152. [CrossRef]
24. García–Díaz, J.C.; Trull, O. Competitive Models for the Spanish Short–Term Electricity Demand Forecasting. In *Time Series Analysis and Forecasting: Selected Contributions from the ITISE Conference*; Rojas, I., Pomares, H., Eds.; Springer International Publishing: Cham, Switzerland, 2016; pp. 217–231. ISBN 978-3-319-28725-6.
25. Trull, O.; García–Díaz, J.C.; Troncoso, A. Application of Discrete–Interval Moving Seasonalities to Spanish Electricity Demand Forecasting during Easter. *Energies* **2019**, *12*, 1083. [CrossRef]
26. Hong, T.; Xie, J.; Black, J. Global energy forecasting competition 2017: Hierarchical probabilistic load forecasting. *Int. J. Forecast.* **2019**, *35*, 1389–1399. [CrossRef]
27. Makridakis, S.; Spiliotis, E.; Assimakopoulos, V. The M4 Competition: Results, findings, conclusion and way forward. *Int. J. Forecast.* **2018**, *34*, 802–808. [CrossRef]
28. Smyl, S. A hybrid method of exponential smoothing and recurrent neural networks for time series forecasting. *Int. J. Forecast.* **2020**, *36*, 75–85. [CrossRef]
29. Choi, T.-M.; Yu, Y.; Au, K.-F. A hybrid SARIMA wavelet transform method for sales forecasting. *Decis. Support Syst.* **2011**, *51*, 130–140. [CrossRef]
30. Sudheer, G.; Suseelatha, A. Short term load forecasting using wavelet transform combined with Holt–Winters and weighted nearest neighbor models. *Int. J. Electr. Power Energy Syst.* **2015**, *64*, 340–346. [CrossRef]
31. Fard, A.K.; Akbari-Zadeh, M.-R. A hybrid method based on wavelet, ANN and ARIMA model for short-term load forecasting. *J. Exp. Theor. Artif. Intell.* **2014**, *26*, 167–182. [CrossRef]
32. Tibshirani, R. Regression shrinkage and selection via the lasso: A retrospective. *J. R. Stat. Soc. Ser. B Stat. Methodol.* **2011**, *73*, 273–282. [CrossRef]
33. Dudek, G. Pattern–based local linear regression models for short-term load forecasting. *Electr. Power Syst. Res.* **2016**, *130*. [CrossRef]
34. Bickel, P.J.; Gel, Y.R. Banded regularization of autocovariance matrices in application to parameter estimation and forecasting of time series. *J. R. Stat. Soc. Ser. B Stat. Methodol.* **2011**, *73*, 711–728. [CrossRef]
35. Ghaderpour, E.; Vujadinovic, T. The potential of the least-squares spectral and cross-wavelet analyses for near-real-time disturbance detection within unequally spaced satellite image time series. *Remote Sens.* **2020**, *12*, 2446. [CrossRef]
36. Ghaderpour, E.; Pagiatakis, S.D. Least-Squares Wavelet Analysis of Unequally Spaced and Non-stationary Time Series and Its Applications. *Math. Geosci.* **2017**, *49*, 819–844. [CrossRef]
37. Taylor, J.W.; Buizza, R. Using weather ensemble predictions in electricity demand forecasting. *Int. J. Forecast.* **2003**, *19*, 57–70. [CrossRef]
38. Shibli, S.M.A.; Meena, B.N.; Remya, R. A review on recent approaches in the field of hot dip zinc galvanizing process. *Surf. Coat. Technol.* **2015**, *262*, 210–215. [CrossRef]
39. Bush, G.W. Developments in the continuous galvanizing of steel. *JOM* **1989**, *41*, 34–36. [CrossRef]
40. Debón, A.; García-Díaz, J.C. Fault diagnosis and comparing risk for the steel coil manufacturing process using statistical models for binary data. *Reliab. Eng. Syst. Saf.* **2012**, *100*, 102–114. [CrossRef]
41. García-Díaz, J.C. Fault detection and diagnosis in monitoring a hot dip galvanizing line using multivariate statistical process control. *Saf. Reliab. Risk Anal. Theory Methods Appl.* **2009**, *1*, 201–204.
42. Ajersch, F.; Ilinca, F.; Hétu, J.F. Simulation of flow in a continuous galvanizing bath: Part II. Transient aluminum distribution resulting from ingot addition. *Metall. Mater. Trans. B* **2004**, *35*, 171–178. [CrossRef]
43. Tang, N.Y. Characteristics of continuous-galvanizing baths. *Metall. Mater. Trans. B* **1999**, *30*, 144–148. [CrossRef]

44. Hippert, H.S.; Pedreira, C.E.; Souza, R.C. Neural networks for short-term load forecasting: A review and evaluation. *IEEE Trans. Power Syst.* **2001**, *16*, 44–55. [CrossRef]
45. Baliyan, A.; Gaurav, K.; Kumar Mishra, S. A review of short term load forecasting using artificial neural network models. *Procedia Comput. Sci.* **2015**, *48*, 121–125. [CrossRef]
46. Xie, H.; Tang, H.; Liao, Y.H. Time series prediction based on narx neural networks: An advanced approach. *Proc. Int. Conf. Mach. Learn. Cybern.* **2009**, *3*, 1275–1279.
47. Liu, Q.; Chen, W.; Hu, H.; Zhu, Q.; Xie, Z. An Optimal NARX Neural Network Identification Model for a Magnetorheological Damper with Force–Distortion Behavior. *Front. Mater.* **2020**, *7*, 1–12. [CrossRef]
48. Deoras, A. Electricity Load and Price Forecasting Webinar Case Study. Available online: https://es.mathworks.com/matlabcentral/fileexchange/28684--electricity--load--and--price--forecasting--webinar--case--study (accessed on 6 July 2020).
49. Moré, J.J. The Levenberg–Marquardt algorithm: Implementation and theory. In *Numerical Analysis. Notes in Mathematics*; Watson, G.A., Ed.; Springer: Berlin/Heidelberg, Germany, 1978; Volume 630, pp. 105–116. ISBN 978-3-540-08538-6.
50. Box, G.E.P.; Jenkins, G.M. *Time Series Analysis: Forecasting and Control*; Holden-Day: San Francisco, CA, USA, 1970.
51. Lu, Y.; AbouRizk, S.M. Automated Box–Jenkins forecasting modelling. *Autom. Constr.* **2009**, *18*, 547–558. [CrossRef]
52. Brockwell, P.J.; Davis, R.A.; Fienberg, S.E. *Time Series: Theory and Methods: Theory and Methods*, 2nd ed.; Springer Science & Business Media: New York, NY, USA, 1991; ISBN 0387974296.
53. Holt, C.C. *Forecasting Seasonals and Trends by Exponentially Weighted Averages*; Carnegie Institute of Technology, Graduate school of Industrial Administration.: Pittsburgh, PA, USA, 1957.
54. Brown, R.G. *Statistical Forecasting for Inventory Control*; McGraw-Hill: New York, NY, USA, 1959.
55. Gardner, E.S., Jr.; McKenzie, E. Forecasting Trends in Time Series. *Manag. Sci.* **1985**, *31*, 1237–1246. [CrossRef]
56. Gardner, E.S., Jr.; McKenzie, E. Why the damped trend works. *J. Oper. Res. Soc.* **2011**, *62*, 1177–1180. [CrossRef]
57. Chatfield, C. The Holt–Winters forecasting procedure. *Appl. Stat.* **1978**, *27*, 264–279. [CrossRef]
58. Gardner, E.S., Jr. Exponential smoothing: The state of the art—Part II. *Int. J. Forecast.* **2006**, *22*, 637–666. [CrossRef]
59. Segura, J.V.; Vercher, E. A spreadsheet modeling approach to the Holt–Winters optimal forecasting. *Eur. J. Oper. Res.* **2001**, *131*, 375–388. [CrossRef]
60. Bermúdez, J.D.; Segura, J.V.; Vercher, E. Improving demand forecasting accuracy using nonlinear programming software. *J. Oper. Res. Soc.* **2006**, *57*, 94–100. [CrossRef]
61. Nelder, J.A.; Mead, R. A Simplex Method for Function Minimization. *Comput. J.* **1965**, *7*, 308–313. [CrossRef]
62. Lagarias, J.C.; Reeds, J.A.; Wright, M.H.; Wright, P.E. Convergence properties of the nelder–mead simplex method in low dimensions. *SIAM J. Optim.* **1998**, *9*, 112–147. [CrossRef]
63. Koller, D.; Friedman, N. *Probabilistic Graphical Models: Principles and Techniques*; MIT Press: Cambridge, MA, USA, 2009; ISBN 0262013192.
64. Durbin, J.; Koopman, S.J. A simple and efficient simulation smoother for state space time series analysis. *Biometrika* **2002**, *89*, 603–615. [CrossRef]
65. Trull, O.; García-Díaz, J.C.; Troncoso, A. Stability of multiple seasonal holt–winters models applied to hourly electricity demand in Spain. *Appl. Sci.* **2020**, *10*, 2630. [CrossRef]
66. Cleveland, R.B.; Cleveland, W.S.; McRae, J.E.; Terpenning, I. STL: A seasonal–trend decomposition procedure based on loess. *J. Off. Stat.* **1990**, *6*, 3–73.
67. Fan, J.; Yao, Q. Characteristics of Time Series. In *Nonlinear Time Series. Nonparametric and Parametric Methods*; Springer: New York, NY, USA, 2003; ISBN 978-0-387-26142-3.
68. Alessio, S.M. *Digital Signal Processing and Spectral Analysis for Scientists*; Springer: Cham, Switzerland, 2016; ISBN 978-3-319-25466-1.
69. Ghaderpour, E.; Ince, E.S.; Pagiatakis, S.D. Least-squares cross-wavelet analysis and its applications in geophysical time series. *J. Geod.* **2018**, *92*, 1223–1236. [CrossRef]
70. Ghaderpour, E.; Pagiatakis, S.D. LSWAVE: A MATLAB software for the least-squares wavelet and cross-wavelet analyses. *GPS Solut.* **2019**, *23*, 1–8. [CrossRef]
71. Gómez, V. SSMMATLAB: A Set of MATLAB Programs for the Statistical Analysis of State Space Models. *J. Stat. Softw.* **2015**, *66*, 1–37. [CrossRef]
72. Hyndman, R.J.; Khandakar, Y. Automatic time series forecasting: The forecast package for R. *J. Stat. Softw.* **2008**, *27*. [CrossRef]
73. Kim, S.; Kim, H. A new metric of absolute percentage error for intermittent demand forecasts. *Int. J. Forecast.* **2016**, *32*, 669–679. [CrossRef]
74. Hyndman, R.J.; Athanasopoulos, G. *Forecasting: Principles and Practice*, 2nd ed.; OTexts: Melbourne, Australia, 2018; Chapter 3.4; ISBN 978-0-9875071-1-2.

Article

Long-Term Forecasting of Electrical Loads in Kuwait Using Prophet and Holt–Winters Models

Abdulla I. Almazrouee [1,*], **Abdullah M. Almeshal** [2], **Abdulrahman S. Almutairi** [3], **Mohammad R. Alenezi** [2] **and Saleh N. Alhajeri** [1]

[1] Department of Manufacturing Engineering Technology, College of Technological Studies, P.A.A.E.T., P.O. Box 42325, Shuwaikh 70654, Kuwait; sn.alhajeri@paaet.edu.kw
[2] Department of Electronics Engineering Technology, College of Technological Studies, P.A.A.E.T., P.O. Box 42325, Shuwaikh 70654, Kuwait; am.almeshal@paaet.edu.kw (A.M.A.); mr.alenezi@paaet.edu.kw (M.R.A.)
[3] Department of Mechanical Power and Refrigeration Technology, College of Technological Studies, P.A.A.E.T., P.O. Box 42325, Shuwaikh 70654, Kuwait; asa.almutairi@paaet.edu.kw
* Correspondence: ai.almazrouee@paaet.edu.kw

Received: 25 July 2020; Accepted: 10 August 2020; Published: 13 August 2020

Abstract: The rapidly increasing population growth and expansion of urban development are undoubtedly two of the main reasons for increasing global energy consumption. Accurate long-term forecasting of peak load is essential for saving time and money for countries' power generation utilities. This paper introduces the first investigation into the performance of the Prophet model in the long-term peak load forecasting of Kuwait. The Prophet model is compared with the well-established Holt–Winters model to assess its feasibility and accuracy in forecasting long-term peak loads. Real data of electric load peaks from Kuwait powerplants from 2010 to 2020 were used for the electric load peaks, forecasting the peak load between 2020 and 2030. The Prophet model has shown more accurate predictions than the Holt–Winters model in five statistical performance metrics. Besides, the robustness of the two models was investigated by adding Gaussian white noise of different intensities. The Prophet model has proven to be more robust to noise than the Holt–Winters model. Furthermore, the generalizability test of the two models has shown that the Prophet model outperforms the Holt–Winters model. The reported results suggest that the forecasted maximum peak load is expected to reach 18,550 and 19,588 MW for the Prophet and Holt–Winters models by 2030 in Kuwait. The study suggests that the best months for scheduling the preventive maintenance for the year 2020 and 2021 are from November 2020 until March 2021 for both models.

Keywords: Prophet model; Holt–Winters model; long-term forecasting; peak load

1. Introduction

Electricity power is an essential part of today's life, and it is the backbone of modern civilization [1]. The generation of power for daily life is crucial in every country. Different challenges worldwide in economics, environment, and growing populations require electrical systems that operate efficiently and continually all around the year. Therefore, electrical load forecasting is one of the critical tools for policymakers to make the right decision in expanding and managing the electric grid and for the management of the existing powerplants. Energy forecasting provides vital information for generating capacity, control and planning, system management, distribution, and maintenance scheduling. Accurate forecasting assures an efficient capacity planning for the growing population and increasing demand for electricity that avoids over or underestimating of utility expansion plans. In addition, it would allow proper and data-driven economic and environmental management and planning. Different planning horizons of electrical load forecasting are investigated in various publications, which are traditionally categorized into short-term, medium-term, and long-term forecasting [2–6]. First, the short-term forecasting investigates the sub-hourly, hourly, daily, and weekly predictions. Second, the medium-term forecasting that includes weekly, monthly, and quarterly forecasting. Lastly, long-term forecasting contains periods of a year or beyond. Each one of these planning horizons is important; however, the long-term forecasting can be considered the most critical horizon due to the consequences of the strategic and costly decisions, such as the expansion of utility plants. An overestimation of electricity demand, especially in the long-term forecasting, will result in a significant increase in the construction of unnecessary electricity generation plants. In contrast, an underestimation of electricity demand forecasting will result in a shortage of electricity production and customer dissatisfaction. Therefore, the study of this research will focus on long-term electricity demand forecasting and the use of models that give the most accurate predictions.

An enormous number of research in electrical load forecasting is found in the literature that tackles the different challenges faced by the power industry and provides a superior forecasting method for predicting the demand of the electrical load. Various types of models and methodologies are implemented for electrical load forecasting in the literature with several parameters in a range of complexity degrees to achieve the best load forecasting accuracy. The methods can be categorized into several groups, but for simplicity, it can be divided into two main groups, namely the group of conventional models and the group of artificial intelligence (AI) models [1–6]. Conventional methods include models, such as regression models, time series models, exponential smoothing, and gray models [2,4]. In contrast, artificial intelligence models include models such as artificial neural network (ANN)-based models, support vector regression (SVR), genetic algorithm (GA) models, machine learning (ML) models, and deep learning (DL) models [1–4]. These models were used as simple or hybrid models or as a combination of more than one method, whether conventional or artificial intelligence models. Generally, the artificial intelligence models are more complex than conventional models. During the last two decades, the application of the AI models in the forecasting processes was rapidly increasing compared to the conventional models, and that can be attributed to the development of different AI models and the advancement of the computers [2]. However, a relatively recent review [3] depicted that the conventional methods, such as regression and/or multiple regression, are still widely efficiently used, especially for long-term forecasting despite their simplicity.

Researchers globally tackled the long-term forecasting challenges by using different models and methodologies to achieve superior and accurate forecasting. For example, Dudic et al. [7] used a linear regression model to forecast the monthly and yearly electricity consumption for the German market, taking into account some factors, especially the higher efficiency of electricity usage from year to year. Filik et al. [8] proposed a nested combination of three subsections for modeling to reduce the forecasting error and can be used for several years ahead. Mohammed [9] examined the correlation of actual load supply with factors, such as population, gross national product, consumer price index, and weather temperature of Iraq using linear logarithmic and ANN models. García-Díaz and Trull [10] presented multiple Holt–Winters models to improve the forecasting electricity demand of the Spanish national electricity market for very short-term forecasting. Taylor [11] showed the superiority of triple seasonal methods of Holt–Winters and auto regressive moving average (ARMA) models for Short-Term Electricity Demand Forecasting. Recently, Trull et al. [12] proposed a new method to initialize the level, seasonality, and trend in multiple seasonal Holt–Winters models. Bianco et al. [13] used a trigonometric grey model with a rolling mechanism and Holt–Winters smoothing method to predict long-term non-residential electricity consumption for ten years up to the year 2020 and showed low average deviation. Hussain et al. [14] employed Holt–Winters and Autoregressive Integrated Moving Average (ARIMA) models using real data from the year 1980 to 2011 to forecast the electricity consumption for Pakistan up to the year 2020 and showed better results for the Holt–Winters model than ARIMA model. Ali et al. [15] employed a fuzzy logic model for long-term load forecasting of one year based on temperature and humidity in addition to historical load data. Ouedraogo [16] developed a scenario-based model for the African power system using the Schwartz methodology in this context and showed an increase in electricity demand of 4% by 2040. Liu et al. [17] proposed a least squares support vector machine optimized by two different models to forecast the demand of electric load in the multi-energy coupling mode. More examples can be found in several reviews carried out by Kuster et al. [3], Wei et al. [4], Ahmad et al. [5], Deb et al. [18], Khuntia et al. [19], Runge and Zmeureanu [20], and Su et al. [21]. A relatively new method called Prophet is introduced by Taylor and Letham [22] for forecasting, which has a high potential to be used in electric load forecasting. Different implementations were found for this model in recent years. For example, Yenidogan et al. [23] compared two models: ARIMA and Prophet in Bitcoin forecasting. The results show that Prophet had an accuracy of about 94.5%, which was much better than ARIMA, which had an accuracy of only 68%. In addition, Ashwini Chaudhari [24] used three models: ARIMA, Prophet, and long-short term memory (LSTM) recurrent neural networks in forecasting the prices of cryptocurrencies: Bitcoin, Ethereum, and Litecoin. The results show that the application of LSTM and Prophet led to very high accuracy between 93% and 99% for the three currencies, while the accuracy of the ARIMA model ranges between 82% and 66% only. In addition, Bianchi et al. [25] carried a comparative for heat short-term demand forecasting methods using the Autoregressive Model (ARM), Non-Autoregressive Model (NARM), and Prophet based on real data of an Italian utility company. The ARM was superior to the other models in short-term forecasting. A thorough recent study carried out by Das [26] where five different forecasting models (Simple Exponential Smoothing, ARIMA, Dynamic Harmonic Regression, Neural Network, and Prophet) were used for prediction of wind speed in two states in India (Tamil Nadu and Maharashtra). The neural network model provided the best results. However, the Prophet model showed promising results, and it was recommended to be used in the future.

Different studies about long-term forecasting for Kuwait were carried out. Almeshaiei and Soltan [27] proposed a methodology to be used as a guide for constructing electric power load forecasting models based on segmentation and decomposition of the load time series and used real daily load data from the Kuwaiti electric network and a model with a mean absolute percentage error (MAPE) value of 3.84% was reported. Al-Rashidi and El-Naggar [28] employed the particle swarm optimization to minimize the error associated with the estimated model parameters for annual peak load forecasting for Kuwaiti and Egyptian powerplants using the least error squares estimation technique to forecast the annual peak load for the years 2006 to 2010. Alhajeri et al. [29] used the cuckoo search algorithm to minimize the error associated with the estimated parameters of three long-term forecasting methods used to forecast the annual peak demands. Al-Hamad and Qamber [30] presented long-term forecasting for peak loads of Gulf Cooperation Council (GCC) countries using Multiple Linear Regression (MLR) and Adaptive Neuro-Fuzzy Inference System (ANFIS) methods. A recent study for the residential sector in Kuwait was carried out by Alajmi, and Phelan [31] created a baseline using a bottom-up approach for the end-use energy profile for the residential sector in Kuwait until 2040.

With reference to the aforementioned relevant literature, research to date has not yet investigated the performance of the Prophet model in long-term forecasting of maximum load. In this paper, real recorded data from the National Control Center (NCC) in Kuwait were used for long-term electric load forecasting using the Prophet model. The proposed method is simple yet powerful in prediction because of its features of adjusting parameters without exploring the specifications of the underlying model [22]. It consists of a decomposable time series model with three main model components: seasonality, trend, and holidays. The model is compared with a well-established Holt–Winters model for evaluation and to obtain the best forecasting model.

This study aims to contribute to the literature by investigating long-term maximum peak load forecasting performance of Kuwait peak loads using the Prophet method based on comparative quantitative analysis with the Holt–Winters forecasting method. To the best of our knowledge, no prior study has investigated the use of Prophet model in long-term forecasting of the maximum electricity load either in Kuwait's electrical national grid or elsewhere. Furthermore, the generalizability and robustness of the Prophet and Holt–Winters methods for the long-term electric peak loads forecasting are explored and presented.

2. Methodologies

A dataset of the maximum load of Kuwait between January 2010 and May 2020 was acquired from the Ministry of Electricity and Water (MEW) to support this research. Figure 1 presents the maximum load (MW) of Kuwait for the past ten years. With reference to Figure 1, a yearly seasonality of the maximum load can be clearly observed. The maximum load peaks are within the summer period between June and August each year due to the subtropical weather nature of Kuwait with extreme temperatures in summer and cold winter seasons. In addition, the maximum load takes an increasing trend. The gradual and steady trend increase is likely to continue for the upcoming years due to the fact of the increasing population, increased factories, and the expansion of the urban and residential areas.

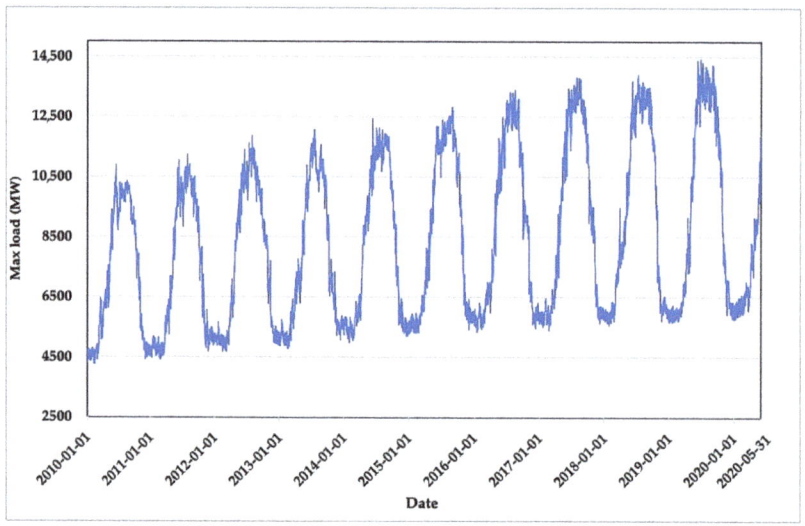

Figure 1. Actual maximum load of Kuwait between January 2010 and May 2020.

In order to forecast the maximum load of Kuwait for the upcoming years, forecasting models that incorporate seasonality and trends are required to ensure a well-fitted model to the actual data. In this work, Facebook's Prophet and Holt–Winters forecasting models have been utilized in this research for the long-term forecasting of the maximum load in Kuwait.

The Prophet forecasting model that is used for forecasting the maximum load is a relatively new modular forecasting method based on various tunable parameters by analyst-in-the-loop, as shown in Figure 2. One of the Prophet forecasting method's strengths is that it was designed to have intuitive tuning of the parameters and does not require knowledge of the underlying model. However, to date, long-term maximum load forecasting using Prophet has not been reported in the literature. Whereas, the Holt–Winters model, or else known as triple exponential smoothing, has been excessively reported in the relevant literature and was proven to be effective in forecasting energy consumption with high accuracy [32–34]. In addition, unlike the Holt–Winters method, the Prophet forecasting method is robust to missing data and does not require data interpolation. Furthermore, seasonality with multiple periods can be incorporated in the Prophet forecasting method to provide flexibility in modeling complex data using an analyst-in-the-loop experience. The Prophet method also enables the user to use extra regressors to present multivariate forecasting to explore the effects of different variables with a very fast-fitting procedure. In the next sections, the implementation of the Prophet and Holt–Winters forecasting methods is presented in detail.

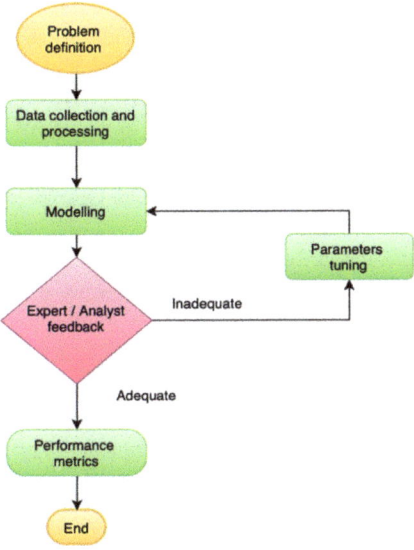

Figure 2. Modelling flowchart with analyst-in-the-loop.

2.1. Prophet Forecasting Method

Prophet forecasting model incorporates data trends, seasonality, and holidays that allow the possibility of modeling complicated time-series features. Multiple seasonality can be fitted as daily, weekly, and yearly patterns. The mathematical representation of the decomposed time series model is hence described as:

$$y(t) = g(t) + s(t) + h(t) + \varepsilon_t \tag{1}$$

where $g(t)$ represents the data trend function, $s(t)$ represents the seasonality, and $h(t)$ represents holidays effect that can be added within specific points of the data. The error term, ε_t, represents any distinctive features of the data that are not fitted by the model.

Prophet trend function, $g(t)$, can be represented by a piecewise linear growth model or a saturating growth model. Since the maximum load data do not exhibit a saturating growth, a piecewise linear growth model is utilized as:

$$g(t) = \left(k + a(t)^T \delta\right)t + \left(m + a(t)^T \gamma\right) \tag{2}$$

where k is the growth rate, δ is adjustment rate, m is the offset parameter, and γ represents the trend changepoints, s_j, and is set as $-s_j\delta_j$, with $a(t)$ defined as:

$$a_j(t) = \begin{cases} 1 & if\ t \geq s_j \\ 0 & otherwise \end{cases} \tag{3}$$

The change points allow the growth model to change the trend and can be utilized by the analyst-in-the-loop to fit the model better and produce reliable data forecasts. The Prophet model allows the user to specify the flexibility of the trend by the adjustment rate. It can also automatically detect the change points, or the data analyst can manually adjust them to describe trend-altering events in the time series.

For the seasonality function, $s(t)$, the time series' multiperiod seasonality can be modeled using the Fourier series to represent the daily, weekly, and yearly seasonality. The seasonality function is hence written as:

$$s(t) = \sum_{n=1}^{N}\left(a_n \cos\left(\frac{2\pi n t}{P}\right) + b_n \sin\left(\frac{2\pi n t}{P}\right)\right) \quad (4)$$

with P = 354.25 for yearly seasonality or P=7 for weekly seasonality. Lastly, to include holiday effects by the holiday function, $h(t)$, the user can define a matrix list of holidays with dates to be incorporated into the time series as a matrix of regressors, $Z(t)$, defined as:

$$Z(t) = [1(t \,\epsilon\, D_1), \ldots, 1(t \,\epsilon\, D_L)] \quad (5)$$

$$h(t) = Z(t)\kappa \quad (6)$$

with D as the set of holiday dates, $\kappa \sim Normal(0, v^2)$ with v as the holiday smoothing parameter.

2.2. Holt–Winters Forecasting Model

There are two variations of the Holt–Winters forecasting method: the additive and multiplicative models of the seasonal variations. The multiplicative model is suitable for a time series with an increasing seasonal pattern that is proportional to the data level. In contrast, the additive model is suitable for fitting a time series with a constant seasonal variation. In this work, the multiplicative method is utilized for forecasting the maximum load of Kuwait.

The Holt-Winters model consists of forecast equation and smoothing equations of the level, trend, and seasonality of the time series. Assuming that s_t represents the seasonality, b_t to represent the trend and that l_t corresponds to the level with smoothing parameters of α, β, and γ. Therefore, the Holt–Winters multiplicative forecast model can be expressed as:

$$\hat{y}_{t+h|t}(k) = (l_t + hb_t)s_{t+h-m(k+1)} \quad (7)$$

$$l_t = \alpha \frac{y_t}{s_{t-m}} + (1-\alpha)(l_{t-1} + b_{t-1}) \quad (8)$$

$$b_t = \beta^*(l_t - l_{t-1}) + (1-\beta^*)b_{t-1} \quad (9)$$

$$s_t = \gamma \frac{y_t}{(l_{t-1} + b_{t-1})} + (1-\gamma)s_{t-m} \quad (10)$$

where m denotes the seasonality period and the smoothing parameters defined as:

$$0 \leq \alpha \leq 1, \qquad 0 \leq \beta \leq 1, \qquad \text{and } 0 \leq \gamma \leq (1-\alpha)$$

In the Holt–Winters multiplicative method, the seasonality component is expressed relatively, and the time series can be seasonally adjusted by dividing through by the seasonality component. Equation (8) corresponds to the level, and it is expressed as a weighted average between the seasonal term and the non-seasonal term $(l_{t-1} + b_{t-1})$. While Equation (9) corresponds to the trend of the time series, which is expressed as a weighted average of the trend between the level and previous slope b_{t-1}. Equation (10) corresponds to the seasonality and is calculated by the weighted average between the current and previous seasonal components of the time series.

2.3. Validation Approach

In order to validate the performance of the prediction of the models, a simulated historical forecast (SMH) approach is conducted. SMH is based on the rolling origin cross-validation approach, or otherwise known as forward chaining, where the data are split into training and testing sets and each day is tested based on the prior training data. However, this method would be computationally intensive due to conducting tests each day and would result in more forecasts that are likely to have correlated estimates of errors. While with SMH, fewer forecasts can be defined at cut-off dates and the total error can be evaluated based on all the forecast horizons. Figure 3 illustrates the process of the rolling origin cross-validation. This approach would allow the models to train on a dataset and test on another unseen dataset of the time series. Moreover, the SMH approach could be used as an indicator of the models' generalizability in forecasting the maximum load.

Train	Train	Test	Data	Data	Data	Data	Data	Data
Train	Train	Train	Test	Data	Data	Data	Data	Data
Train	Train	Train	Train	Test	Data	Data	Data	Data
Train	Train	Train	Train	Train	Test	Data	Data	Data
Train	Train	Train	Train	Train	Train	Test	Data	Data
Train	Train	Train	Train	Train	Train	Train	Test	Data
Train	Train	Train	Train	Train	Train	Train	Train	Test

Figure 3. Rolling origin cross-validation process.

In addition, to assess the performance of each model in terms of accuracy, various statistical metrics were adopted, such as root mean square error (RMSE), the mean absolute percentage error (MAPE), coefficient of determination (R^2), mean absolute error (MAE), and coefficient of variation of root mean square error (CVRMSE) that can be expressed as in the following equations:

$$RMSE = \frac{\sqrt{\sum_{i=1}^{n}(\hat{y}_i - y_i)^2}}{n} \qquad (11)$$

$$CVRMSE = \frac{\sqrt{\sum_{i=1}^{n}(\hat{y}_i - y_i)^2}}{\breve{y}} \qquad (12)$$

$$MAE = \frac{1}{n}\sum_{i=1}^{n}|y_i - \hat{y}_i| \qquad (13)$$

$$MAPE = \frac{1}{n}\sum_{i=1}^{n}\left|\frac{\hat{y}_i - y_i}{y_i}\right| \times 100\% \qquad (14)$$

$$R^2 = 1 - \frac{\sum_{i=1}^{n}(y_i - \hat{y}_i)^2}{\sum_{i=1}^{n}(y_i - \breve{y})^2} \qquad (15)$$

where y, $\hat{y}$ and $\breve{y}$ represent the measured, predicted, and averaged values respectively.

3. Results and Discussion

The Prophet and Holt–Winters models are implemented in R and Python, using real data of electrical daily peak load from Kuwaiti powerplants from 2010 to 2020. The two models' outputs are plotted in Figures 4 and 5, along with the real electrical peak of daily loads. The data include Kuwait's peak loads from 2010 to 2020. Moreover, the forecasted from 2020 to 2030, along with a 99% confidence interval, are included. The forecasted region of this period is enlarged and presented in Figure 6, along with the 99% confidence interval for both models.

The graphs in the previous figures demonstrate that there has been a steady increase in the values of daily peak loads with a yearly seasonality for both models. The two models share several key features, such as trend similarity of the forecasted maximum and minimum peaks. However, the Holt–Winters model generally shows a higher magnitude of the forecasted maximum and minimum peaks than the Prophet model. The superiority of the models is assessed from different aspects by three indicators: accuracy, generalization, and robustness. Also, the future peak loads forecasting for Kuwait is discussed, and the maximum capacity needed by 2030 is investigated.

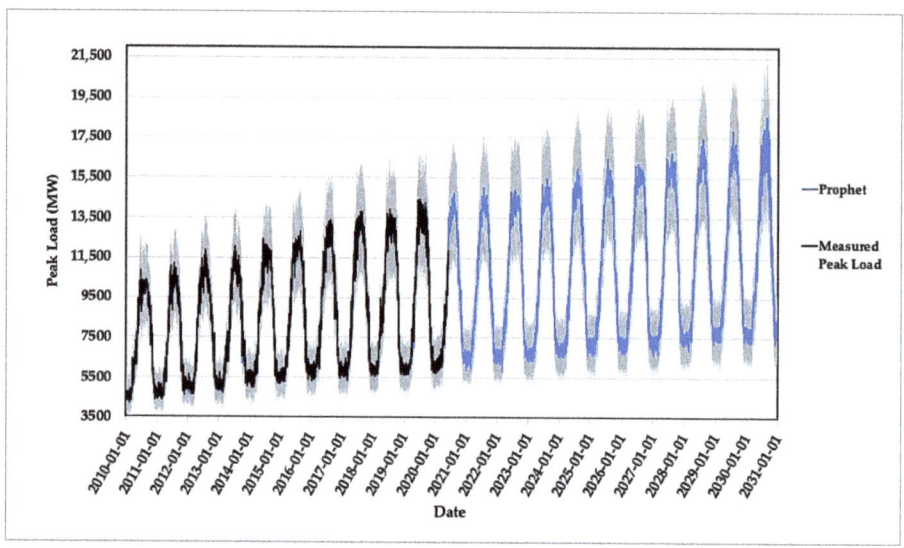

Figure 4. The measured peaks of daily loads data in Kuwait: the trained, predicted, and forecasted data using the Prophet model with a 99% confidence interval.

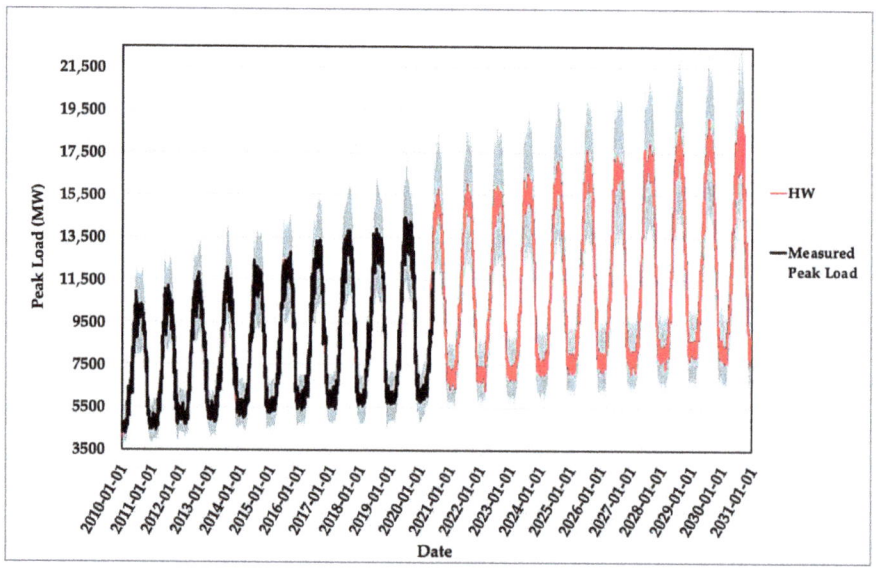

Figure 5. The measured peaks of daily loads data in Kuwait: the trained, predicted, and forecasted data using the Holt–Winters model with a 99% confidence interval.

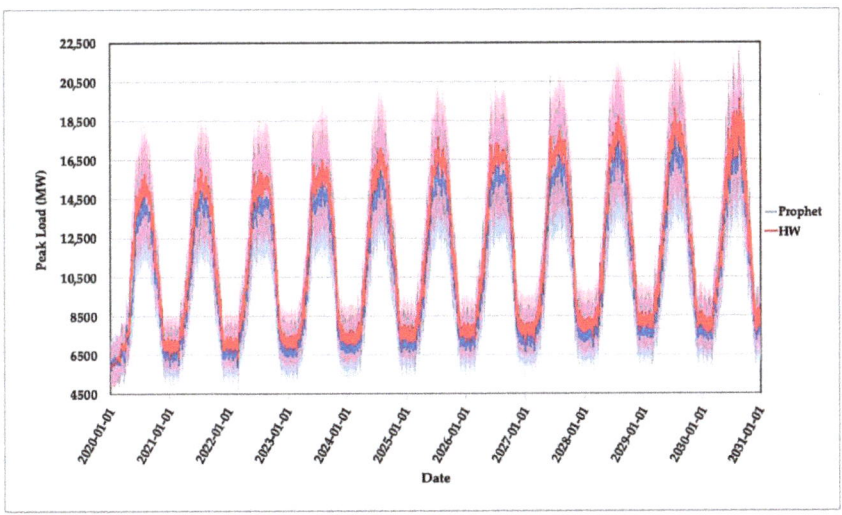

Figure 6. Enlarged forecast portion for both models along with the 99% confidence interval for the years 2020–2030.

3.1. Model Accuracy

Various accuracy and statistical performance metrics were used in this study, which include MAPE, MAE, RMSE, CVRMSE, and the coefficient of determination R^2. MAE demonstrates the gap between the estimated value and the real value using the absolute error. RMSE assesses the instability of model response regarding variance and sensitivity to large errors. CVRMSE normalizes the forecasted error and provides a unitless metric that evaluates the variability of the errors between real and predicted values. The advantage of using these statistical indicators is to explore various aspects of the presented models.

Table 1 presents the calculated values of five statistical performance metrics (MAPE, MAE, RMSE, CVRMSE, and R^2) for both the Prophet and Holt–Winters models using the equations aforementioned in the methodology section. MAPE is one of the most used tools for measuring the accuracy of models [35]. MAPE is proposed in [4] as a reference range for evaluating the performance of energy consumption forecasting at different horizons. Highly accurate models are considered when the MAPE is less than 10%, as benchmarked in [36]. The highly accurate models were divided into levels into four sublevels for each planning horizon. For example, the long-term forecasting is divided into these sublevels: I (≤1.2%), II (1.2–2.8%), III (2.8–4.6%), and IV (4.6–10%) [4].

Table 1. The calculated values of different performance statistical metrics for both models.

Criteria	Prophet	Holt–Winters
MAPE	1.75%	4.17%
MAE	147.89	343.33
RMSE	205.64	475.76
CVRMSE	7.61%	17.59%
R^2	0.9942	0.9694

Accurate values of MAPE were achieved by the Prophet and Holt–Winters methods with superiority by the Prophet model. The values of MAPE were 1.75% and 4.17% for Prophet and Holt–Winters models, respectively. Both values indicate an accurate prediction of the values of both models with relatively low MAPE values. Based on the sublevels of accuracy mentioned above and in [4], the Prophet model falls within sublevel II, whereas the Holt–Winters model falls within sublevel III accuracy.

Figure 7 depicts the coefficient of determination, R^2, and illustrates the variations between the forecasted and real data values for both the Prophet and Holt–Winters models. Both models achieved high values of the coefficient of determination R^2 equal to 0.9942 and 0.9694 for the Prophet and Holt–Winters models, respectively. The MAE of the Prophet model is reported as 147.89, whereas the value of MAE for Holt–Winters model is 343.33, which is approximately more than the double of the Prophet model MAE. In addition, the Prophet model results in a better RMSE value than the Holt–Winters model with a value of 205.64. Moreover, the CVRMSE percentage of the Prophet model is less than the Holt–Winters model with values of 7.61% and 17.59%, respectively.

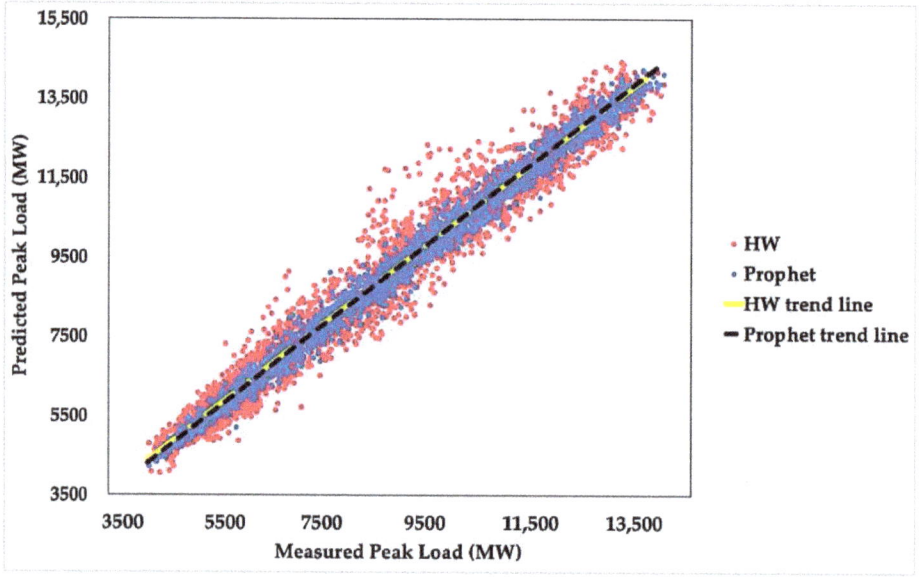

Figure 7. The coefficient of determination R^2 and the fitting characteristics of real and simulated data for both models.

It is clear that the Prophet model has a superior fitting to the real data and has better performance and accuracy than the Holt–Winters model. From the five different statistical metrics, both the Prophet and Holt–Winters models show high accuracy with the superiority of the Prophet model over the Holt–Winters model.

Another measure to assess the accuracy of the models is to use the simulated historical forecast (SHF) [22,37], as depicted in Figure 8. The Prophet model forecasts have a considerably lower prediction error than the Holt–Winters model. The Prophet model's MAPE values are limited within the range between 1.3 and 2.1 approximately, and there is no clear trend of MAPE with the forecast window. The MAPE values of the Holt–Winters model across the different forecasting periods were generally good but higher than the Prophet model. The Holt–Winters model showed a generally increasing trend of MAPE values with the increase in the forecast horizon. These results are evidence that both models exhibit a great extent of accuracy in long-term energy forecasting.

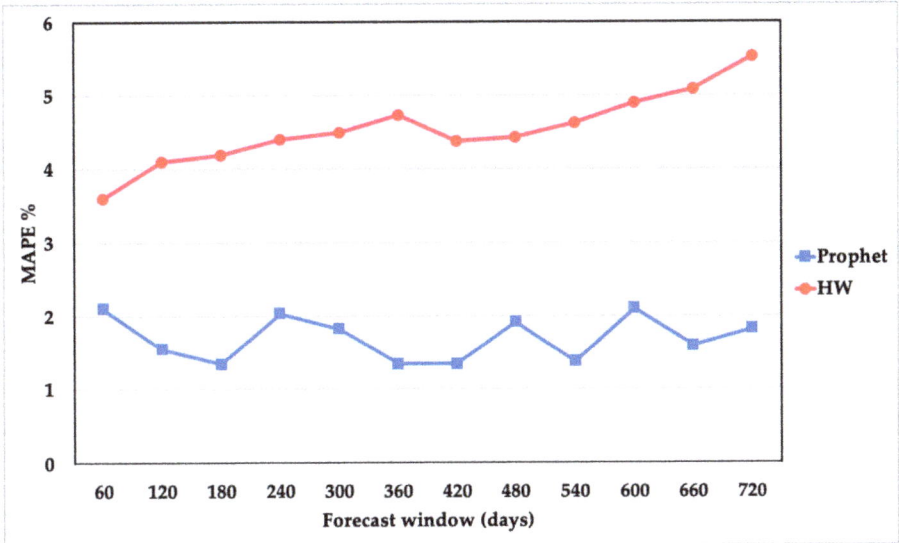

Figure 8. Smoothed mean absolute percentage errors for the Prophet and Holt–Winters models.

3.2. Model Generalization

The model's generalization is assessed by the model's ability to forecast samples beyond the training range. Figure 9 depicts the relative error variation in each of the Prophet and Holt–Winters models. The relative error percentage of the Prophet model outperforms the Holt–Winters model. The percentage of maximum relative error in the Prophet model is less than 16%, whereas the Holt–Winters model's relative error reached 30%. Besides, the SHF results can be used to show the generalizability of both models. The Prophet model shows better generalizability than the Holt–Winters model, as suggested by the MAPE values and the relative error percentage.

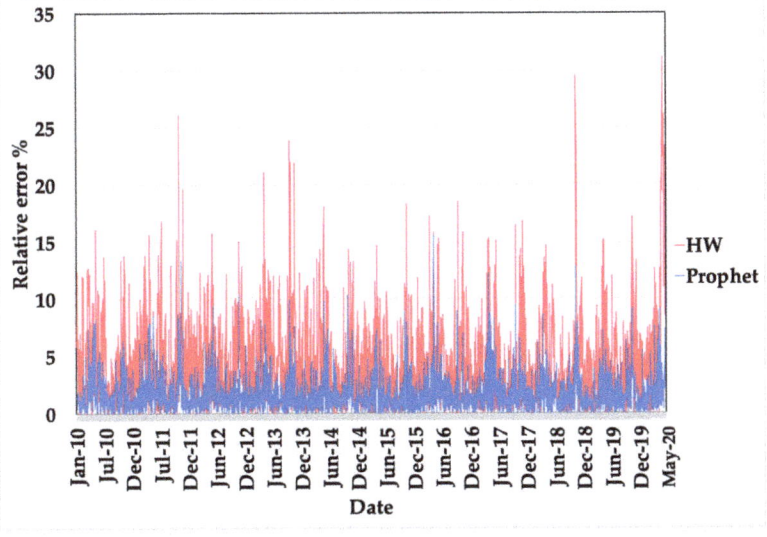

Figure 9. Relative errors percentage for Prophet and Holt–Winters models.

3.3. Model Robustness

To test the model robustness, Gaussian white noise with different intensities is utilized and added into testing data sets of actual data. This approach has been utilized by relevant literature, such as in [38,39]. The data is split into training dataset and multiple testing sets with each set corresponding to a defined noisy intensity. Gaussian white noise is generated with four different intensities of 20%, 40%, 60%, and 80% to assess the robustness of the Prophet and Holt–Winter models. The generated Gaussian white noise samples are distributed randomly at each testing data set, with the corresponding noise intensity, and model robustness is evaluated by the effect of the noise intensity over the accuracy of the model, measured by the coefficient of determination R^2. Low variance in R^2 indicates high robustness where high variance indicates low robustness. Table 2 presents the results of the R^2 of both models under various noise intensities.

Table 2. The accuracy reduction of different models under various noise intensities.

Noise Intensity	Prophet	Holt–Winter
0%	0.9942	0.9694
20%	0.9892	0.9483
40%	0.9795	0.9275
60%	0.9708	0.9014
80%	0.9604	0.8883

A reduction in the coefficient of determination is associated with the increase in the noise level, as depicted in Figure 10. The Prophet model showed high R^2 values across the different noise intensities with a minimum value of 0.9604 at 80% noise intensity. On the other hand, the Holt–Winters model showed high values of R^2 but relatively lower than the Prophet model. The minimum value of R^2 for Holt–Winters was 0.8883 at 80% noise intensity. The results indicate that the Prophet model is more robust than the Holt–Winters model under various Gaussian white noise intensities.

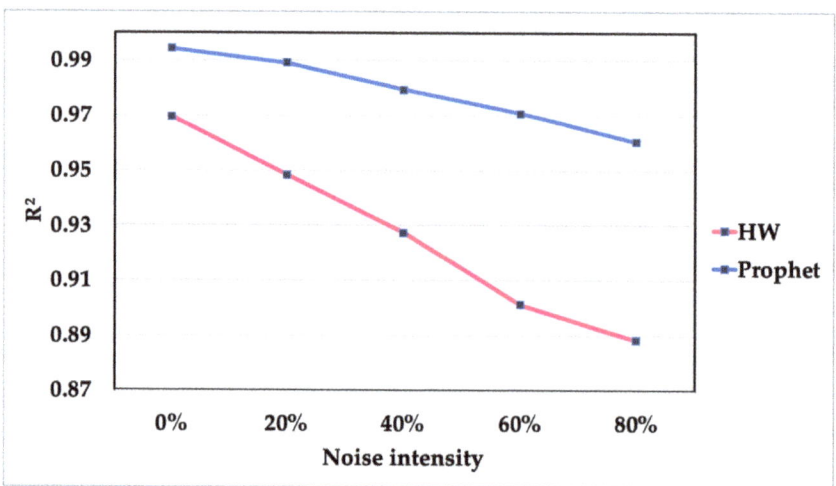

Figure 10. Variations of the coefficient of determination at different noise intensities for both models.

3.4. Future Peak Loads Forecasting

According to the assessment of the two models, the Prophet model outperforms the Holt–Winters model and, therefore, should provide more reliable forecasting. The real data of daily peak loads consumption from 2010 to the end of May 2020 are used to forecast the daily peak load from June

2020 to 31-12-2030, with results plotted in Figures 4 and 5. The forecasting plots also provide essential information about the yearly maximum peak demand. Estimating the maximum peak demand is crucial for long-term strategic decisions in terms of electricity capacity expansion plans to withstand the foreseen maximum loads. Soares et al. [40] reported that the electric peak demand is expected to reach 30,000 MW by 2030. Al-Hamad and Qamber [30] applied the Adaptive Neuro-Fuzzy Inference System (ANFIS) and Multiple Linear Regression (MLR) methods to forecast the peak loads for Kuwait in three scenarios according to the expected growth rates of the gross domestic product (GDP) for the years 2014–2024. The three sceneries were associated with high, average, and low growth of GDP. The high, average, and low growth of GDP models were increasing in different rates reaching maximum forecasted loads of 18,700, 27,300, and 44,500 MW, respectively, for the year 2024. Alhajeri et al. [41] showed that the expected demand in Kuwait is increasing by an average of 2.8% annually by 2030, and the installed capacity should be higher than 21.8 GW. Past studies [30,40–43] about the maximum peak loads forecasting showed a clear increasing trend for peak loads in the coming years, reaching about 30 GW by 2030. On the other hand, the recent study and the new forecast of MEW show a similar trend but lower in magnitude.

The long-term forecasting provides daily, monthly, and annual maximum peaks. Table 3 presents a comparison between actual maximum peak load data and forecasted demand from the MEW in different years (2017–2019) [42–44], Prophet, and Holt–Winters models. The MEW forecasting showed variations in the percentage increase in annual maximum load from 2017 to 2019 with a decreasing trend. In the year 2017, there was a yearly increase in the maximum peak load by an average of 5.4%. The average increase was reduced in the forecast for 2018 to reach 4.7% annually. However, the growth became more conservative in the statistical book of the year 2019 and reached 1% only. The forecasting for years between 2020 and 2030 by the Prophet and Holt–Winters models showed an increasing trend with varying percentages for each year, reaching a maximum peak load of 18,550 and 19,588 MW by the year 2030, respectively. The magnitude of the increase in the Prophet model is between the value of the maximum peaks of MEW in the year 2019 and the Holt–Winters model that suggests the Prophet model is more reliable when compared with the actual data. It is a common practice to have a capacity reservoir to withstand any sharp increase in the daily consumption of electricity. Accordingly, the 99% confidence interval can be used to be the capacity reservoir. As a result, the capacity reservoir should reach up to 22.1 and 23.3 GW for the Prophet and Holt–Winters models to tolerate any failure or disruption of the electrical system during the maximum peak load time by 2030.

On the other hand, Table 4 presents the monthly forecasted maximum load peaks for 17 months from August 2020 to December 2021. The data provided in Table 4 are essential for monthly planning in the powerplants. It offers a clear vision for the expected maximum consumption of power by proposing the monthly maximum load peaks, which is essential for planning activity in powerplants, such as maintenance scheduling. Optimum planning for the maintenance schedule is vital for unit availability and avoiding any unexpected failures or shutdowns. Preventive maintenance is a cost-effective option that can be implemented when planning is accurate. The monthly maximum load peaks indicate that the best months for scheduling maintenance are from November 2020 until March 2021 for both models. Even with 99% confidence interval, the maximum peaks do not exceed 10,000 MW and 10,500 MW for the Prophet and Holt–Winters models. Additional months can be alternatives, such as October 2020 and April 2021 but with some low risk.

Table 3. Comparison between the maximum load of actual data, forecasted maximum peaks from Ministry of Electricity and Water and the Prophet and Holt–Winters models.

Year	Actual	MEW [44]	Prophet	Max 99% CI	Holt–Winters	Max 99% CI
2010	10,890		10,648	12,817	10,195	12,123
2011	11,220		10,925	13,057	11,050	13,146
2012	11,850		11,618	13,996	11,278	13,521
2013	12,060		11,700	13,995	11,882	14,164
2014	12,410		11,982	14,233	11,662	14,015
2015	12,810		12,617	15,048	12,393	14,725
2016	13,390		13,214	15,979	12,933	15,420
2017	13,800		13,646	16,482	13,500	16,088
2018	13,910		13,866	16,634	13,834	16,570
2019	14,420	14,049	14,235	17,197	14,438	17,314
2020		14,190	14,727	17,561	15,758	18,894
2021		14,331	14,900	17,771	15,943	19,026
2022		14,475	14,975	17,875	16,024	19,200
2023		14,620	15,431	18,538	16,511	19,860
2024		14,766	15,978	19,157	17,096	20,547
2025		14,913	16,184	19,208	17,316	20,858
2026		15,063	16,451	19,751	17,602	21,188
2027			16,746	20,240	17,918	21,594
2028			17,446	21,084	18,668	22,485
2029			17,836	21,372	19,085	22,972
2030			18,550	22,061	19,558	23,305

Table 4. Comparison between the monthly maximum load of forecasted maximum peaks from the Prophet and Holt–Winters models.

Month/YY	Prophet		Holt–Winters	
	Max	Upper 99% CI	Max	Upper 99% CI
Aug-20	14,727	15,887	15,758	17,292
Sep-20	13,744	15,036	14,706	16,031
Oct-20	10,951	11,813	11,718	12,552
Nov-20	8771	9568	9384	10,313
Dec-20	6930	7619	7415	8034
Jan-21	6828	7534	7306	7823
Feb-21	6866	7504	7347	7962
Mar-21	8095	8684	8661	9424
Apr-21	10,079	11,120	10,785	11,814
May-21	12,821	13,873	13,719	14,743
Jun-21	14,571	15,986	15,591	16,836
Jul-21	14,899	16,263	15,942	17,436
Aug-21	14,628	16,002	15,652	16,779
Sep-21	14,173	15,180	15,165	16,363
Oct-21	11,500	12,375	12,305	13,528
Nov-21	9190	10,028	9834	10,861
Dec-21	6972	7492	7460	8122

4. Conclusions

Long-term energy forecasting plays a pivotal role in providing insights for policymakers' decisions, such as the need to expand the electrical power utilities. In this study, two forecasting models were utilized for long-term maximum electrical load forecasting of Kuwait; the Prophet and Holt–Winters forecasting models. Both models performed outstandingly in three performance metrics: accuracy, generalization, and robustness and provided essential knowledge for planning as follows:

1. The Prophet model achieved excellent values for MAPE, MAE, RMSE, CVRMSE, and R^2 with values of 1.75%, 147.89, 205.64, 7.61, and 0.9942, respectively. The Holt–Winters model performance

metrics were 4.17, 343.33, 475.76, 17.59%, and 0.9694 for MAPE, MAE, RMSE, CVRMSE, and R^2, respectively. The superiority of the Prophet model in these values indicates higher accuracy when compared to the Holt–Winters model.
2. The Prophet model exhibits better generalizability than Holt–Winters, as suggested by the simulated historical forecast investigation.
3. The robustness of the two models was assessed by adding white noise and found that the Prophet model is more robust than the Holt–Winters.
4. The forecasted maximum peak load reached 18,550 and 19,588 MW for the Prophet model and Holt–Winters model, respectively, by 2030. An additional capacity reservoir should be available to tolerate any failure or disruption of the electrical system.
5. The study suggests that the best months for scheduling the preventive maintenance for the years 2020 and 2021 are from November 2020 until March 2021 for both models.

It is believed that the insights concluded from this study would be of assistance to policymakers in estimating the future electricity demands and the strategic development plan of the State of Kuwait in addition to the maintenance schedule.

Author Contributions: Conceptualization, A.I.A. and A.M.A.; methodology, A.M.A. and A.I.A.; software, A.M.A.; validation, A.M.A., A.I.A., M.R.A., and S.N.A.; formal analysis, A.M.A. and A.I.A.; investigation, A.M.A. and A.I.A.; resources, A.M.A., A.I.A., A.S.A., M.R.A, and S.N.A.; data curation, A.I.A. and A.M.A.; writing—original draft preparation, A.I.A., A.M.A., A.S.A., M.R.A., and S.N.A.; writing—review and editing, A.I.A., A.M.A., A.S.A., M.R.A., and S.N.A.; visualization, A.I.A., A.M.A., A.S.A., M.R.A., and S.N.A. All authors have read and agreed to the published version of the manuscript.

Funding: This research received no external funding.

Conflicts of Interest: The authors declare no conflict of interest.

References

1. Weron, R. *Modeling and Forecasting Electricity Loads and Prices: A Statistical Approach*; John Wiley & Sons: Chichester, UK, 2007; Volume 403.
2. Alfares, H.K.; Nazeeruddin, M. Electric load forecasting: Literature survey and classification of methods. *Int. J. Syst. Sci.* **2002**, *33*, 23–34. [CrossRef]
3. Kuster, C.; Rezgui, Y.; Mourshed, M. Electrical load forecasting models: A critical systematic review. *Sustain. Cities Soc.* **2017**, *35*, 257–270. [CrossRef]
4. Wei, N.; Li, C.; Peng, X.; Zeng, F.; Lu, X. Conventional models and artificial intelligence-based models for energy consumption forecasting: A review. *J. Pet. Sci. Eng.* **2019**, *181*, 106187. [CrossRef]
5. Ahmad, T.; Zhang, H.; Yan, B. A review on renewable energy and electricity requirement forecasting models for smart grid and buildings. *Sustain. Cities Soc.* **2020**, *55*, 102052. [CrossRef]
6. Hammad, M.A.; Jereb, B.; Rosi, B.; Dragan, D. Methods and Models for Electric Load Forecasting: A Comprehensive Review. *Logist. Sustain. Transp.* **2020**, *11*, 51–76. [CrossRef]
7. Dudić, B.; Smolen, J.; Kovač, P.; Savkovic, B.; Dudic, Z. Electricity Usage Efficiency and Electricity Demand Modeling in the Case of Germany and the UK. *Appl. Sci.* **2020**, *10*, 2291. [CrossRef]
8. Filik, Ü.B.; Gerek, O.N.; Kurban, M. A novel modeling approach for hourly forecasting of long-term electric energy demand. *Energy Convers. Manag.* **2011**, *52*, 199–211. [CrossRef]
9. Mohammed, N.A. Modelling of unsuppressed electrical demand forecasting in Iraq for long term. *Energy* **2018**, *162*, 354–363. [CrossRef]
10. García-Díaz, J.C.; Trull, Ó. *Competitive Models for the Spanish Short-Term Electricity Demand Forecasting. Time Series Analysis and Forecasting*; Springer: Cham, Switzerland, 2016; pp. 217–231.
11. Taylor, J.W. Triple seasonal methods for short-term electricity demand forecasting. *Eur. J. Oper. Res.* **2010**, *204*, 139–152. [CrossRef]
12. Trull, O.; Garcia-Diaz, J.C.; Troncoso, A. Initialization Methods for Multiple Seasonal Holt–Winters Forecasting Models. *Mathematics* **2020**, *8*, 268. [CrossRef]
13. Bianco, V.; Manca, O.; Nardini, S.; Minea, A.A. Analysis and forecasting of nonresidential electricity consumption in Romania. *Appl. Energy* **2010**, *87*, 3584–3590. [CrossRef]

14. Hussain, A.; Rahman, M.; Alam Memon, J. Forecasting electricity consumption in Pakistan: The way forward. *Energy Policy* **2016**, *90*, 73–80. [CrossRef]
15. Ali, D.; Yohanna, M.; Puwu, M.; Garkida, B. Long-term load forecast modelling using a fuzzy logic approach. *Pac. Sci. Rev. A Nat. Sci. Eng.* **2016**, *18*, 123–127. [CrossRef]
16. Ouedraogo, N.S. Modeling sustainable long-term electricity supply-demand in Africa. *Appl. Energy* **2017**, *190*, 1047–1067. [CrossRef]
17. Wang, L.; Qin, G.; Liu, D.; Liu, M. Power Load Demand Forecasting Model and Method Based on Multi-Energy Coupling. *Appl. Sci.* **2020**, *10*, 584. [CrossRef]
18. Deb, C.; Zhang, F.; Yang, J.; Lee, S.E.; Shah, K.W. A review on time series forecasting techniques for building energy consumption. *Renew. Sustain. Energy Rev.* **2017**, *74*, 902–924. [CrossRef]
19. Khuntia, S.R.; Rueda, J.L.; Van Der Meijden, M.A. Forecasting the load of electrical power systems in mid- and long-term horizons: A review. *IET Gener. Transm. Distrib.* **2016**, *10*, 3971–3977. [CrossRef]
20. Runge, J.; Zmeureanu, R. Forecasting Energy Use in Buildings Using Artificial Neural Networks: A Review. *Energies* **2019**, *12*, 3254. [CrossRef]
21. Su, P.; Tian, X.; Wang, Y.; Deng, S.; Zhao, J.; An, Q.; Wang, Y. Recent Trends in Load Forecasting Technology for the Operation Optimization of Distributed Energy System. *Energies* **2017**, *10*, 1303. [CrossRef]
22. Taylor, S.J.; Letham, B. Forecasting at Scale. *Am. Stat.* **2017**, *72*, 37–45. [CrossRef]
23. Yenidoğan, I.; Çayir, A.; Kozan, O.; Dağ, T.; Arslan, Ç. Bitcoin forecasting using ARIMA and prophet. In Proceedings of the 2018 3rd International Conference on Computer Science and Engineering (UBMK), Sarajevo, Bosnia and Herzegovina, 20–23 September 2018; pp. 621–624.
24. Chaudhari, A. Forecasting Cryptocurrency Prices using Machine Learning. Master's Thesis, National College of Ireland, Dublin, Ireland, 11 June 2020.
25. Bianchi, F.; Castellini, A.; Tarocco, P.; Farinelli, A. Load Forecasting in District Heating Networks: Model Comparison on a Real-World Case Study. In Proceedings of the 5th International Conference, Siena, Italy, 10–13 September 2019; pp. 553–565.
26. Das, S. Forecasting the Generation of Wind Power in the Western and Southern Regions of India: Comparative Approach. Master's Thesis, National College of Ireland, Dublin, Ireland, 10 June 2020.
27. Almeshaiei, E.; Soltan, H. A methodology for Electric Power Load Forecasting. *Alex. Eng. J.* **2011**, *50*, 137–144. [CrossRef]
28. AlRashidi, M.R.; El-Naggar, K. Long term electric load forecasting based on particle swarm optimization. *Appl. Energy* **2010**, *87*, 320–326. [CrossRef]
29. AlHajri, M.; AlRashidi, M.; EL-Naggar, K. Long-term electric load forecast in Kuwaiti and Egyptian power systems. *J. Eng. Res.* **2018**, *6*, 116–135.
30. Al-Hamad, M.Y.; Qamber, I.S. GCC electrical long-term peak load forecasting modeling using ANFIS and MLR methods. *Arab. J. Basic Appl. Sci.* **2019**, *26*, 269–282. [CrossRef]
31. Alajmi, T.; Phelan, P. Modeling and Forecasting End-Use Energy Consumption for Residential Buildings in Kuwait Using a Bottom-Up Approach. *Energies* **2020**, *13*, 1981. [CrossRef]
32. Tratar, L.F.; Strmčnik, E. The comparison of Holt–Winters method and Multiple regression method: A case study. *Energy* **2016**, *109*, 266–276. [CrossRef]
33. Qiuyu, L.; Qiuna, C.; Sijie, L.; Yun, Y.; Binjie, Y.; Yang, W.; Xinsheng, Z. Short-term load forecasting based on load decomposition and numerical weather forecast. In Proceedings of the 2017 IEEE Conference on Energy Internet and Energy System Integration (EI2), Beijing, China, 26–28 November 2017; pp. 1–5.
34. Lago, J.; De Ridder, F.; De Schutter, B. Forecasting spot electricity prices: Deep learning approaches and empirical comparison of traditional algorithms. *Appl. Energy* **2018**, *221*, 386–405. [CrossRef]
35. Kim, S.; Kim, H. A new metric of absolute percentage error for intermittent demand forecasts. *Int. J. Forecast.* **2016**, *32*, 669–679. [CrossRef]
36. Lewis, C.D. *Industrial and Business Forecasting Methods: A Practical Guide to Exponential Smoothing and Curve Fitting*; Butterworth-Heinemann: London, UK, 1982.
37. Tashman, L.J. Out-of-sample tests of forecasting accuracy: An analysis and review. *Int. J. Forecast.* **2000**, *16*, 437–450. [CrossRef]
38. Wang, R.; Lu, S.; Feng, W. A novel improved model for building energy consumption prediction based on model integration. *Appl. Energy* **2020**, *262*, 114561. [CrossRef]

39. Cai, M.; Pipattanasomporn, M.; Rahman, S. Day-ahead building-level load forecasts using deep learning vs. traditional time-series techniques. *Appl. Energy* **2019**, *236*, 1078–1088. [CrossRef]
40. Soares, N.; Reinhart, C.F.; Hajiah, A. Simulation-based analysis of the use of PCM-wallboards to reduce cooling energy demand and peak-loads in low-rise residential heavyweight buildings in Kuwait. *Build. Simul.* **2017**, *10*, 481–495. [CrossRef]
41. Alhajeri, N.S.; Al-Fadhli, F.M.; Aly, A.Z. Unit-Based Emissions Inventory for Electric Power Systems in Kuwait: Current Status and Future Predictions. *Sustainability* **2019**, *11*, 5758. [CrossRef]
42. Ministry of Electricity and Water. *Statistical Year Book*; State of Kuwait Ministry of Electricity and Water: Shuhada, Kuwait, 2017.
43. Ministry of Electricity and Water. *Statistical Year Book*; State of Kuwait Ministry of Electricity and Water: Shuhada, Kuwait, 2018.
44. Ministry of Electricity and Water. *Statistical Year Book*; State of Kuwait Ministry of Electricity and Water: Shuhada, Kuwait, 2019.

© 2020 by the authors. Licensee MDPI, Basel, Switzerland. This article is an open access article distributed under the terms and conditions of the Creative Commons Attribution (CC BY) license (http://creativecommons.org/licenses/by/4.0/).

MDPI
St. Alban-Anlage 66
4052 Basel
Switzerland
Tel. +41 61 683 77 34
Fax +41 61 302 89 18
www.mdpi.com

Applied Sciences Editorial Office
E-mail: applsci@mdpi.com
www.mdpi.com/journal/applsci

www.ingramcontent.com/pod-product-compliance
Lightning Source LLC
LaVergne TN
LVHW070553100526
838202LV00012B/453